I0795894

IMAGES
of America

FRANKLIN

IMAGES
of America

FRANKLIN

Geoffrey G. Gorsuch

ARCADIA
PUBLISHING

ISBN 978-0-7385-3419-0

Published by Arcadia Publishing
Charleston, South Carolina

Printed in the United States of America

Library of Congress Catalog Card Number: 2005902266

For all general information contact Arcadia Publishing at:
Telephone 843-853-2070
Fax 843-853-0044
E-mail sales@arcadiapublishing.com
For customer service and orders:
Toll-Free 1-888-313-2665

Visit us on the Internet at www.arcadiapublishing.com

On the cover: **SOUTHWEST CORNER OF MAIN AND SECOND STREETS.** This scene takes place on a sunny autumn morning between 1903 and 1907. The single-story wood structure in the distance on the left contains the offices of the local newspaper, the *Franklin Chronicle*. Three unknown citizens lounge against the iron-railed fence that surrounds the residence at right. The complete photograph and caption are found on page 10.

CONTENTS

ACKNOWLEDGMENTS

This book was only possible because of the donations of old photographs to the Franklin Area Historical Society made over the last 40 years by members and other preservation-minded citizens. The backbone of this book is composed of these photographs and of illustrations contained in early histories of the community. Unfortunately the names of most of these original donors are now lost. For those who have generously donated their photographs or old books to our collection in the distant past, I am deeply indebted, as is the historical society.

Since this project was envisioned, many current and past residents of Franklin, and other nice people with no connection to the community, have offered additional photographs for inclusion in this book. Among these are Liz Buchanan, Bob Croll (now of Moreno Valley, California), Mary Sue Edwards, Dennie Fitzgerald, Harriet Foley, Tom Foley, Patty Frazee, Jackie Lane (of Lebanon), William Moses, Richard Norvell, Weesie Polley, Beverly Rossman, Larry Strayer (of Oakwood), and Dick Tracy. I am very grateful for their photographs and information, which contributed substantially to this book. My sincere apologies to any whose names I have forgotten or left off.

I must also express my special and continuing appreciation to Harriet Foley for her book, *Franklin in the Great Miami Valley*, which I found an invaluable resource for many aspects of the history of the city.

I am grateful to Valerie Elliot of the Lane Public Library in Oxford for setting an example for excellence in her book about Oxford, Ohio, and for her help and encouragement in my compiling this.

Lastly I am indebted to Brian and Cricket Pohanka of Alexandria, Virginia, who, with their great knowledge of 19th-century costuming, provided timely assistance in dating some of the photographs.

—Geoffrey Gorsuch
Franklin, Ohio
April 22, 2005

INTRODUCTION

Laid out by two surveyors, one of whom was William C. Schenck, in 1796, Franklin began its existence as a collection of cabins along the Great Miami River, surrounded by forests of black walnut, ash, hickory, cherry, oak, and beech. Slowly at first, the village grew away from the river banks, and surrounding farms flourished. With the completion of the Miami Canal through the village in 1829, the first industries—a pork slaughterhouse, sawmill, barrel manufacturer, and whiskey distillery—were established. With the arrival of the railroad in nearby Carlisle in 1851, both manufacturing and farming grew and prospered. In 1872, the railroad came through Franklin itself, and the downtown was quickly filled with fine brick and stone residences, businesses, churches, and public buildings. By the early 1890s, paper making dominated the manufacturing life, with no less than five different factories operating in and around the village.

But with progress, there were setbacks. Amid the prosperity of the early 1890s, the community became enthralled by the racing success of a trotting horse named Nightingale, owned by two local businessmen, Derrick Anderson and Charles Harding. Many locals let their optimism get the better of their responsibilities and bet more than they should have on the horse. When the trotter was eventually defeated, these solid citizens sustained losses they could not afford. By 1895, the national recession had caused several local factories to close, including one managed by Anderson. The only local bank also crashed in 1896, after it was discovered that William Boynton, a trusted longtime teller and son of a Baptist minister, had been embezzling deposits. Among the accounts he looted were private, corporate, and government funds. Though he was imprisoned for his crimes by federal judge William H. Taft, several prominent local families were nearly ruined by Boynton's theft.

The community, however, recovered. On the western edge of Franklin's suburbs, the village fairgrounds were established, and there in 1896 these became home of the Miami Valley Chautauqua. Though by 1901 it had moved to a new location to the north, just inside Montgomery County, the citizens of Franklin thronged to the Chautauqua to enjoy the nationally known speakers, religious inspiration, entertainment, and summer weather.

Business, work, and school continued along the streets shaded by the boughs of great trees that arched over them. Inside the homes, with their dark-colored, ornately detailed porches, covered with vines, and surrounded by white-picket or spiked-iron fences, the familiar steady rhythms of life went on. The children of the well-to-do rode their ponies, while the other children had to be satisfied with dogs and cats. Men of substance wore butterfly collars, frock coats, or tailored suits, and sometimes even top hats, but even working men looked dignified in their jackets and bowlers. Respectable, older women wore heavy, long, dark dresses all year long. Younger ladies, though, might wear tightly collared blouses and even white dresses in the summer. Though little boys might wear sailor suits or short jackets with lace collars, by adolescence they would be playing football without pads.

From the village emerged a few people whose influence would be felt throughout the state, and even the nation. Among these were Robert Cumming Schenck, son of the village's founder, and Lewis Davis Campbell. Both were born in log cabins near the river and both went on to become powerful members of the House of Representatives. Schenck, especially, achieved national renown by also becoming a general in the Civil War and a diplomat. Many men from Franklin and the surrounding farms served in the nation's wars. The Civil War, particularly, cost the community dearly, killing 10 men in battle and 17 by disease, and wounding 19 more. Yet most citizens were content to remain at home, laboring for the success of local businesses or institutions or the comfort of their families, all the while enjoying life in their beautiful village along the river.

As the community grew and prospered through the 19th century, so did its sense of pride in itself and its accomplishments. This sense of community led its leaders to proclaim a grand celebration of its past, present, and envisioned future, in the Franklin Homecoming of July 1910. Just three years later, Franklin and its environs were struck by the greatest calamity in local history, the March 1913 flood of the Great Miami River. And though Franklin quickly recovered, it soon left its past behind as it became a modern city in a rapidly changing nation.

This book is intended as a visual portrayal of Franklin and its life around the turn of the 20th century. This portrayal is limited to the time prior to 1920 for several reasons. The first is that Franklin was especially pretty, even charming, during these years. The second is that very few photographs after 1920 contain anything like the visual details found in earlier photographs. The last reason is that the book was intended to reveal the past, and to not flatter or offend anyone in the present. Had I chosen to continue the story to the present or even close to it, somebody or many might have thought themselves slighted by their treatment in the book. Only by limiting the portrayal to early Franklin would we be assured of keeping it truly a book of history.

Even in limiting the subject to early history, there were many more images available for publication than could be fit into just one book, so many had to be left out. Among those not included are photographs of buildings that appear entirely unchanged over the years. Examples of these include the Methodist church, St. Mary Catholic Church, the Conover Hardware Store building, and the historic residence at 225 Oxford Road.

Lastly, in the group portraits contained in the book, usually most or all faces can be identified. However I have chosen not to list all of the names in the captions. This was done because of the inevitable trade off between illustrations and words. The more words, the fewer photographs the book could contain. I chose to include the maximum number of photographs accompanied by a general description of the image. If a reader has a special interest in the identity of any individual in a group photograph, he or she may contact the historical society, and in most cases this information can be provided.

One

DOWNTOWN

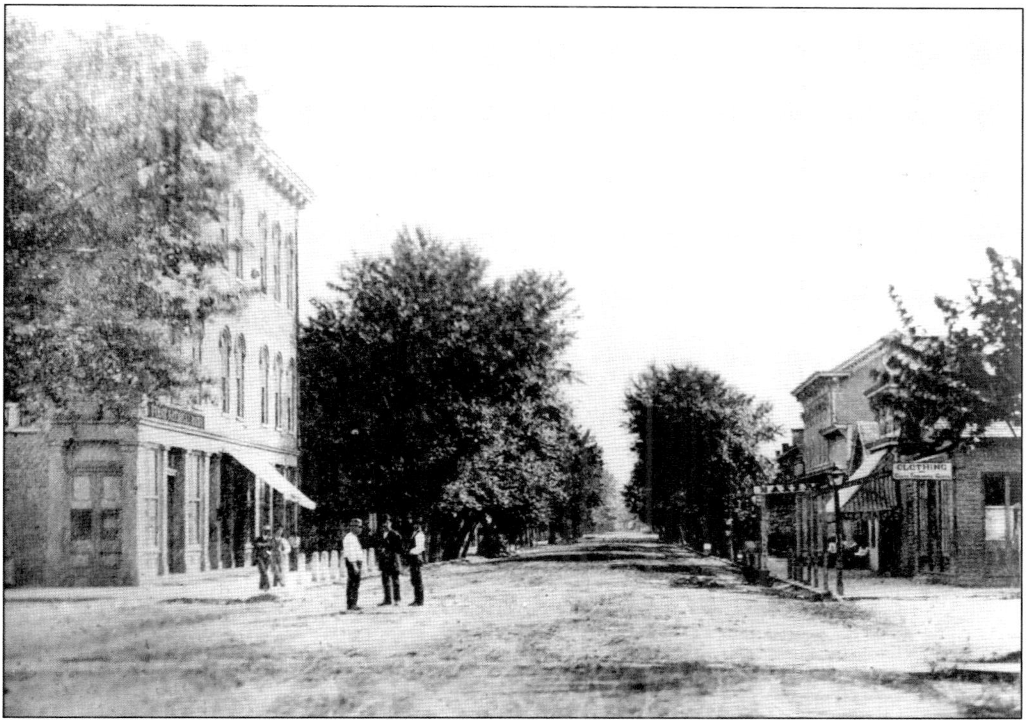

MAIN STREET, C. 1880. This is probably the oldest-known photograph of downtown Franklin. The view is looking south on Main Street, just south of its corner with Fourth Street. Judging from the clothes the men are wearing, the buildings present, and the structures not yet constructed, the photograph was probably taken in the 1880s. The three-story Odd Fellows building, on the corner of Main and Fourth Streets stands at left. The one-story wooden structures on the right constitute one of the village's two Merchant's Rows.

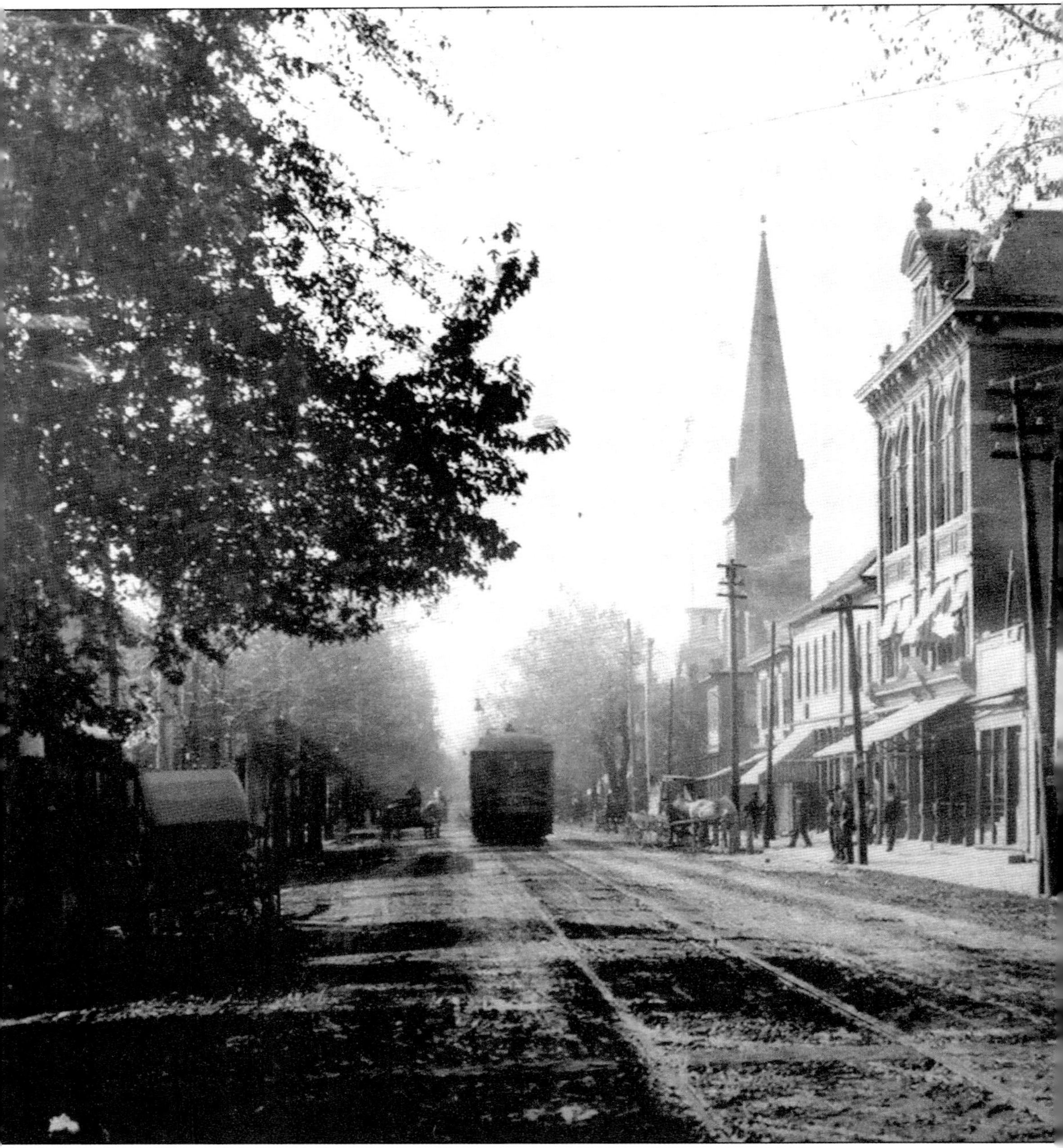

DOWNTOWN FRANKLIN. The view is looking south from the corner of Main and Second Streets. In the center distance are the tall Second Empire–style Elite Hotel and the steeple of the Methodist church. The vaguely discernible name on the trolley car in the distance—Cincinnati, Dayton and Toledo Traction Company—dates the photograph between 1903 and 1907, when that company was in operation through the village. The two-story structure with eight windows, under the steeple of the church and connected to the hotel, is the Woodward Block. The single-story structure connected to the north side of the hotel is the office of the local newspaper, the *Franklin Chronicle*. This wooden building was replaced

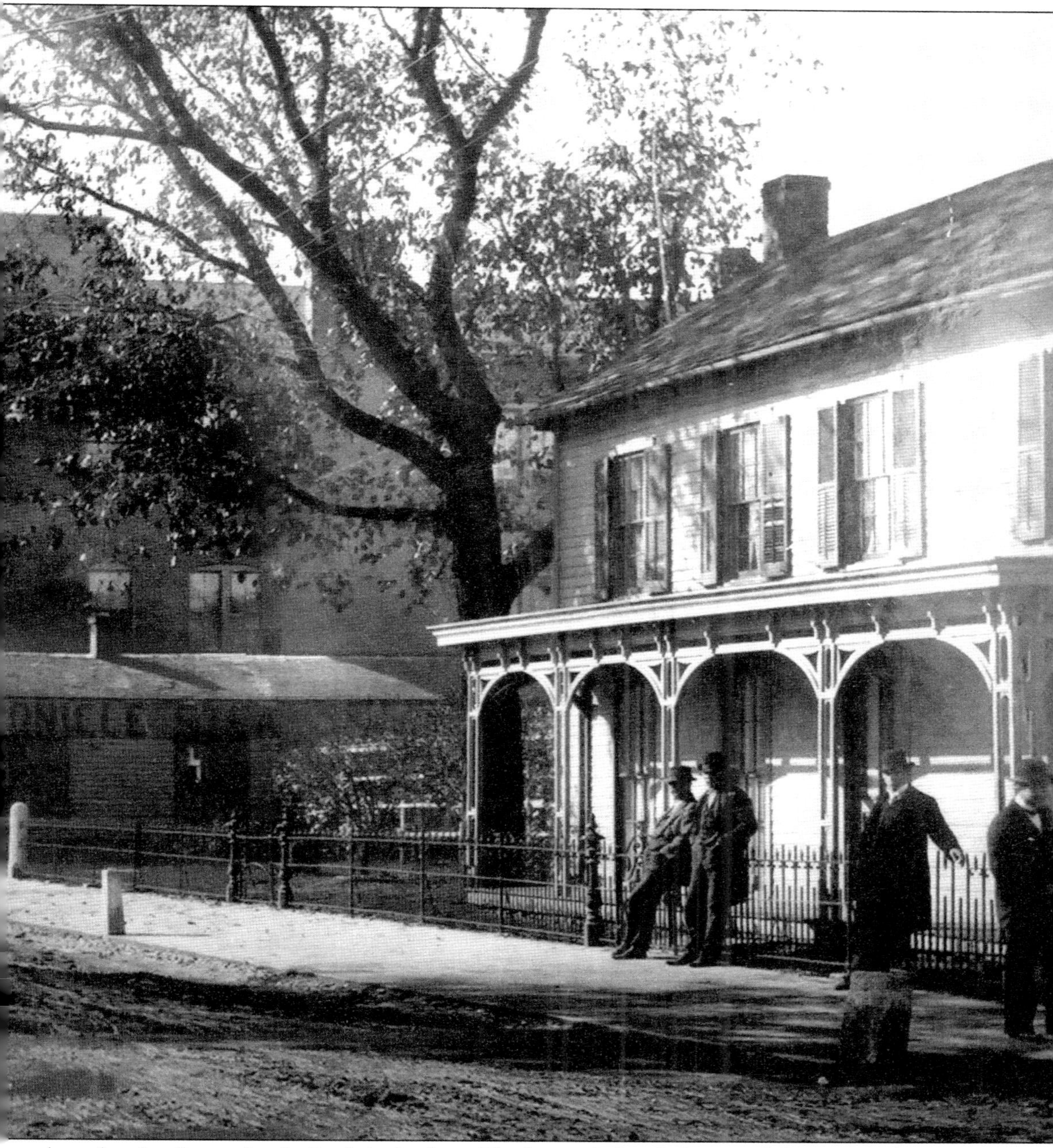

later by the Oscar Apple Ford dealership. The house behind the metal fence at right was originally owned by Dr. Washington L. Schenck, who served during the Civil War and also as the village's mayor. Later it was the home of Phillip and Margaret Hans Weber, the builders of the Elite Hotel, and after that was the residence of their daughter, Louise, and her husband, Jim Governey. Oscar Apple then lived in the house. The home was demolished between the 1920s and 1940s. The small, mustached man at right, in the dark suit and derby hat, is George Rossman, owner of the grocery store that operated on the other side of Second Street.

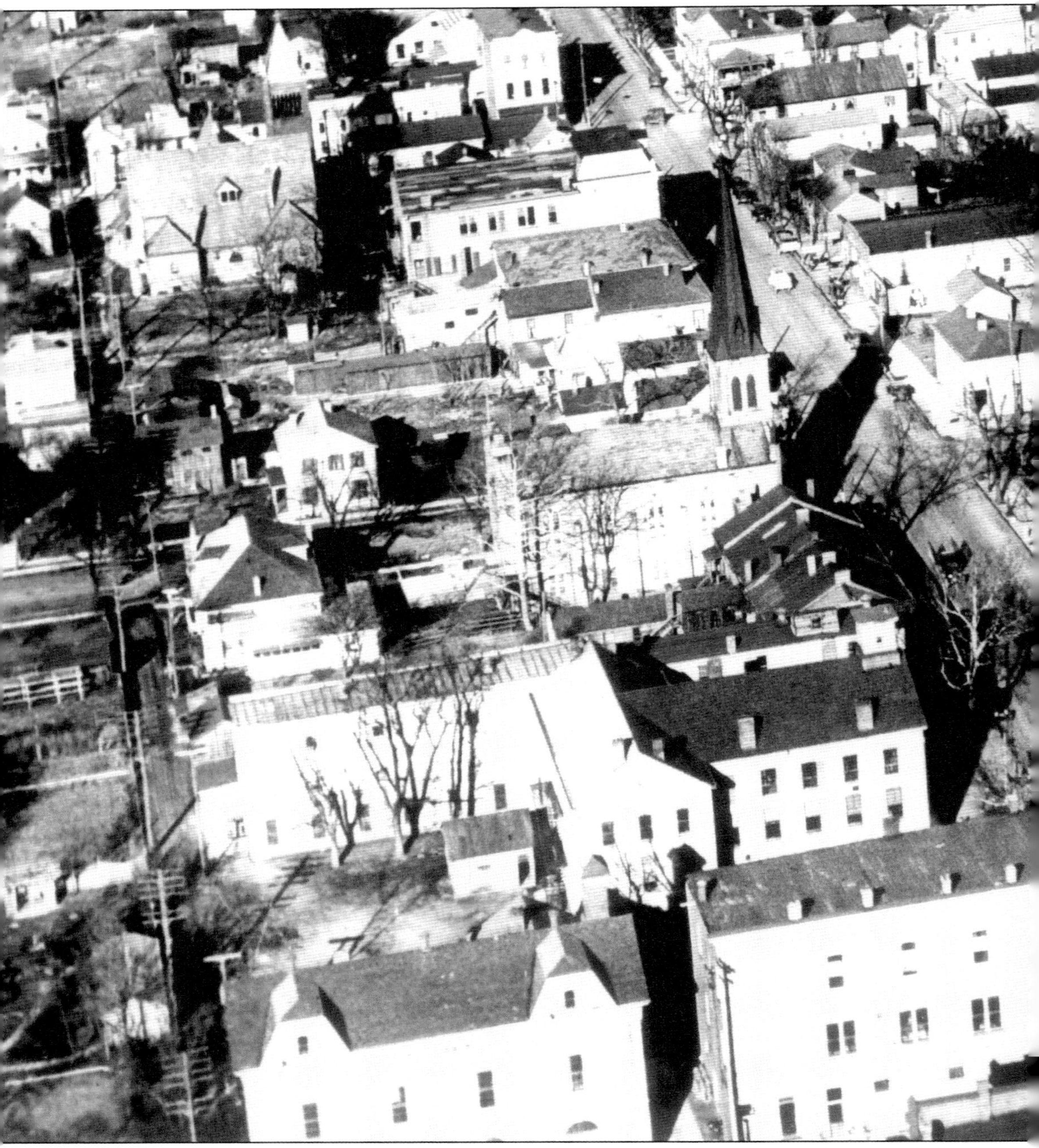

AERIAL VIEW OF DOWNTOWN FRANKLIN. The camera is looking north about 1920. Main Street runs diagonally from the bottom center of the photograph to the left corner. Fourth Street is just visible at the bottom right. Diagonally from the middle of the right side of the page to the upper left corner is the Miami-Erie Canal, then still filled with water. Just east of the canal and parallel with it is the Big Four Railroad. Second Street runs diagonally from the upper right side to the canal, then horizontally to the middle left edge of the page. Many prominent buildings of the time are visible in the image. The large building located at the northeast corner

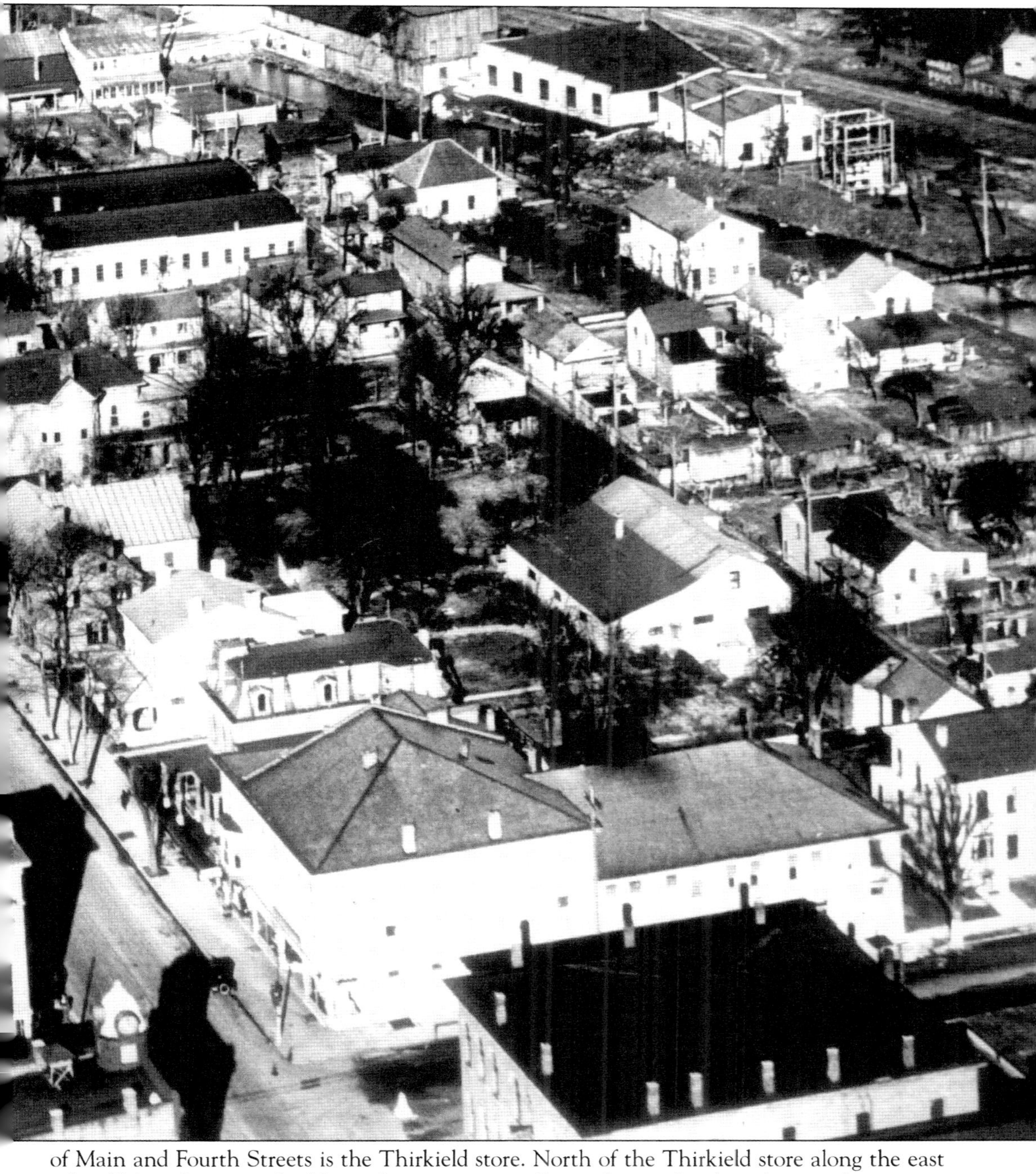

of Main and Fourth Streets is the Thirkield store. North of the Thirkield store along the east side of Main Street are buildings that were originally residences, but later became businesses. Among these are the Adams House, adjacent to the store, and the Dr. Otho Evans House, on the southeast corner of Main and Third Streets. All of these were demolished between the 1950s and 1980s. On the west side of Main Street are many buildings that still stand, including the Conover Building, the old Central School, the Methodist church, the Rossman Store, the First Baptist Church, and St. Mary Church.

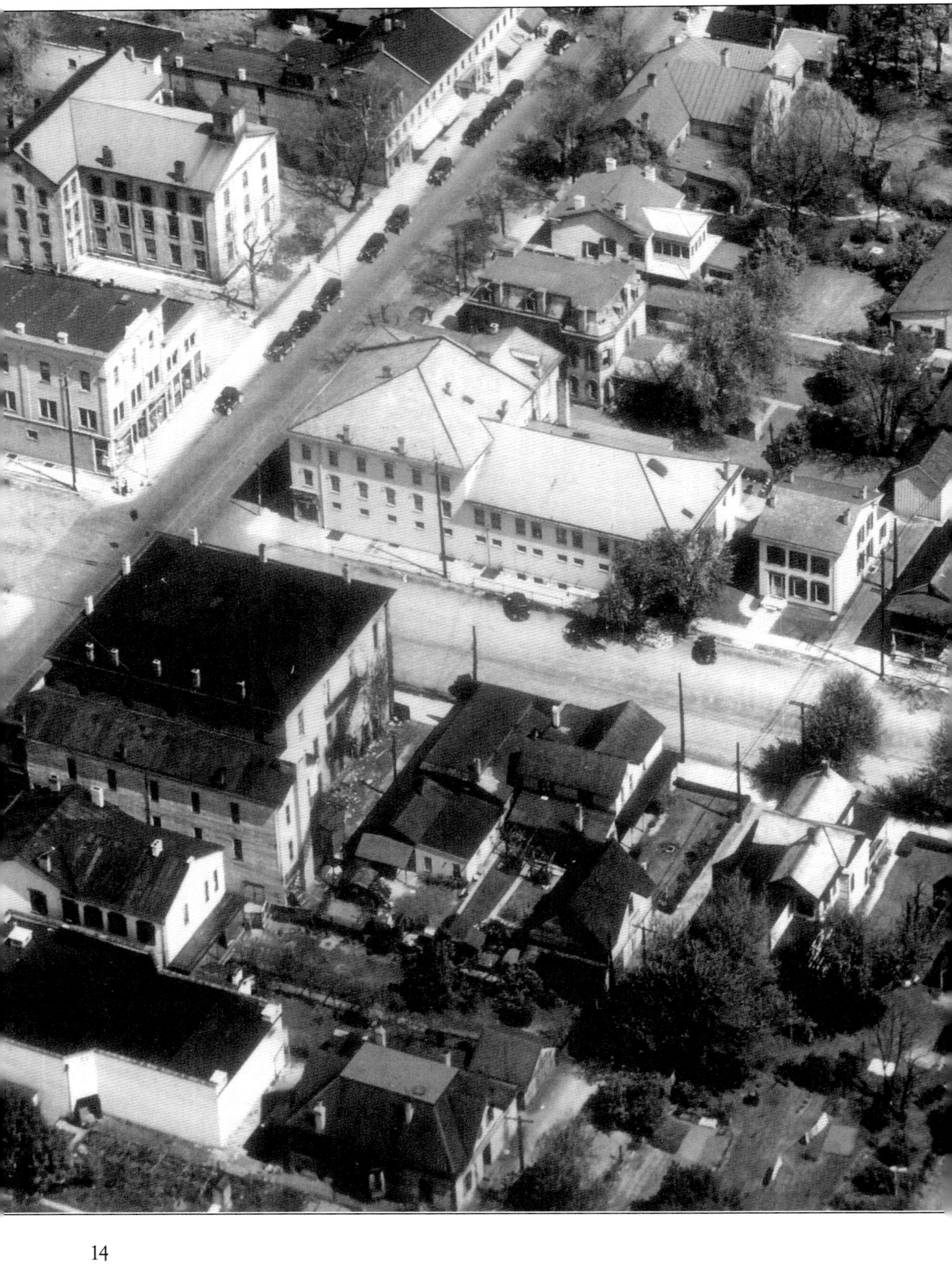

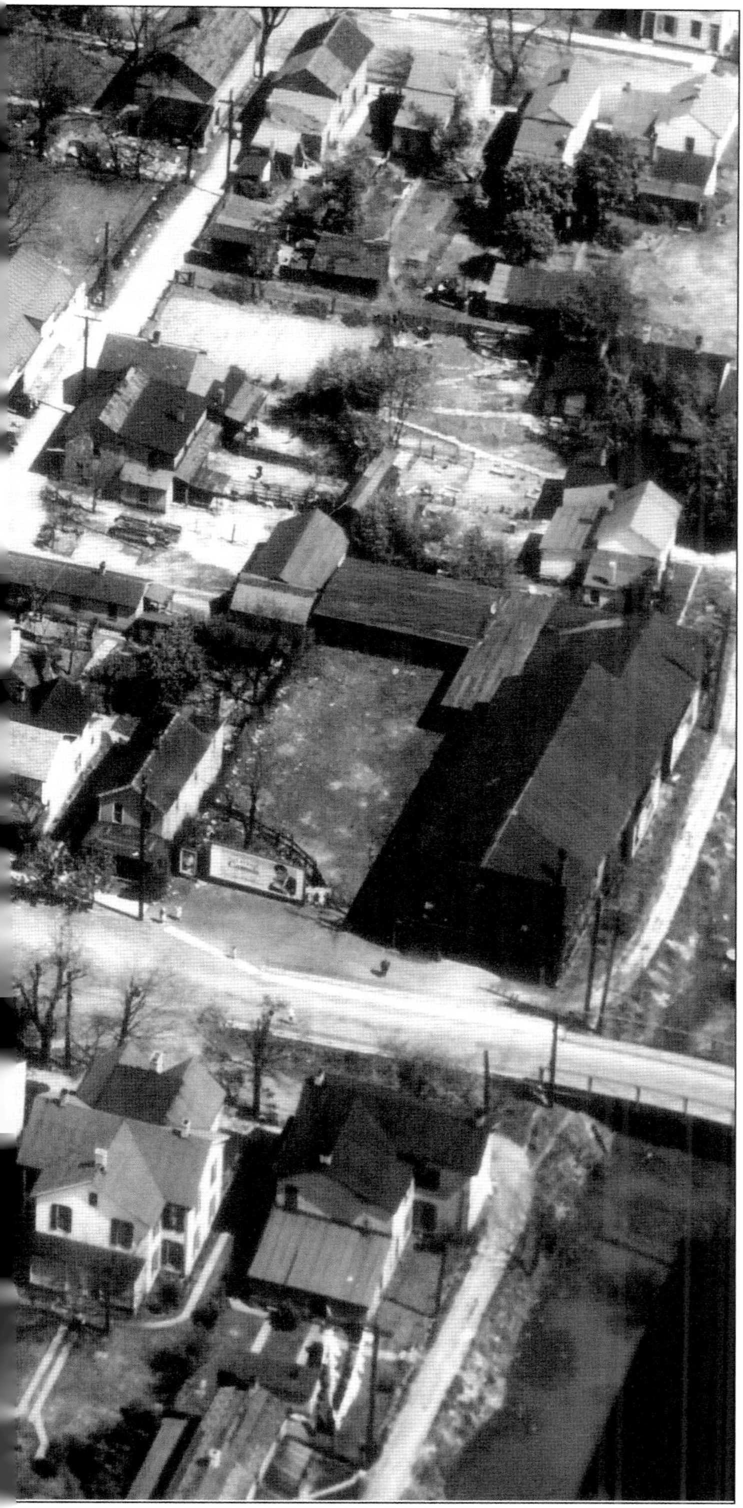

AERIAL VIEW OF DOWNTOWN, C. 1920. The view is to the north. Running diagonally from the lower left to upper right corner is Main Street. The road that cuts across the middle of the photograph is Fourth Street. The canal is in the right corner. Adjacent to it, along the north side of Fourth Street, is a livery, one of at least three that served the village during its horse-and-buggy days. Half a block west on the same side of Fourth Street is the house originally owned by the Thirkield family that later became the village's telephone exchange. To the west of it is the L-shaped Thirkield Department Store. This business operated at this corner from 1850 until the 1970s. The building was demolished in 1980. Across Main Street from Thirkield's is the Conover Hardware Store, and behind it is the old city building. Across the street from Conover's is the Hamilton Building, and across from Thirkield's is the Odd Fellows building. North of Conover's is the old T-shaped Central School Building. To its north stands the northernmost of two Merchant's Row buildings that were constructed as the village's original stores in 1838. To their north stands the First Methodist Church, erected in 1859. Across Main from the church is the residence built for Dr. Otho Evans. To its south stands the Unglesby residence and the house that became the Unglesby Funeral Home after 1913.

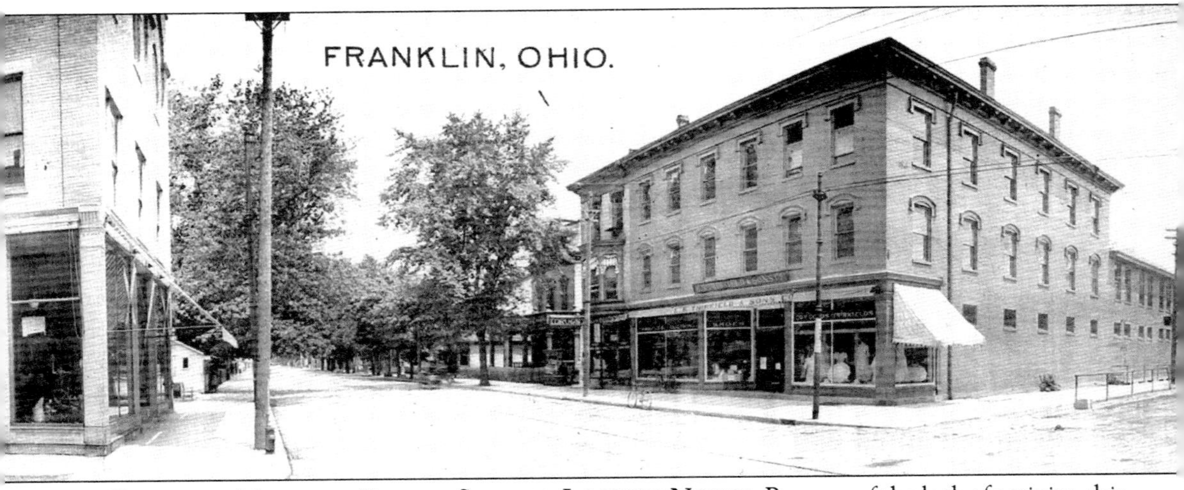

CORNER OF MAIN AND FOURTH STREETS, LOOKING NORTH. Because of the lack of activity, this panoramic image was probably taken in the early morning. Visible at far left, on the northwest corner of the intersection, is the new Conover Hardware Building, erected in 1906 on the site of the village's Union Church. Across the street from Conover's is the Thirkield Department Store, constructed on this site in 1850. To the left of Thirkield's is the Adams Building, which originally contained the Farmer's National Bank on its first floor. At the time of this photograph, the first floor contained Earhart's Drug Store. It was in front of Earhart's in October 1906 that village marshal George Basore was shot and mortally wounded by a burglary suspect, who was waiting for Earhart's to open so he could purchase a ticket for the traction trolley car so he could get out of town. Behind the picket fence to the left of Earhart's is the Second Empire–style home originally owned by David Adams, the founder of the Farmer's National Bank. The home was later owned by the Lake family, who still operate a jewelry business on Main Street.

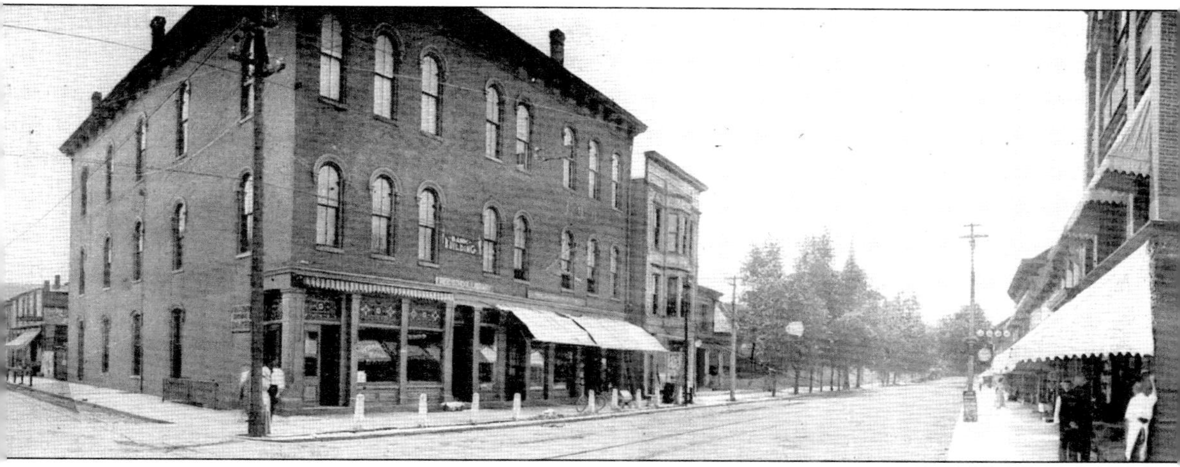

CORNER OF MAIN AND FOURTH STREETS, LOOKING SOUTH. At far right in this panoramic photograph stands the Hamilton Building, which was built about 1890 and replaced a wooden structure on the corner that housed a billiard hall, grocery, and saloon. The second floor of the Hamilton Building contained the law office of Perry Rue, who also served as mayor and owned a house on the West Side. His practice was later sold to longtime Franklin mayor, judge, and power broker J. T. Riley, who occupied the same office. Across Main Street is the three-story Odd Fellows building, constructed about 1865. Originally Lodge 11 of the Odd Fellows occupied the south half of the building's third floor while the north half was filled by the Eastern Star Lodge 55 of the Free and Accepted Masons. By 1874, the north half of the second floor was occupied by the YMCA library, which became the village's own library. The south half of the second floor was occupied by the law office of J. D. Miller, a prominent Democrat, who hosted nationally known members of that party at his 258 Hill Avenue home (called Valeridge) when they were visiting Franklin. The north half of the first floor was originally occupied by the First National Bank. This institution failed in 1895 after its longtime cashier was discovered to have embezzled its deposits. After 1897 the Franklin National Bank occupied these spaces. Around the beginning of the 20th century, the south side of the first floor was occupied by businesses selling dry goods, clothing, boots, and wallpaper. In 1898, these were replaced by what eventually became known as the Albaugh Drug Store.

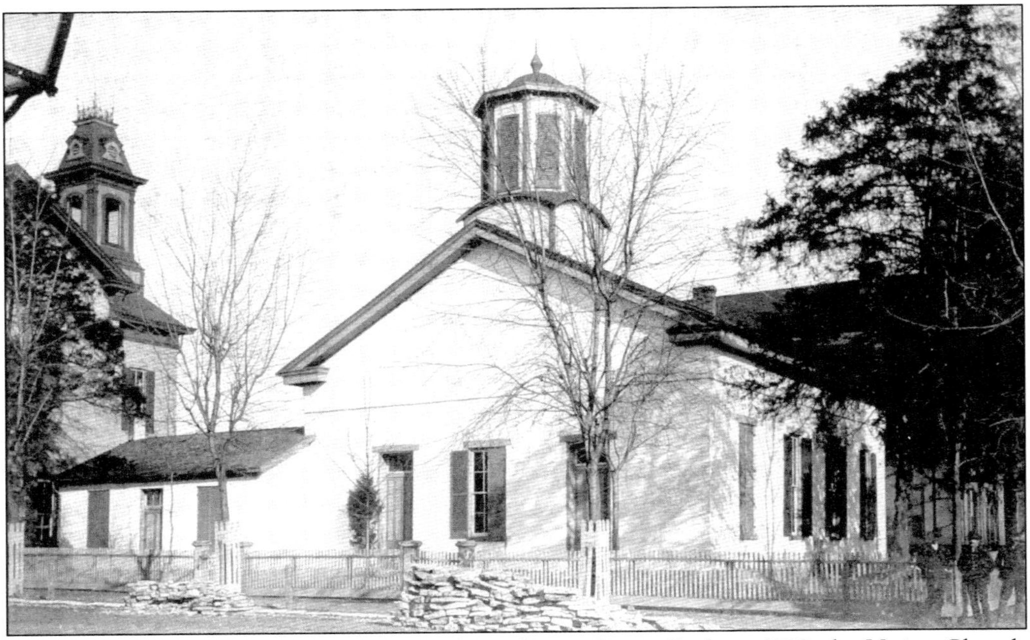

THE OLD UNION CHURCH. The view is from the southeast. Built in 1823, the Union Church stood at the northwest corner of Main and Fourth Streets, and originally housed Franklin's Methodist, Presbyterian, and Christian churches. The tower at left is part of the village's city building. The Union Church was demolished in 1904 and was replaced by the Conover Hardware building, which still stands.

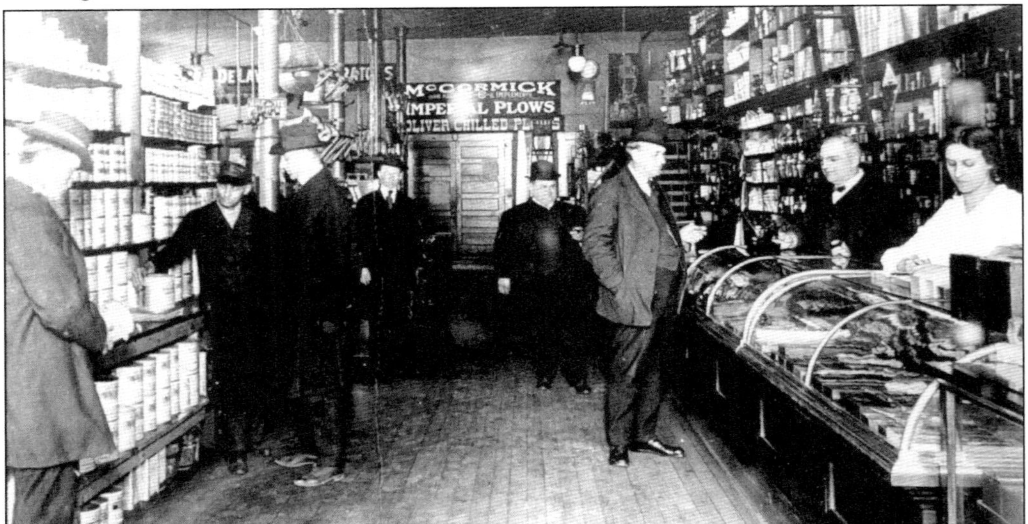

INTERIOR OF THE CONOVER HARDWARE STORE. The Conover store opened in its new building on this site in 1906. Then, as today, paints (seen at left) were among a hardware store's wares. The plows, however, seen advertised here, are now less in demand. The three men at left are unidentified. The stout man is Toby Dechant. The customer looking down at the glass case is Bert Vail. Serving him is Howard Conover, the store's owner. The female employee is Helen Robison.

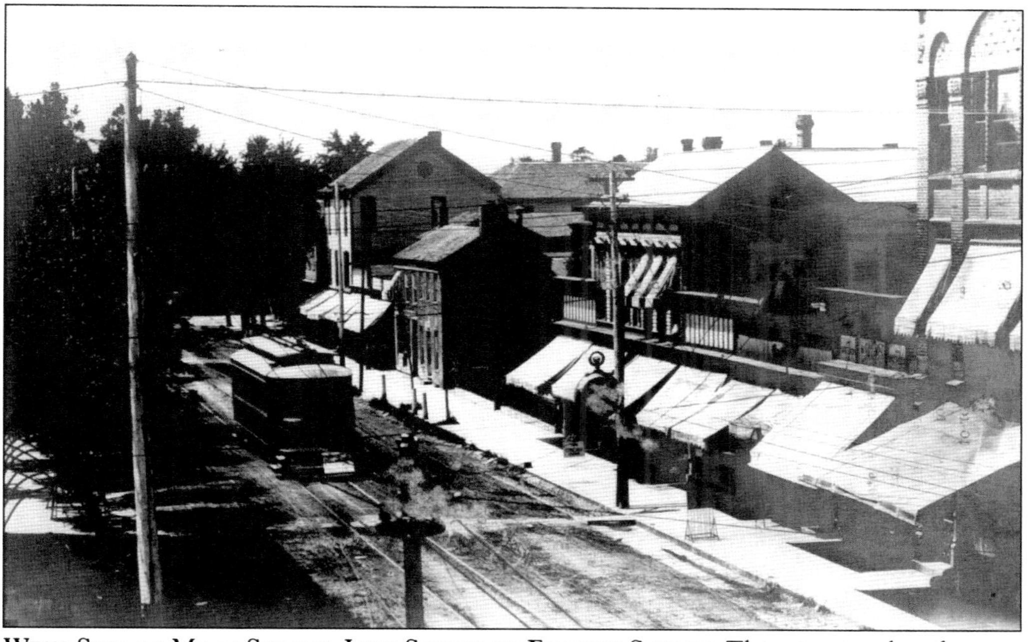

WEST SIDE OF MAIN STREET, JUST SOUTH OF FOURTH STREET. This view is taken from an upper floor of the Thirkield store, located at the northeast corner of Fourth and Main. Visible at right is the Hamilton Building; its characteristic bell tower is out of view. The wooden structures at right center constituted one of the village's two Merchant's Rows, which contained over the years such businesses as billiard halls, milliners, bakeries, and shoemakers.

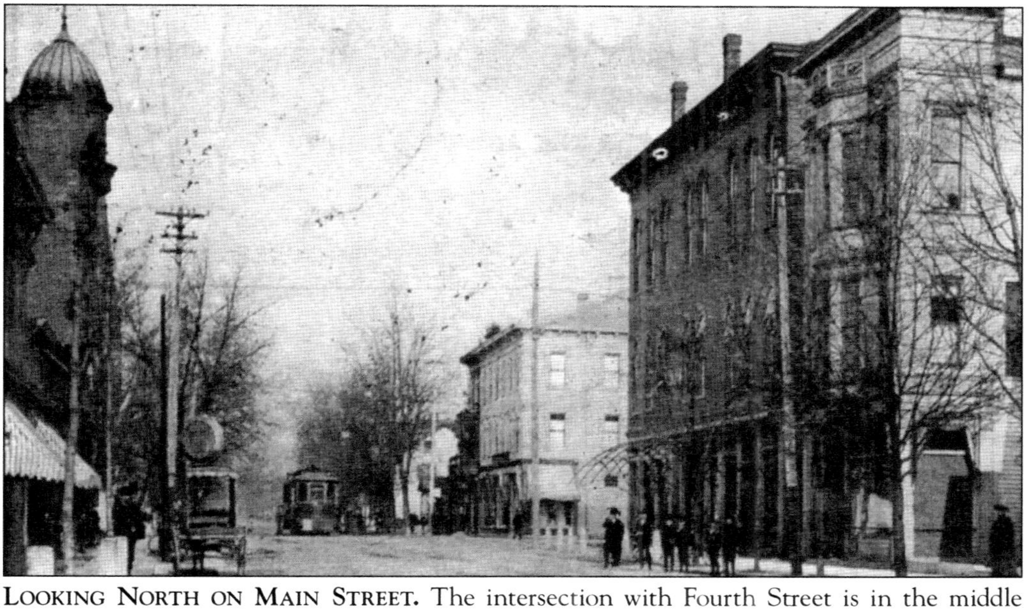

LOOKING NORTH ON MAIN STREET. The intersection with Fourth Street is in the middle distance. At right is the Odd Fellows building, with the current Fitzgerald building to the right of it. That building's façade is made of cast iron, galvanized with zinc to protect it from the weather. For much of its life, its second floor was occupied by a dentist's office. Across Fourth Street from the Odd Fellows building is Thirkield's. (Courtesy of Liz Buchanan.)

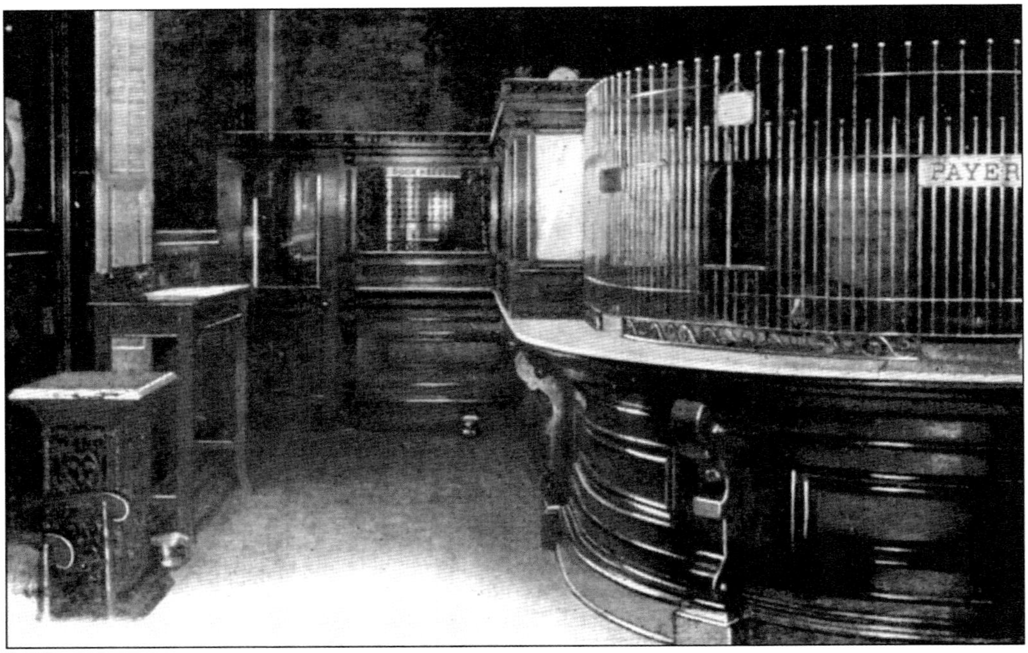

INTERIOR OF THE FRANKLIN NATIONAL BANK. This institution was the second bank to operate on this site, opening in 1897 and replacing the First National Bank that closed its doors in 1895. That bank crashed after the discovery that its longtime teller, William A. Boynton, had embezzled huge sums from the depositor's accounts, destroying the fortunes of several families. Boynton was sentenced to prison by federal judge (and later president) William H. Taft in 1896. Note the spittoon at left.

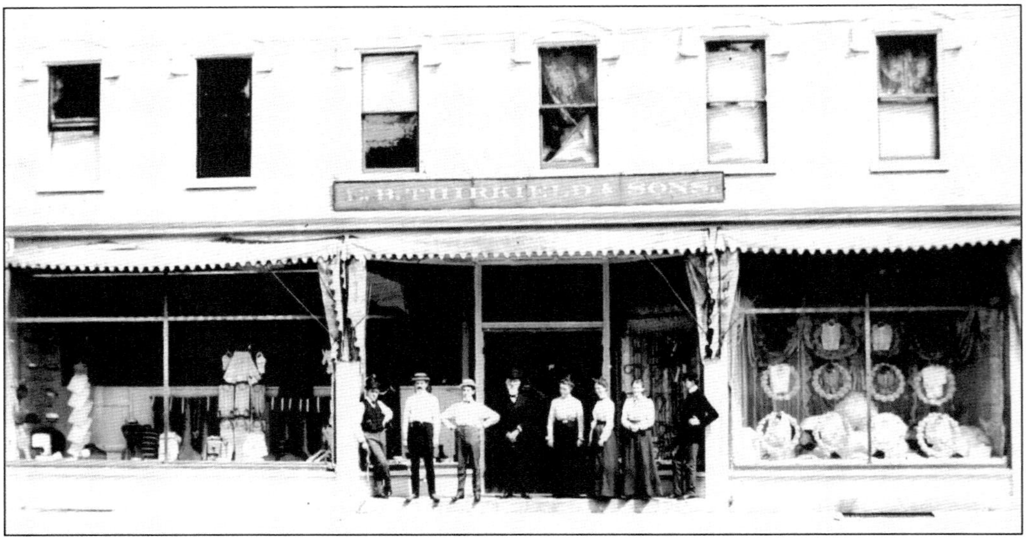

PICTURE WINDOWS OF THE THIRKIELD DEPARTMENT STORE. This photograph, showing the store's enticingly displayed wares, illustrates the true meaning of the term "window shopping." In front of the windows stand the store's employees. The white-bearded man is Eden Thirkield, the owner of the store, who lived a block away, in a large house located at the northeast corner of River and Fourth Streets.

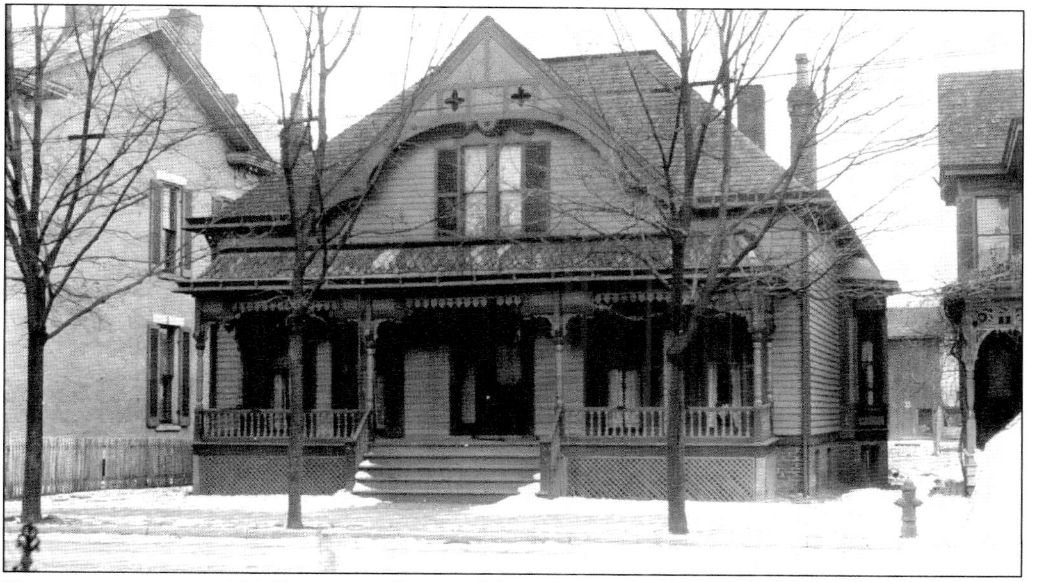

RESIDENCE IN THE 400 BLOCK OF SOUTH MAIN STREET. This small home, with its ornately carved trim, was among three homes that stood mid-block on the east side of Main, between Fourth and Fifth Streets. To its north was a Federal-period brick home, and to its south a small wooden Queen Anne. These houses began to disappear after World War I, when Main Street was increasingly given over to businesses.

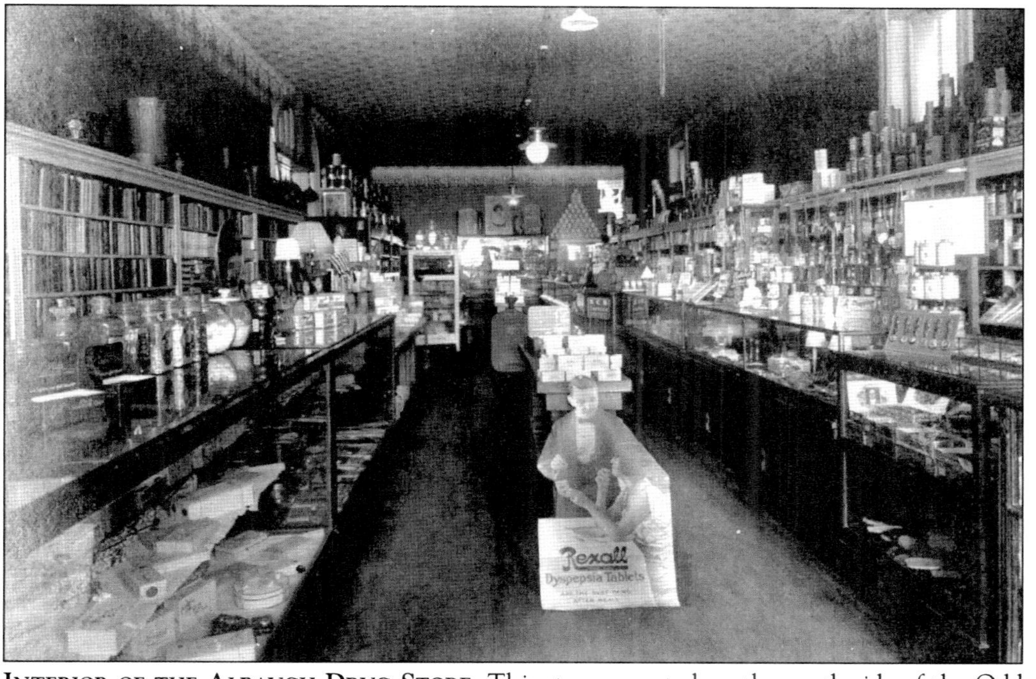

INTERIOR OF THE ALBAUGH DRUG STORE. This store operated on the south side of the Odd Fellows building beginning in 1898. It acquired its name in 1907 under the ownership of Herbert and Grace Albaugh, who ran the store until 1945. Among the items sold in the store were china, paper, cigars, and pharmaceuticals.

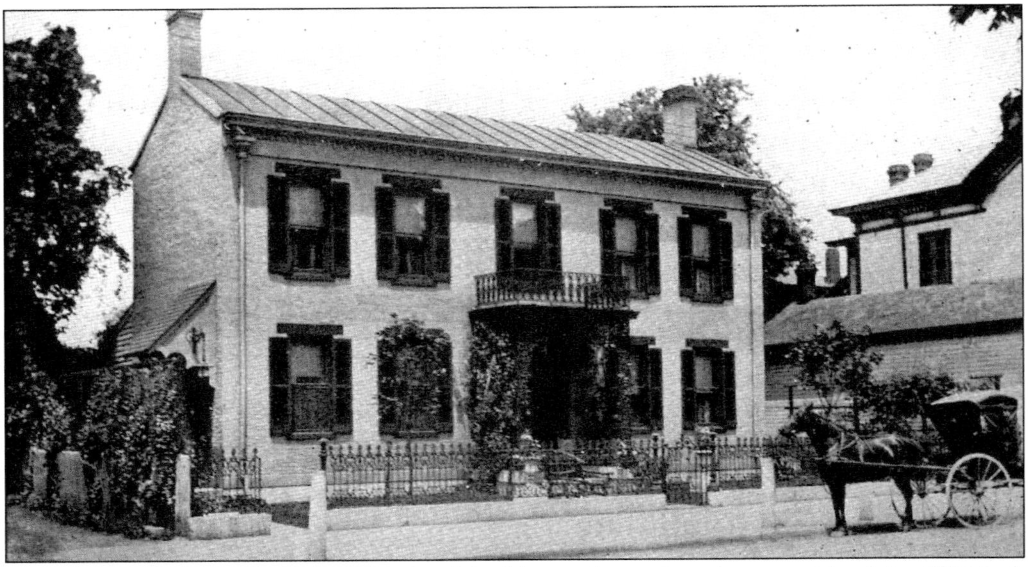

The Dr. Hugh Death Home. This brick building is located on the west side of the 400 block of South Main Street. The home also contained Dr. Death's medical office. The dapper and affable Hugh Death was the second physician in the village's history to practice under that menacing surname. Only the roofline and chimneys of the building are visible today behind the tile façade of a modern business.

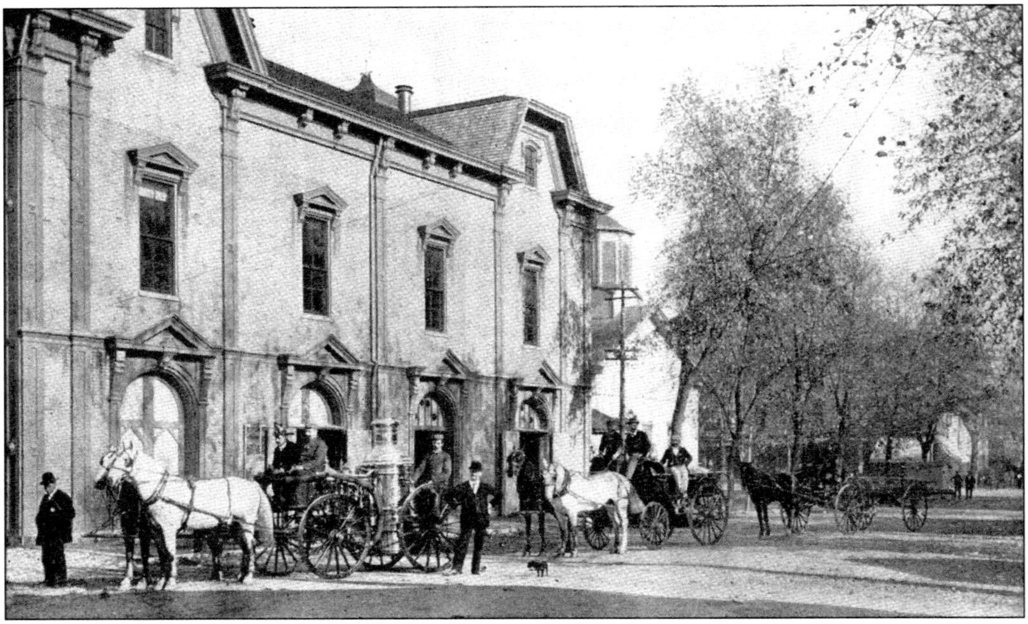

Franklin's City Building. This building that stood on the north side of West Fourth Street is seen in a view to the northeast. Here village residents proudly show off their state-of-the-art fire engines. The building was constructed in 1877. Its upstairs contained an opera house that could seat 600. Entertainments and ceremonies, such as graduations, were held there. Over the years, many of the functions were moved to other locations, and the city building was demolished in 1973.

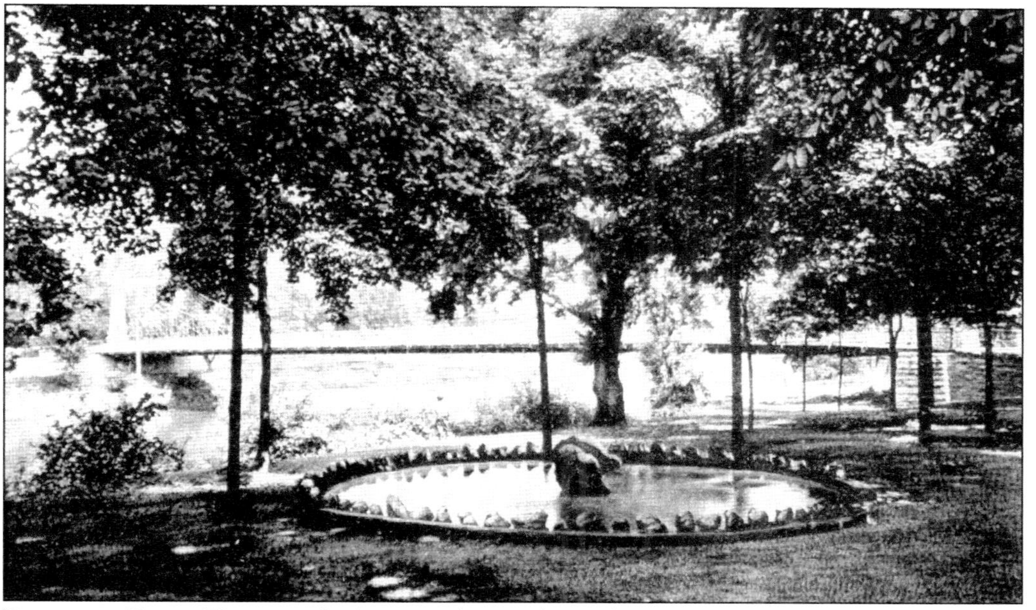

RIVERSIDE PARK. This view, looking northwest, shows the fountain the way it appeared about 1910. The suspension bridge in the distance was built in 1873 by the Shipman Company of Cincinnati, under the supervision of Roebling and Sons of Trenton, New Jersey, the builders of New York's Brooklyn Bridge. (Courtesy of William Moses.)

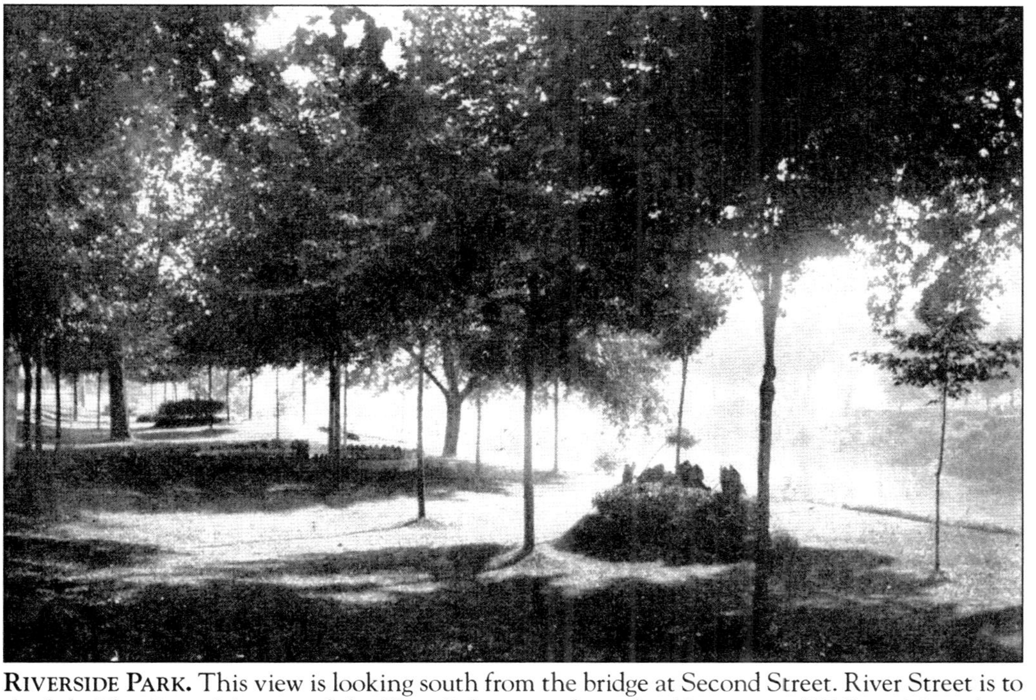

RIVERSIDE PARK. This view is looking south from the bridge at Second Street. River Street is to the left. The Great Miami and the West Side are to the right. (Courtesy of William Moses.)

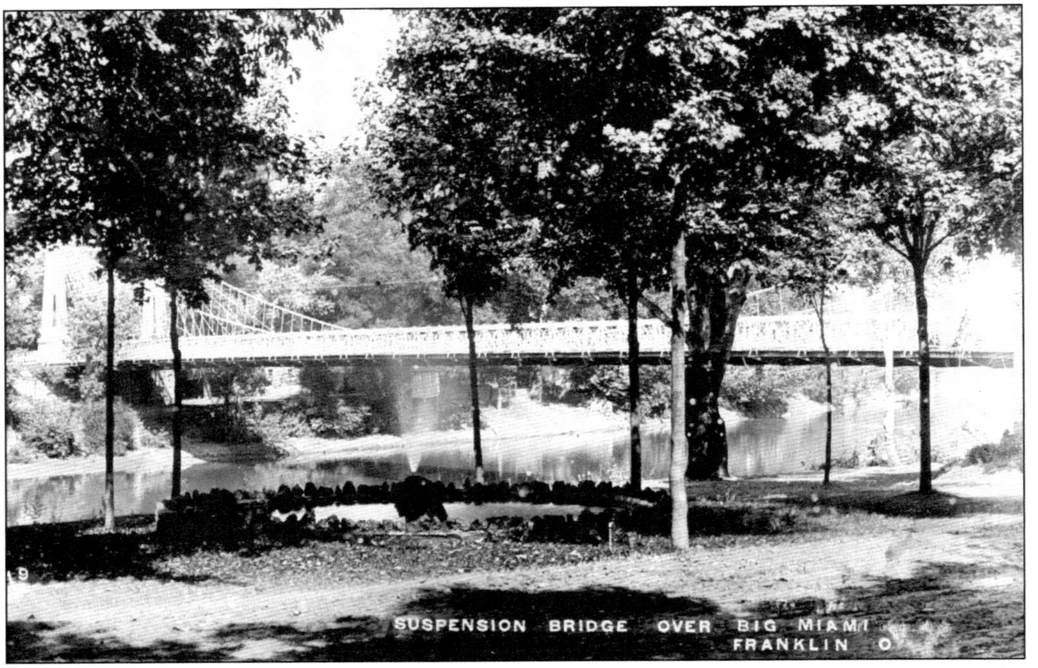

THE PARK ALONG RIVER STREET. The view is looking northwest from the fountain. Notice the abundant vegetation growing along the west bank of the Great Miami prior to the construction of the levee after the flood of 1913. (Courtesy of William Moses.)

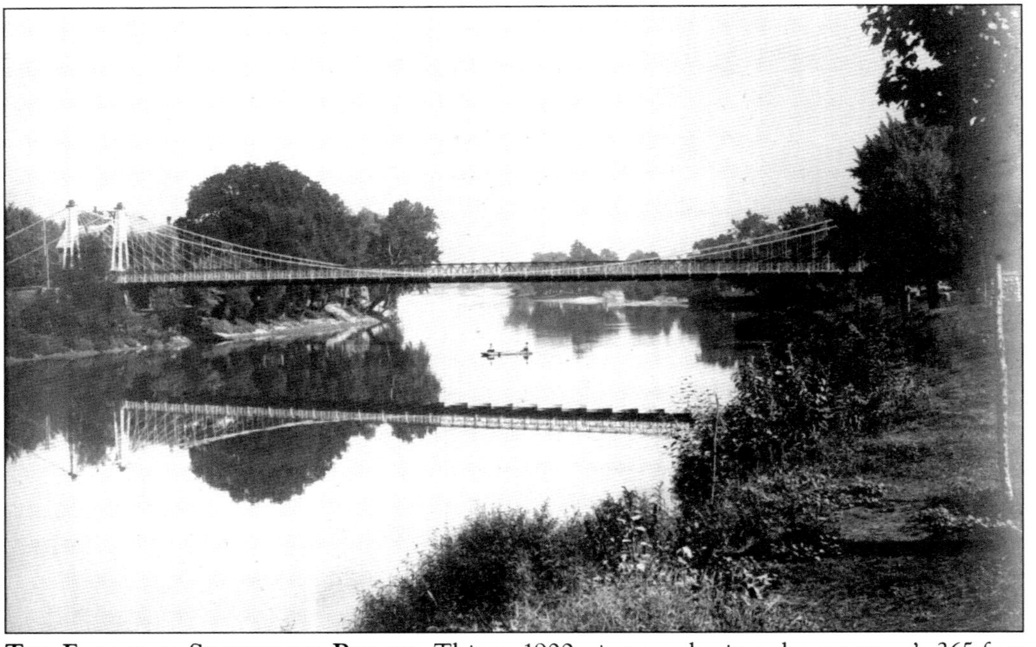

THE FRANKLIN SUSPENSION BRIDGE. This *c.* 1900 view emphasizes the structure's 365-foot length. Built in 1873, the Franklin bridge replaced an earlier wooden covered bridge constructed in 1857. The sturdy remains of the wooden bridge were incorporated into a business block that still stands at 227–233 South Main Street.

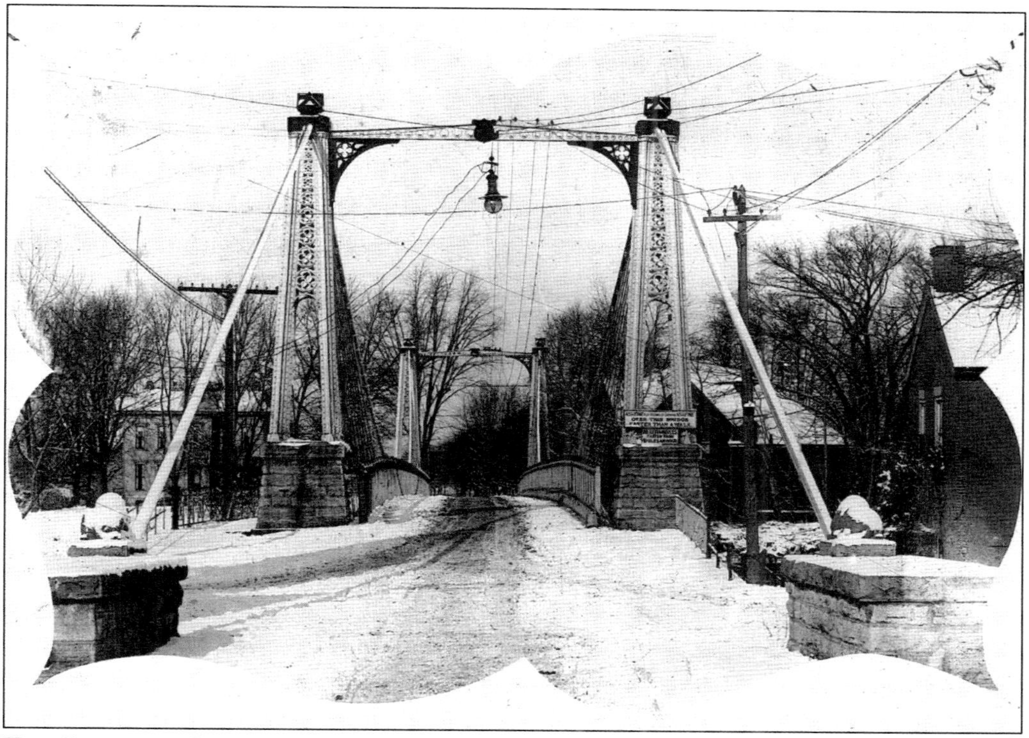

The Franklin Bridge in Winter. This scene, viewed from the east, clearly shows the inviting pedestrian path along the south side of the structure. The image also emphasizes the 38-foot height of the bridge's towers. The signs at right warn of fines for "riding or driving over this bridge faster than a walk" and that automobiles should not go faster than 4 miles per hour when crossing the bridge. The presence of these posted warnings suggests these rules were violated regularly.

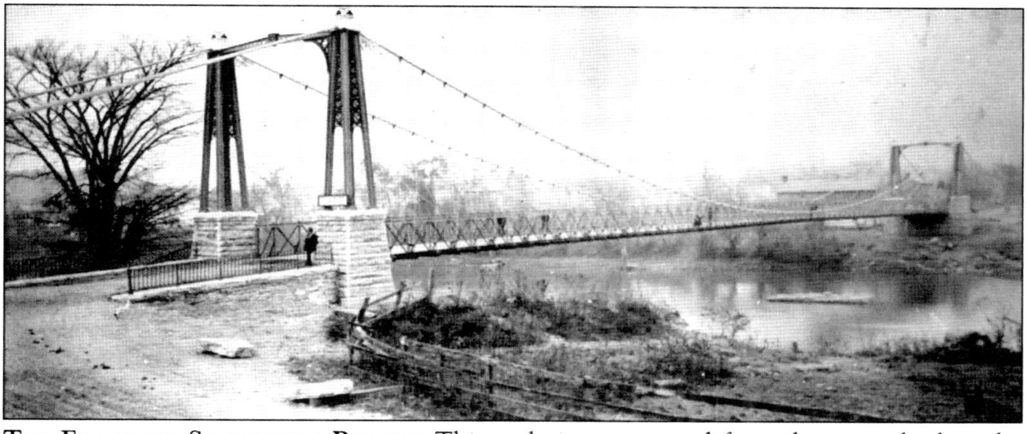

The Franklin Suspension Bridge. This early image, viewed from the west, displays the bridge's grace and elegance. These same aesthetic qualities made it unsuited to the heavy vehicular traffic of the modern world. Years of overuse by heavy trucks badly weakened the Franklin Bridge and it failed structurally. The current Lion Bridge replaced it in 1933.

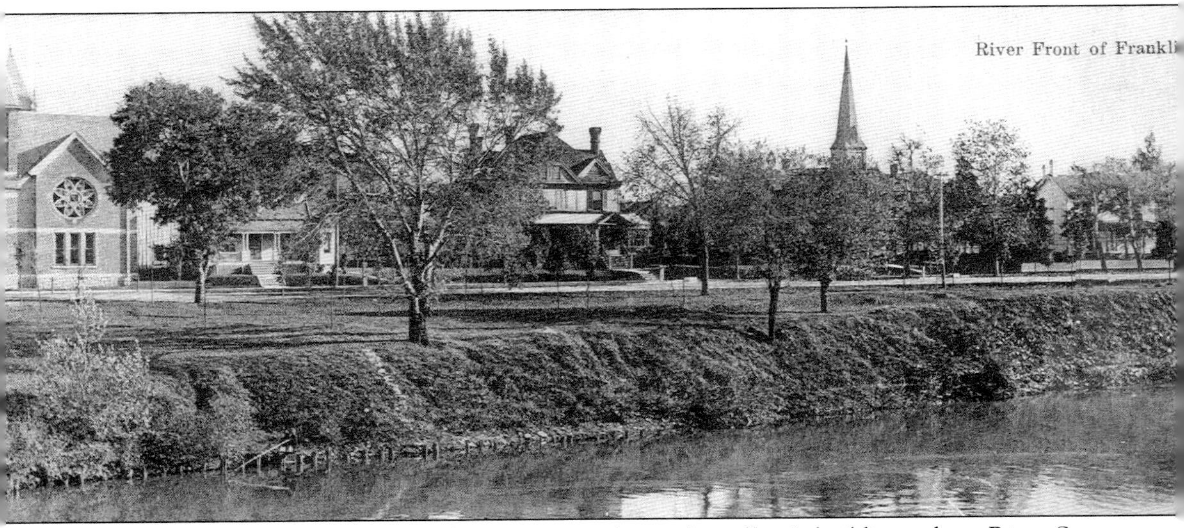

FRANKLIN FROM THE WEST. This panorama shows the village's buildings along River Street. The charming building at the far left is St. Paul Lutheran Church, built in 1893. The building to its right (partially hidden behind a tree) is the Victorian Eclectic–style home of King Carson. The structure to its right is the Eastlake-style home of Dr. Firman Evans. The church was razed in 1961, the Dr. Evans home in 1962, and the Carson home about 2001. To the right of the Evans home, behind the picket fence, stands a frame house built on or around the site of one of the village's original cabins. The prominent steeple belongs to the First Methodist Church, at the corner of Main and Third Streets. To the right of the house behind the picket fence is the former Methodist parsonage, on the southeast corner of River and Third Streets. The tower rising behind the roof of the parsonage is on the city building, located on the north side of

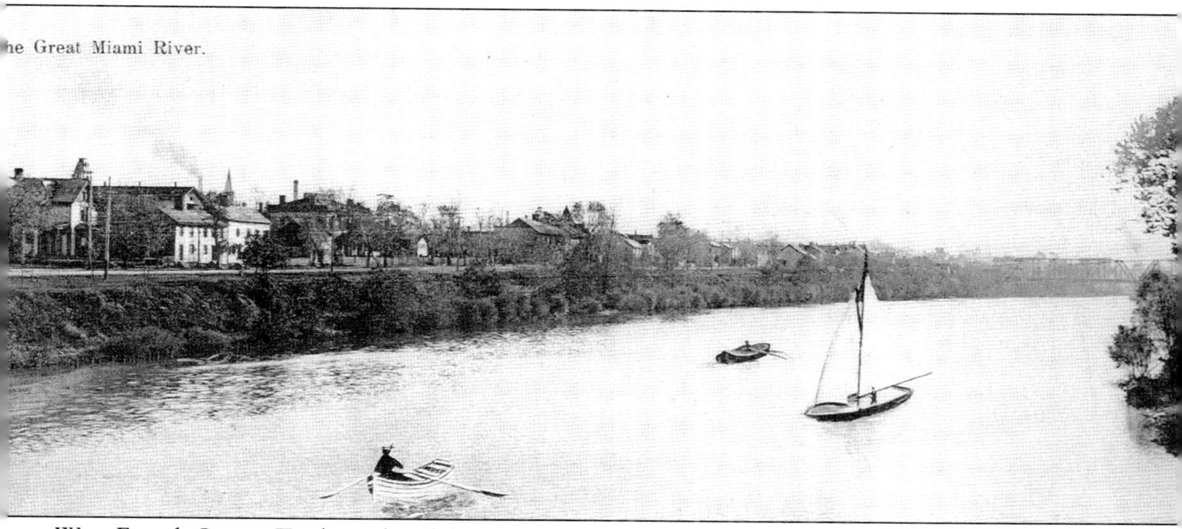

West Fourth Street. To the right of the parsonage stands the twin white buildings that used to contain what is today the Old Log Post Office, now moved to the other side of River Street at the intersection with Fifth Street. Above these buildings is the old steeple of the First United Church of Christ on Main Street. To the right (with the industrial smokestack behind it) is the Eden Thirkield House. Just to the right of it, facing the river at the corner of Fourth Street, is the Miller House, one of the village's residential hotels that operated in the 1800s and early 1900s. In the 1920s, the old hotel was replaced by a large brick Georgian Revival home built for Dr. Orville Layman. Rising above the southwest corner of the Miller House is the low peak of the tower of the South School, located at the southwest corner of River and Eighth Streets. At far right is the Big Four Railroad Bridge.

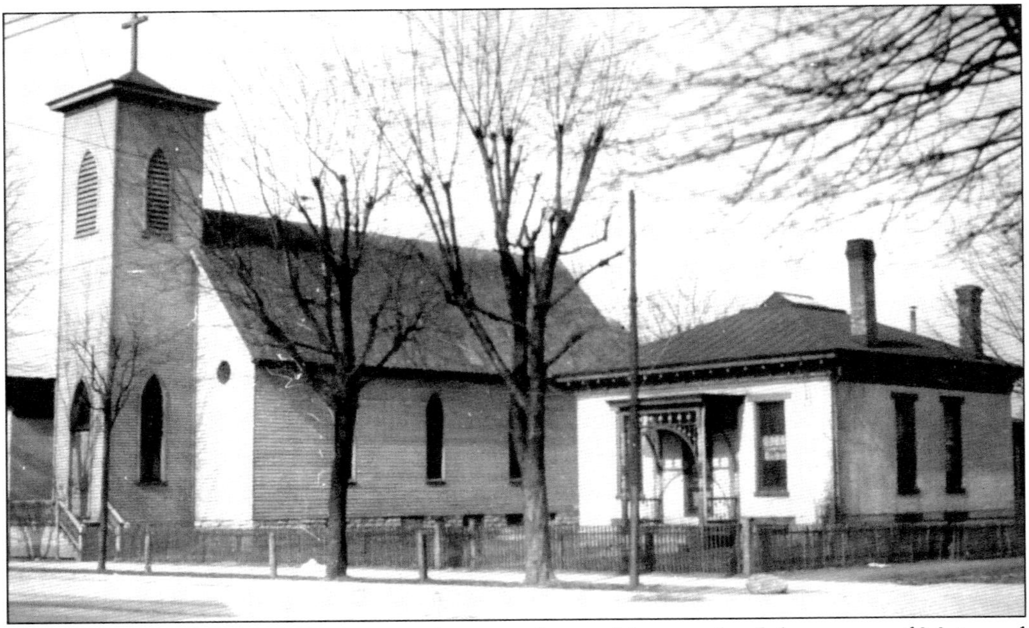

THE VILLAGE'S ORIGINAL CATHOLIC CHURCH. It stood just south of the corner of Main and First Streets. The building on the corner was the home of Edward Rossman, who owned a blacksmith shop on River Street, to the rear of the property. In 1913, the new brick St. Mary Church was built on the site of the Rossman home and the church's parsonage was constructed on the site of the earlier original wooden church. (Courtesy of Harriet Foley.)

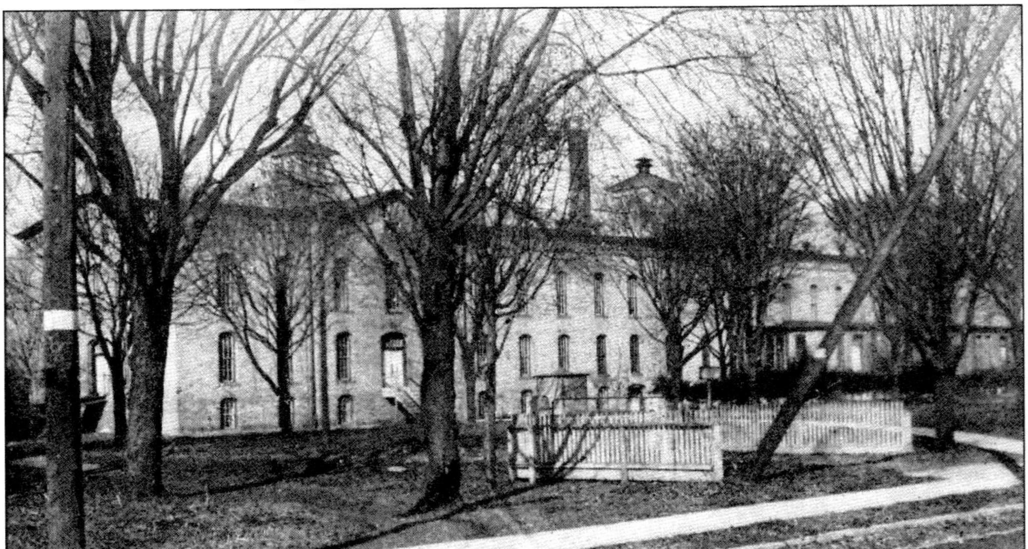

THE HARDING PAPER COMPANY BUILDINGS. These buildings were constructed in 1879, to replace the 1873 structures lost to fire. The company was known for the fine quality of writing paper it produced. In 1899, the business was purchased by the American Writing Paper Company. When that company failed in 1923, it was acquired by the Howard Maxwell Company, subsequently operating under the Howard or Maxwell names until 1976, when it was acquired by the Georgia-Pacific Company.

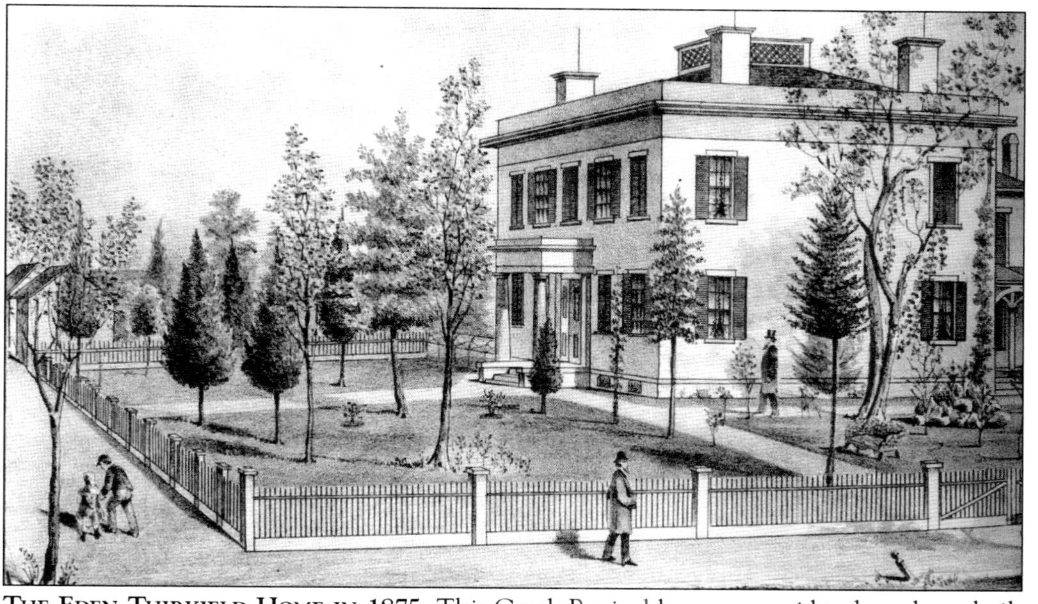

THE EDEN THIRKIELD HOME IN 1875. This Greek Revival house was said to have been built in 1848 for a riverboat captain, Henry C. Storms, who was so bedeviled by the children in the Old Central School, behind his house, that he sold to Thirkield, co-owner of the Main Street department store. After Thirkield's death, a two-story south wing was added, the porch was extended, and the house was shared by two of his children and their families.

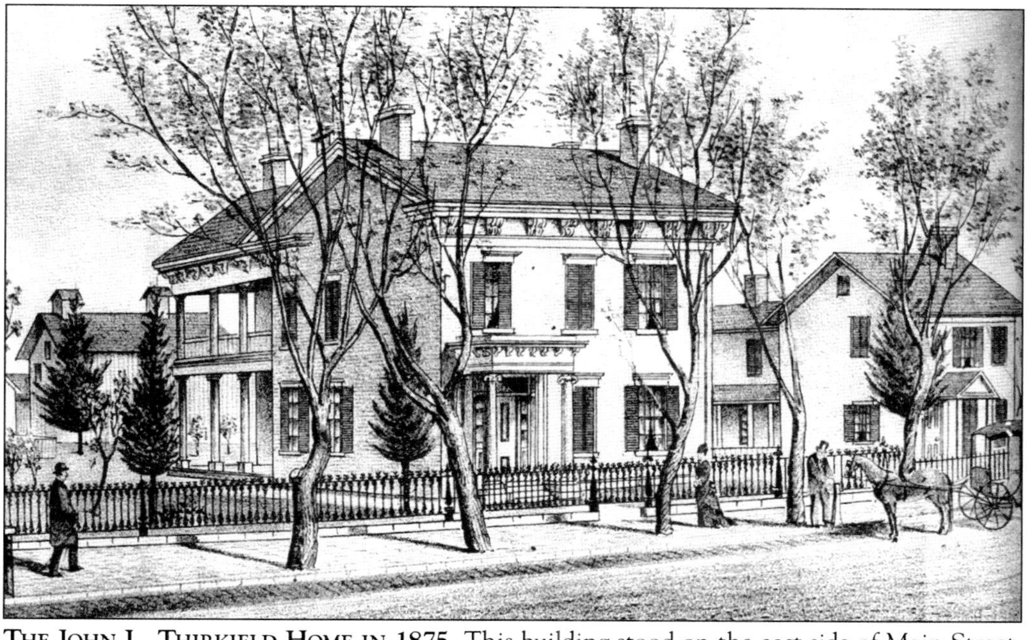

THE JOHN L. THIRKIELD HOME IN 1875. This building stood on the east side of Main Street, just south of the Odd Fellows building. Thirkield established his department store on Main Street in 1832. Around 1905 the building became the village's telephone exchange, housing the system's female telephone operators. In response to the need for more downtown parking, the building was demolished in 1955.

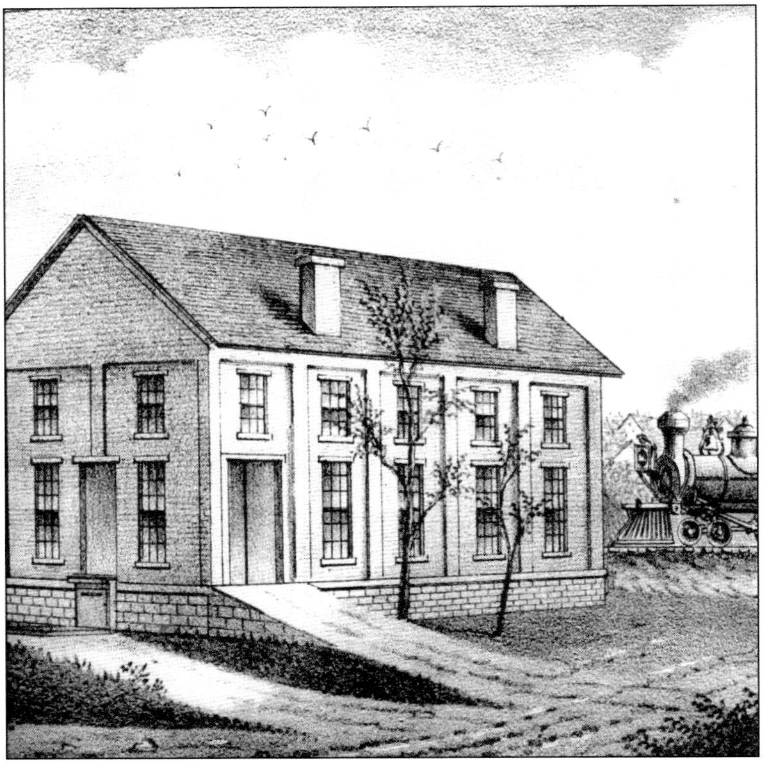

The Antrim Tobacco Warehouse in 1875. This large building stood on the west side of Anderson Street, one-half block south of Fourth Street, and was the home of Franklin's Christian Church until the congregation moved into its new church on South Main Street in 1872. The old church/warehouse stood until 2000, when it was demolished to expand vehicle access to the new Franklin Public Library.

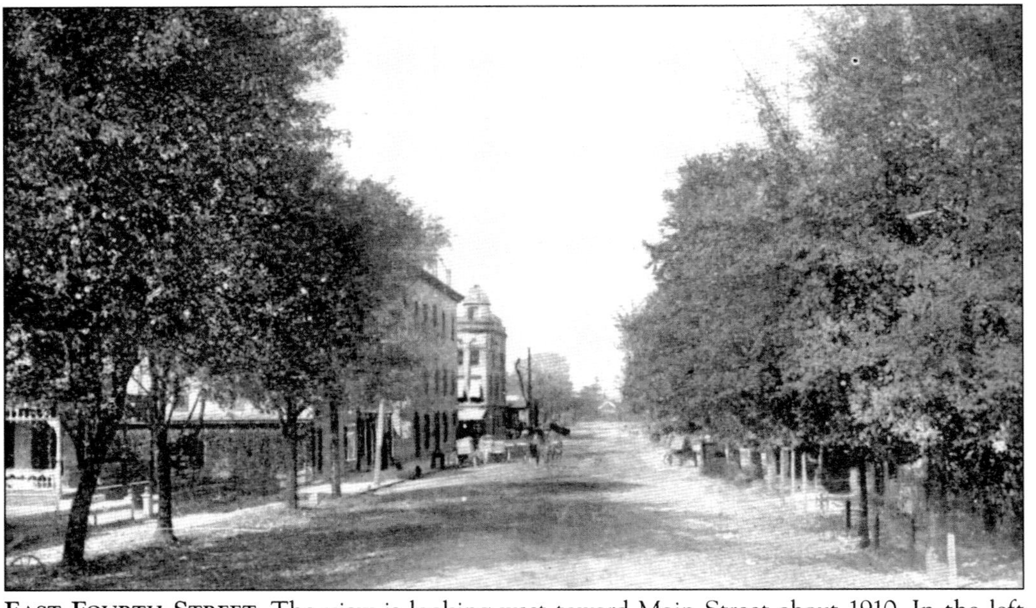

East Fourth Street. The view is looking west toward Main Street about 1910. In the left distance are the Odd Fellows building, and across Main, the domed and towered Hamilton Building. Notice the horse-drawn wagons, hitching posts, and beautiful trees shading both the street and sidewalk. At left is the gingerbread porch of a Queen Anne–style home that still stands at 25 East Fourth Street.

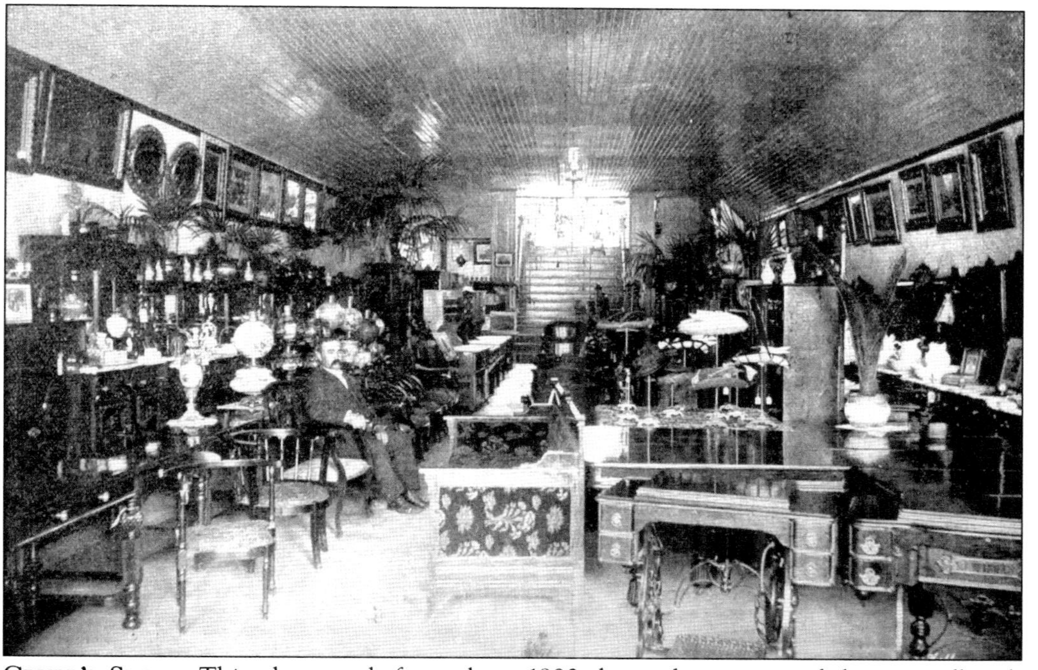

Grubb's Store. This photograph from about 1900 shows the interior of this secondhand-furniture business that was located on the east side of Main, between Fifth and Sixth Streets. Charles Grubb, the owner, is seen in the chair amongst his wares that today might be valuable antiques. Grubb lived conveniently around the corner at 26 East Fifth Street. His home still stands, but the building that contained the store is hidden by a modern façade.

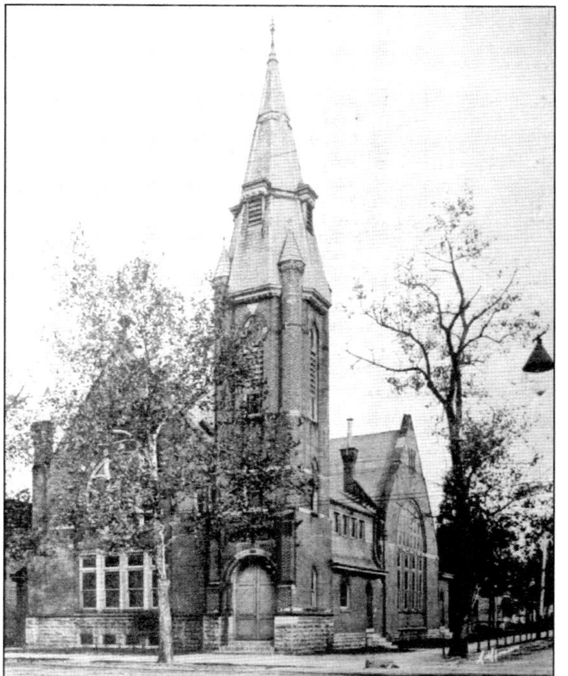

The First Presbyterian Church. This view of the brick Gothic-style structure, seen from the southwest, shows the church as it appeared about 1900. Constructed around 1885, it was so scarred by a 1919 fire that a well-meaning parishioner paid for the church to be coated with stucco and painted to improve its appearance. At the beginning of the 20th century, the church was led by energetic clergyman and orator Rev. Calvin Dill Wilson.

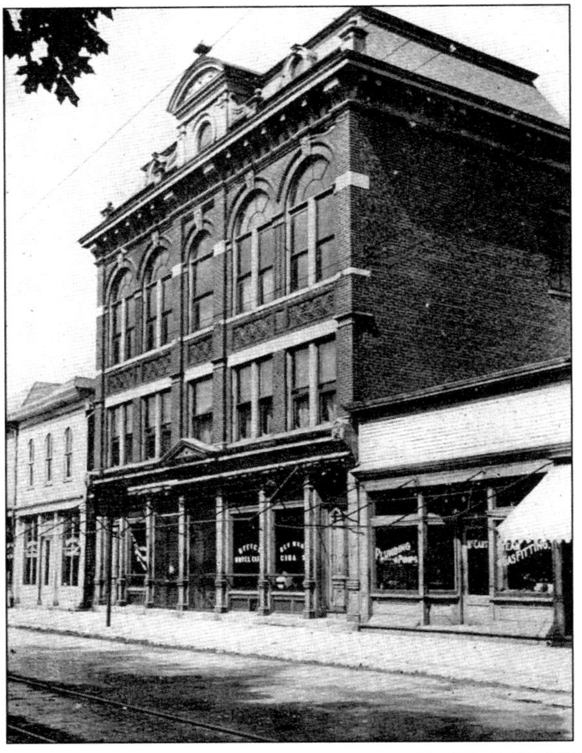

THE ELITE HOTEL. This Second Empire–style building still dominates the downtown from its post at today's 219–223 South Main Street. The fanciest of the village's early hotels, it was built for Margaret Hans Weber in 1886. She was the widow of a successful barber and billiard-hall keeper, Philip Weber, who had operated similar businesses in a small wooden structure on the same site. The hotel contained 20 guest rooms upstairs, and a bar, restaurant, and cigar store downstairs.

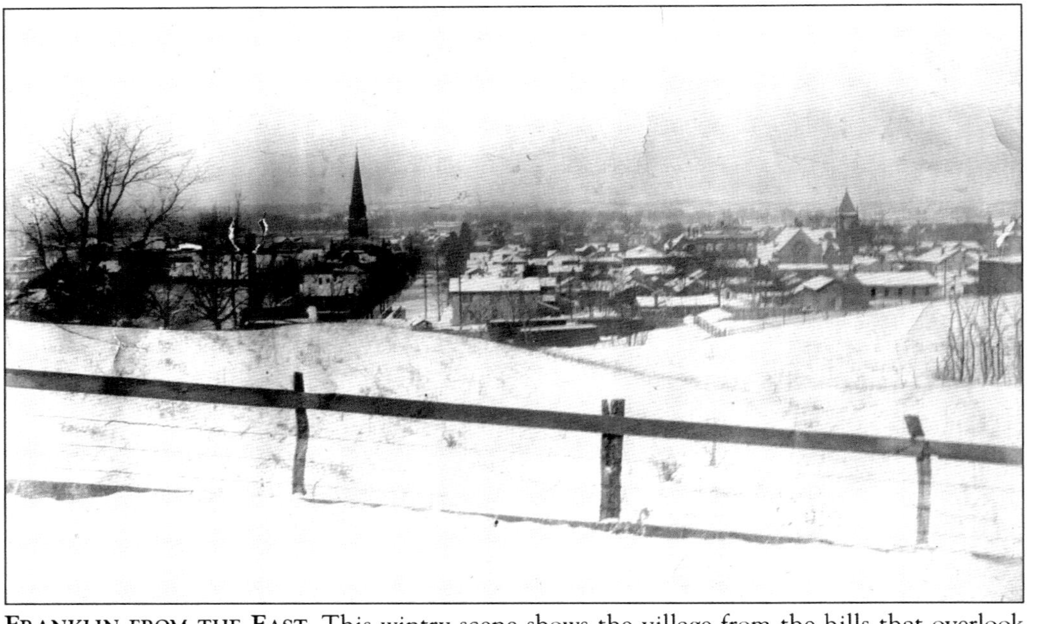

FRANKLIN FROM THE EAST. This wintry scene shows the village from the hills that overlook it. Third Street is in the center of the image, coming directly at the camera. The spires of the Methodist Church (at Third and Main) and the First Baptist Church (on Second) are clearly visible in the middle distance. Just over the brow of the ridge in the foreground is seen the Miami-Erie Canal, lined with industrial buildings.

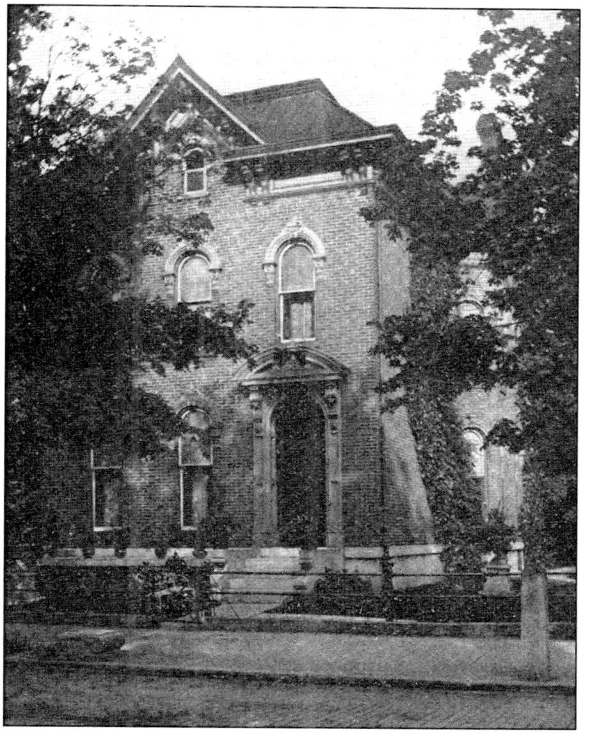

The Dr. Otho Evans Jr. House. This Italianate brick residence was built on the southeast corner of Third and Main Streets in 1870 for Dr. Evans, one of six members of the family, over three generations, to practice medicine. After Otho Evans died in 1902, his nephew Dr. Rice Evans is believed to have lived here for a short time before it became the property of William F. Schenck. Like most other Main Street homes, this one eventually became a business. In 1973, it was demolished.

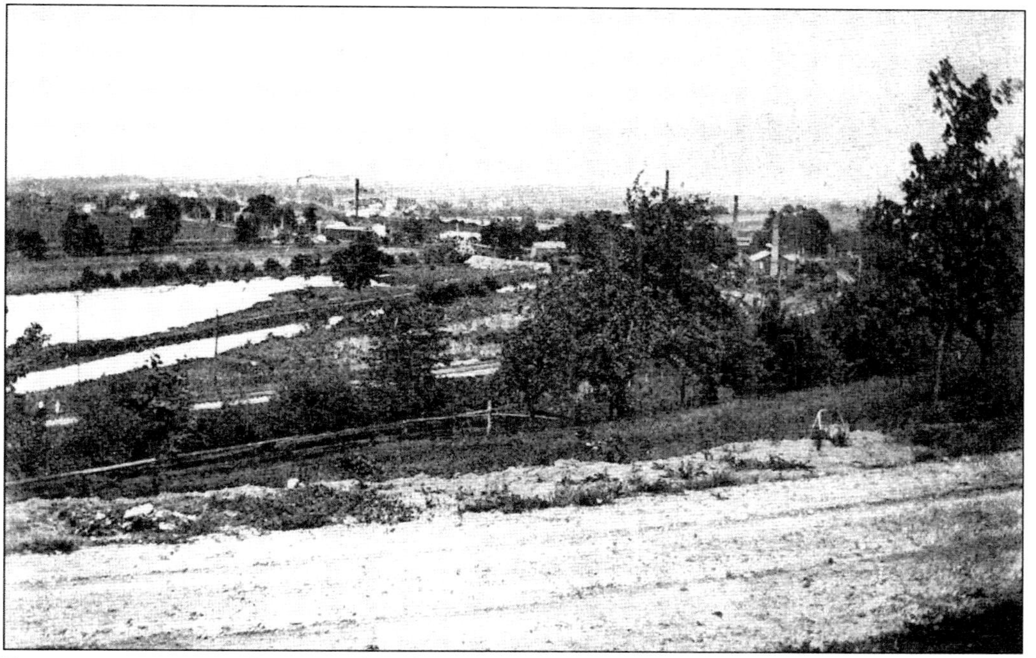

Franklin from the South. This photograph, taken from Woodhill Cemetery, appeared in a 1907 calendar and shows the many industrial smokestacks that dominated the skyline of the southern end of the village. At left is the Great Miami River, with the Miami-Erie Canal just this side of it.

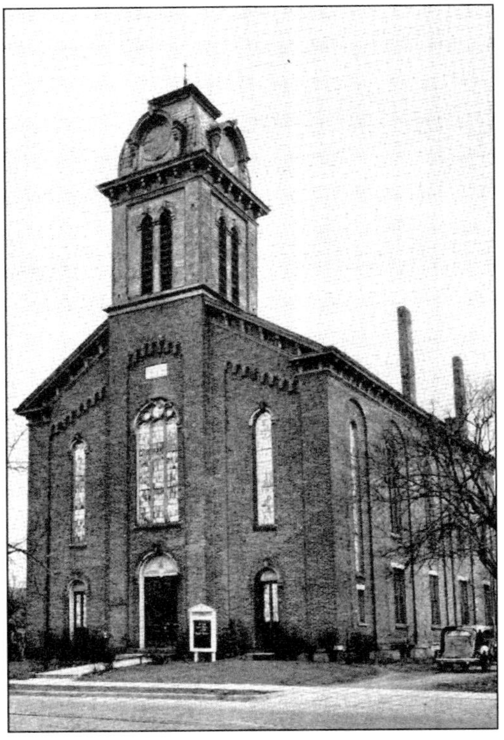

The First United Church of Christ. This impressive structure at 632 South Main Street was constructed in 1872. It was the third home to a congregation that was amongst the longest-enduring in the community, having originally worshipped at Union Church on Main Street. Prior to the construction of this building, the congregation gathered for services at another structure, located at 417 Anderson Street, which later became a warehouse.

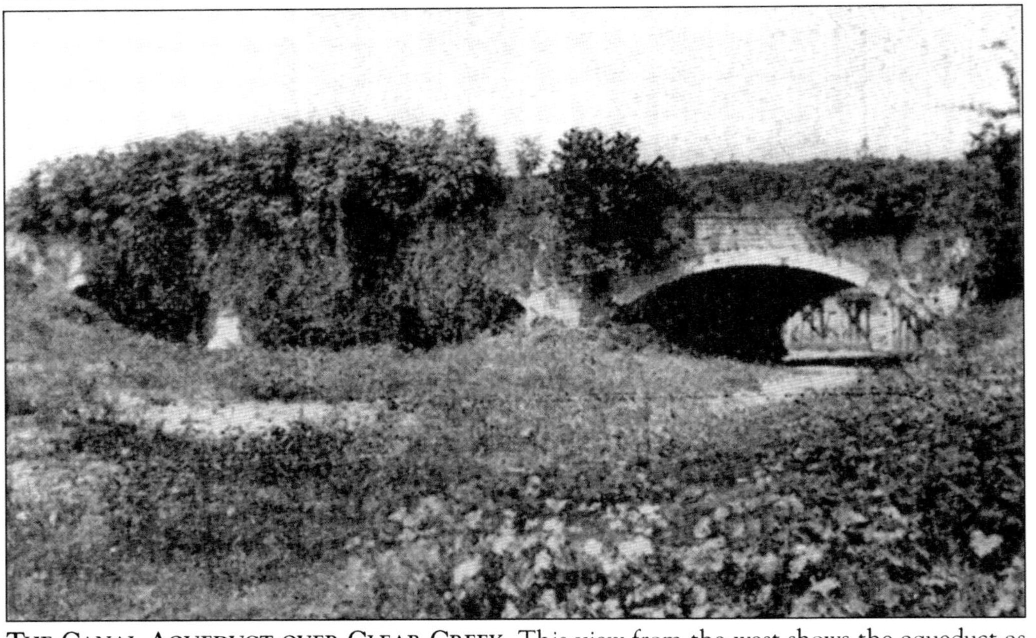

The Canal Aqueduct over Clear Creek. This view from the west shows the aqueduct as it appeared about 1900. The massive three-arched stone structure was completed by 1829 to carry the water of the Miami-Erie Canal over the creek below. In the early 1930s, the canal bed was filled in, becoming first Canal Street, then renamed as Riley Boulevard. The aqueduct was removed in 1948.

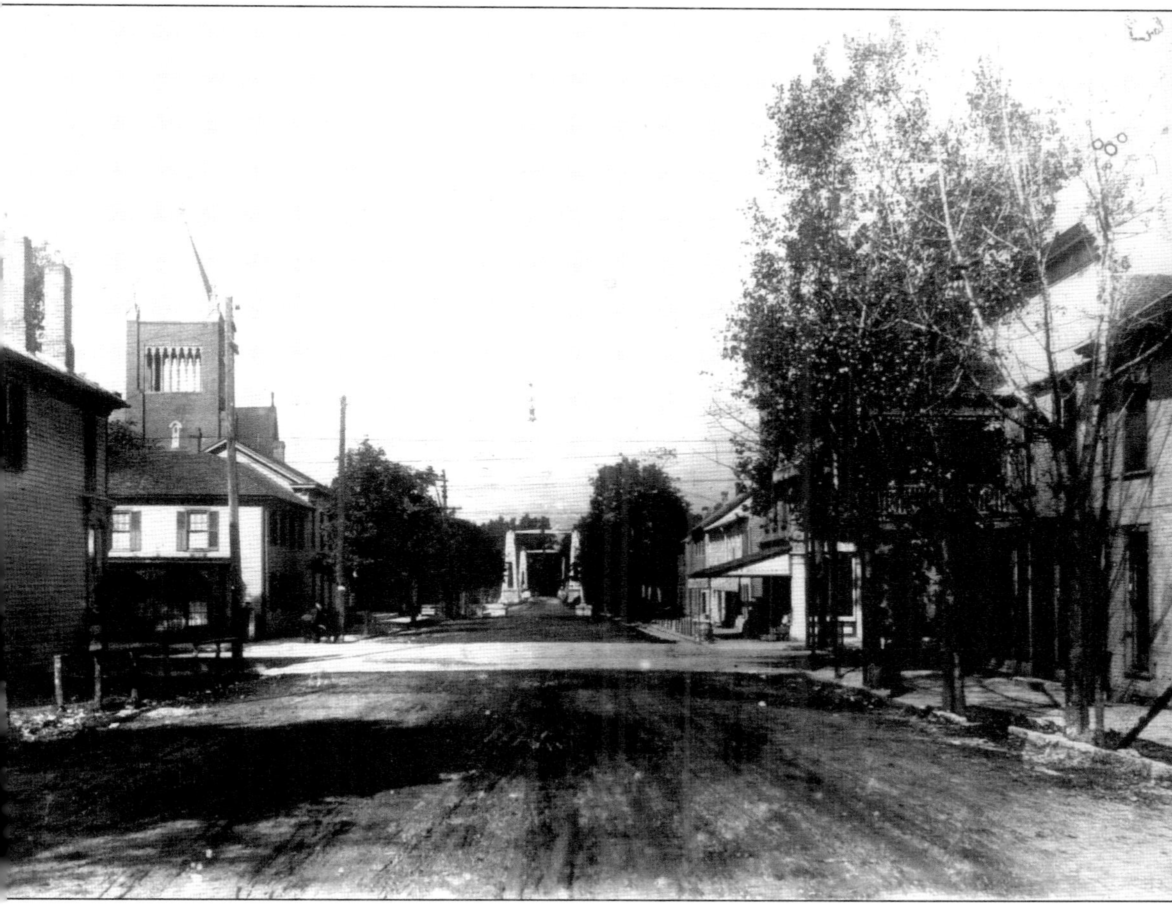

SECOND STREET, LOOKING WEST. Seen here is a view of Second Street, through the intersection with Main Street, looking toward the Suspension Bridge. The overhead cables that powered the traction cars are seen hanging over Main Street. On the southwest corner can be seen the wooden house that, over the years, belonged to Washington Schenck, the Webers, and the Governeys. Behind this home is the steeple of the First Baptist Church. Across Second Street, on the northwest corner, stands the Rossman Grocery building. To Rossman's right, running west along the north side of Second, stand several houses fronted with trees. These were removed from the 1930s to 1950s. On the northeast corner of the intersection stood Unglesby's Corner. The building at this corner contained first a furniture and cabinet business, then a funeral home, and later, a tavern. Across from it on Second Street, on the southeast corner of the intersection, stood a grocery store. In 1999, the buildings at right were destroyed to build a chain drugstore, and in 2000 the building at left was razed to allow for the expansion of a gasoline station.

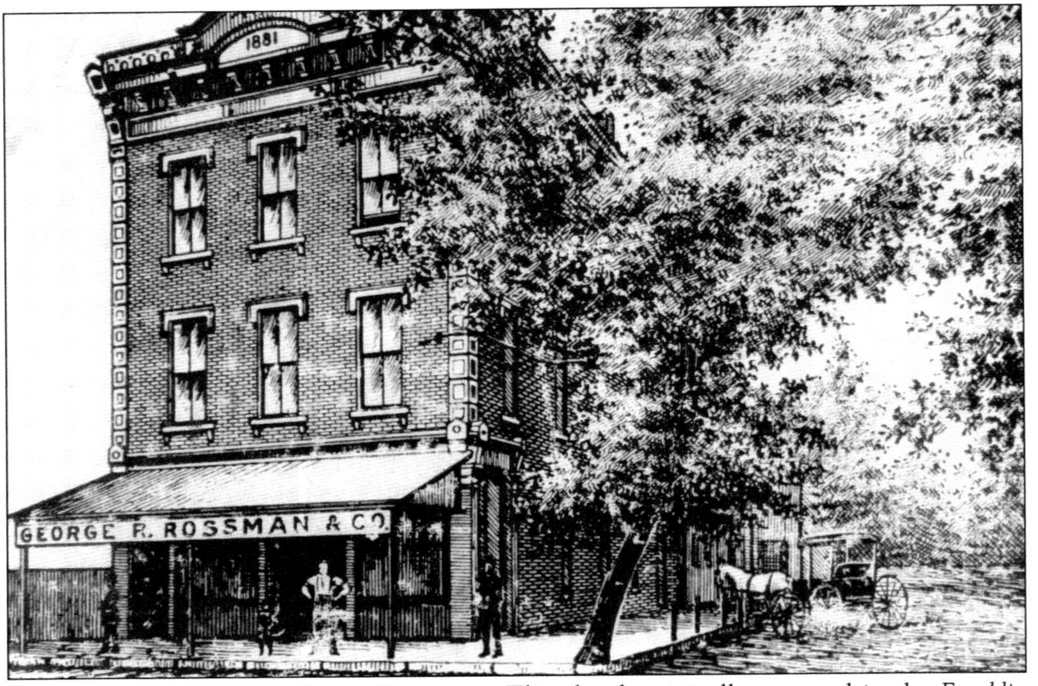

The Rossman Grocery Store Building. This sketch originally appeared in the *Franklin Chronicle* about 1890. This Italianate structure was constructed by George Rossman in 1881 as the replacement for an earlier grocery established by his father, James. Formerly on the site of this building stood the log cabin built about 1796 for the Campbell family, in which Lewis D. Campbell, a member of the House of Representatives in the 1850s, was born in 1811.

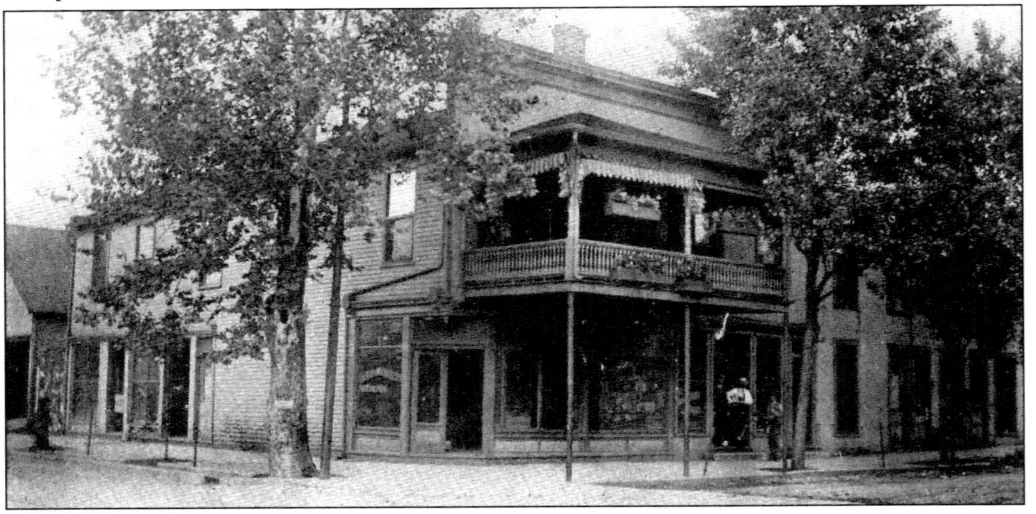

Unglesby's Corner. This photograph shows the northeast corner of Main and Second Streets. It was here, in 1865, that Edward Crist established a furniture and cabinet business, which quickly included the lucrative and more dependable line of coffins and undertaking. In 1897, the business was sold to Wilson Unglesby, whose undertaking business operated at the corner until 1913, when it relocated to Main Street. Later this building contained a popular and somewhat shady tavern, the Amber Lantern.

THE FIRST BAPTIST CHURCH. This magnificent Romanesque Gothic–style church was built about 1890 on a plot purchased by Main Street banker and resident David Adams. The church was one of several dominating public and private structures constructed by William Roof. In 1965, the church burned down and was replaced by one of a thoroughly modern design in 1969.

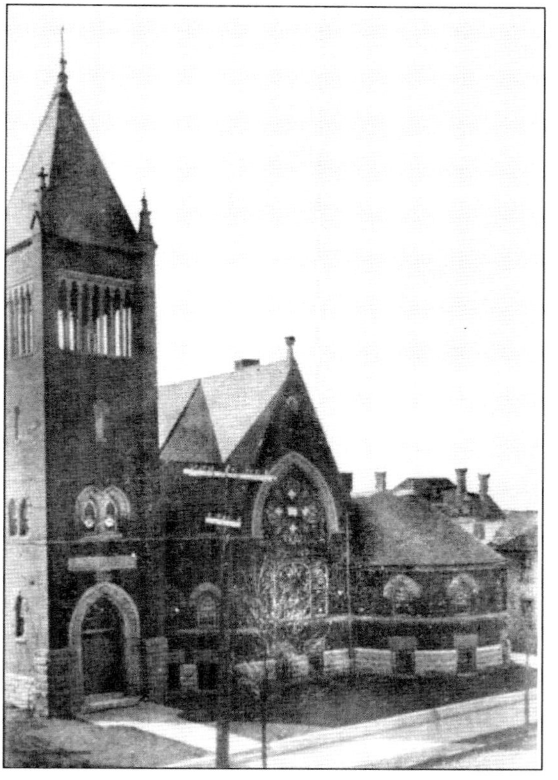

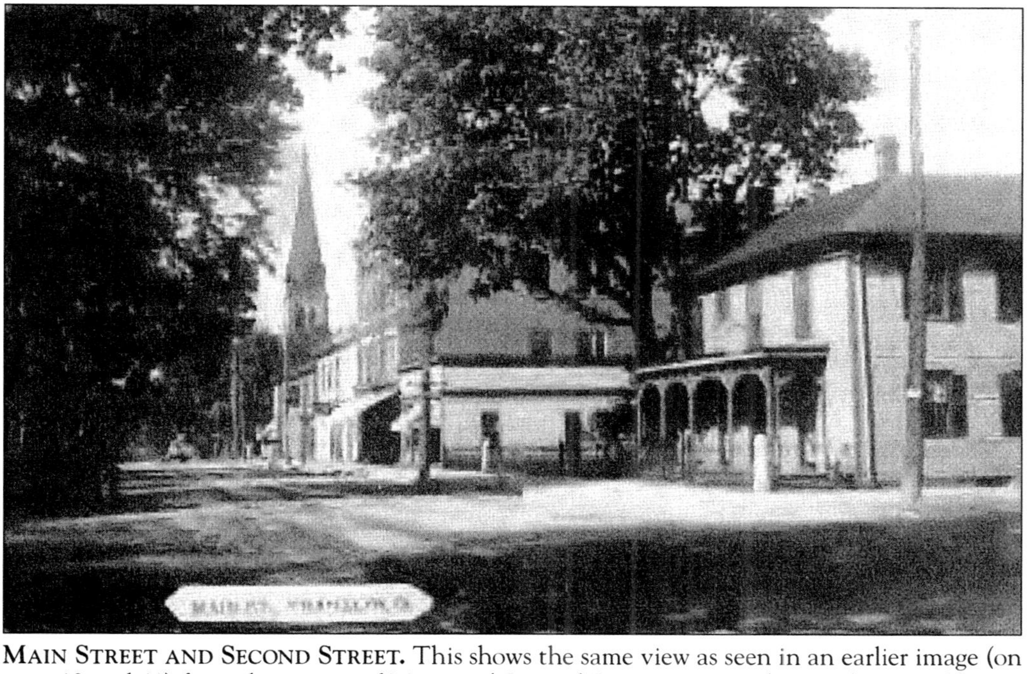

MAIN STREET AND SECOND STREET. This shows the same view as seen in an earlier image (on page 10 and 11) from the corner of Main and Second Streets, except that in this one the tree which dominates both photographs is in full leaf. (Courtesy of Liz Buchanan.)

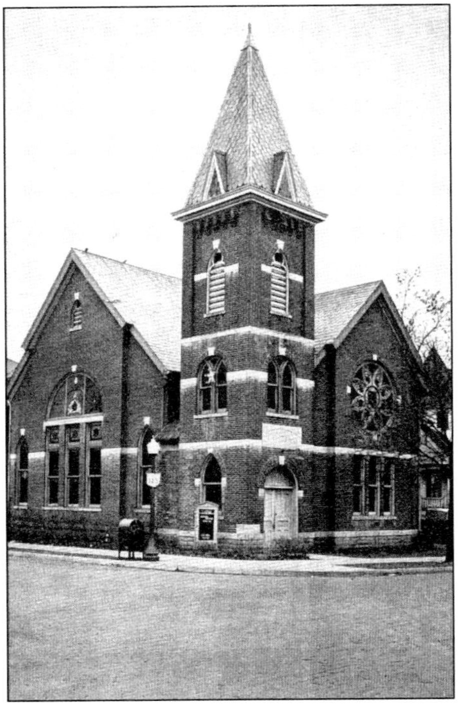

ST. PAUL LUTHERAN CHURCH. This small Gothic Revival–style church stood at the southeast corner of River and Second Streets and was constructed there in 1893. From 1877 onward, the site had been occupied by the Lewis Eisenminger shop, where farm machinery and other apparatus were repaired. In 1961, the congregation moved to 500 East Second Street, sold this site, and the church was razed to make room for a service station.

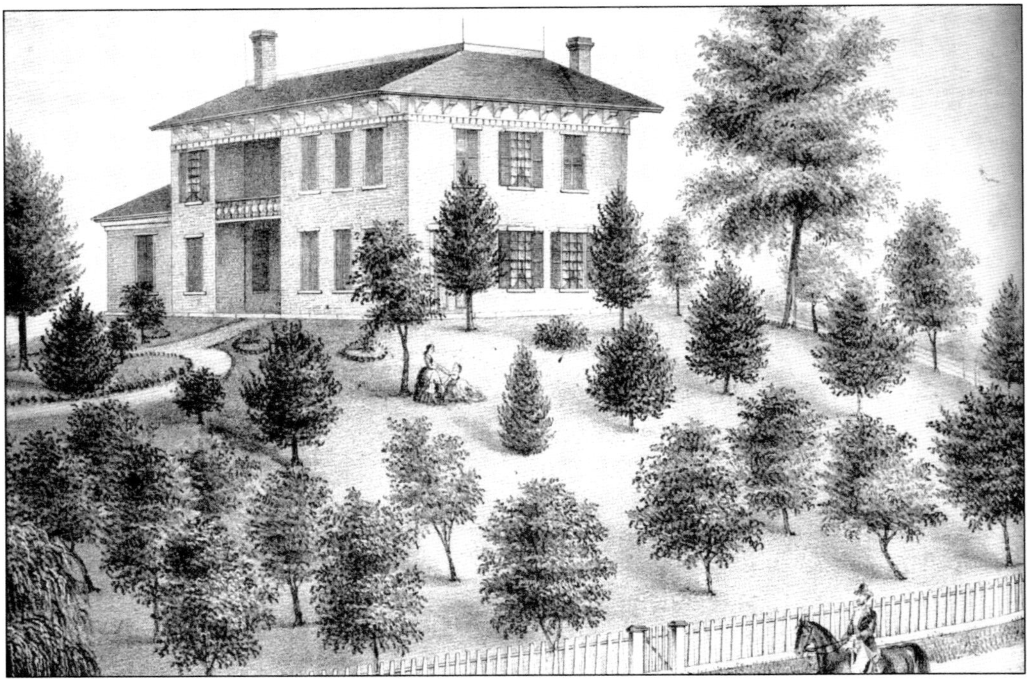

THE FRANKLIN ACADEMY IN 1875. Standing on the hill that overlooks the village, the academy was built in the 1840s to house a private, coeducational institution. The building later became the home of a retired blacksmith named George L. Denise, who lived there from 1859 to the 1880s. In 1945, the building became the Eaton Funeral Home.

Two

HOME AND NEIGHBORHOOD

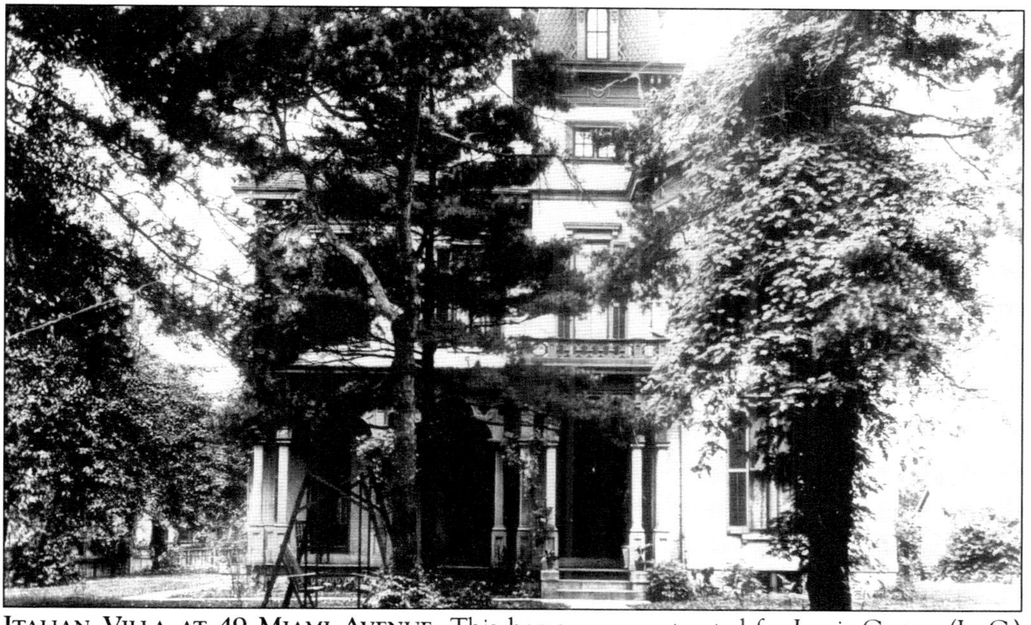

ITALIAN VILLA AT 49 MIAMI AVENUE. This home was constructed for Lewis Gaston (L. G.) Anderson in the 1860s as the centerpiece of his 156-acre farm that covered most of what is today's Mackinaw Historic District. Because of the leaves on the ground, the photograph would appear to have been taken in the autumn. The white picket fence that surrounded the entire front yard is visible at left. In pleasant weather, the home's residents could spend relaxing hours on the swing in the foreground. The house still stands, but much of its original outdoor decorative detail—including the porches, brackets under the eaves, and mansard roof on its tower—were removed between the 1920s and the 1940s. Though the evergreens seen in the foreground are long dead, many other original trees still stand, probably by now almost 150 years old.

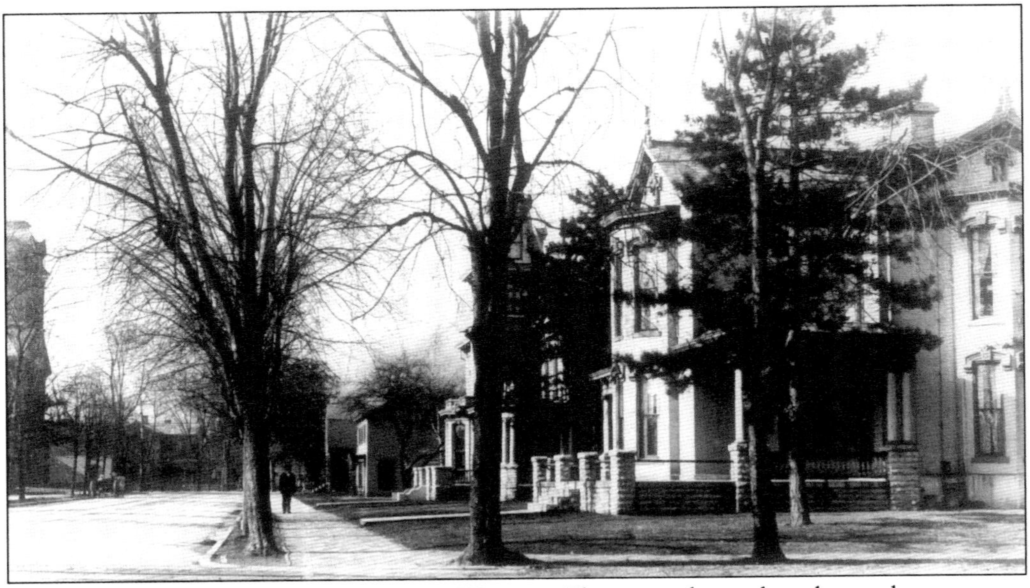

THE GALLAHER AND JACKSON HOMES IN WINTER. These were located on the southwest corner of Main and Sixth Streets and were both built in 1875. At the time of this photograph, in the early 20th century, the Italianate townhouse in the foreground was owned by C. S. Jackson. The Second Empire house to its right was owned by J. J. Gallaher, an independently wealthy music professor. The tall building at left is the First United Church of Christ.

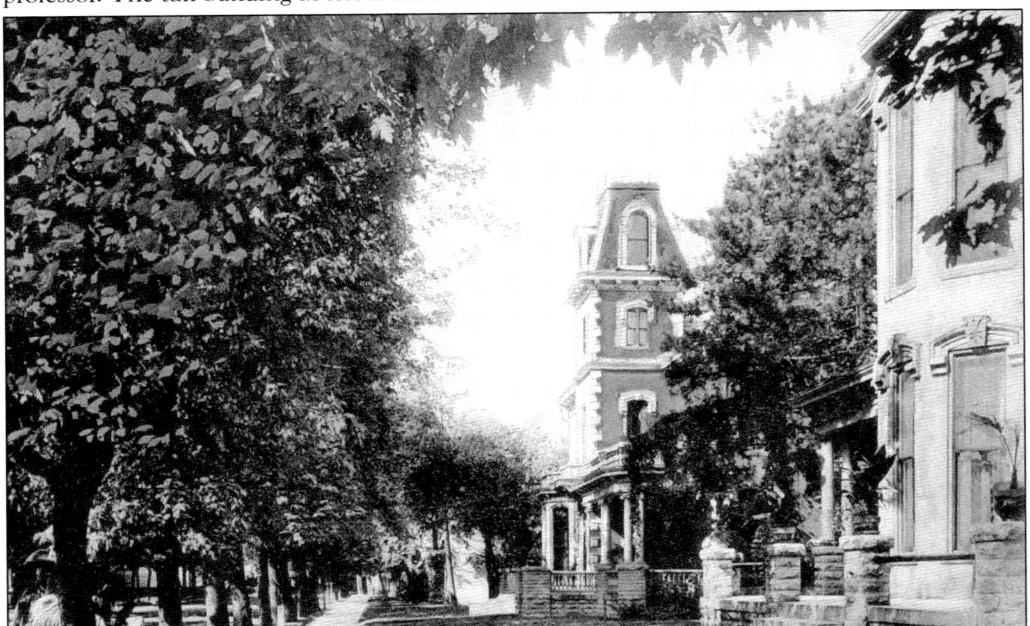

THE GALLAHER AND JACKSON HOMES IN SUMMER. This postcard gives the viewer an idea of how beautiful South Main Street was with its trees, some of them American chestnuts, in full leaf. Unfortunately tastes changed and both beautiful structures were swept away in 1964 to make room for a drive-in restaurant. (Courtesy of William and Paula Moses.)

THE DEARDOFF-GALLAHER HOUSE. This fine residence was built just south of the intersection of Main and Sixth Streets about 1875, by Frank Deardoff, a dry goods merchant. After its construction, the home was described in the local paper as "one of the most imposing and splendid mansions in the county. Its imposing tower commands a view of the beautiful Miami and rich valley." When Deardoff went bankrupt, the house was sold to J. J. Gallaher.

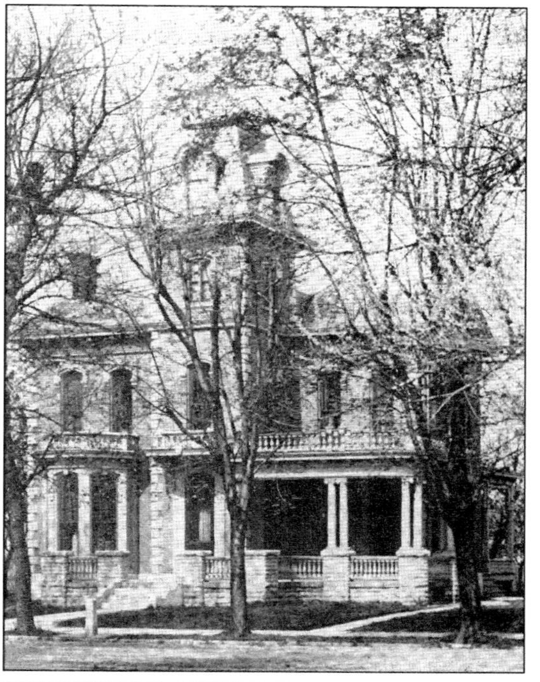

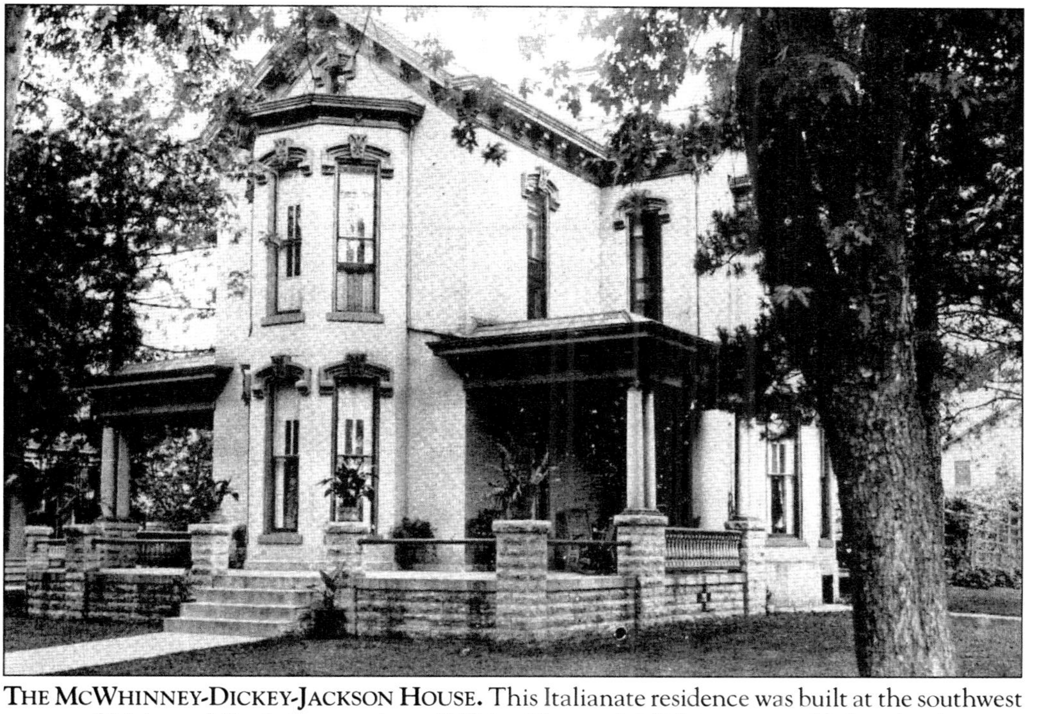

THE MCWHINNEY-DICKEY-JACKSON HOUSE. This Italianate residence was built at the southwest corner of Main and Sixth Streets about 1875 by Thomas McWhinney, a publisher, land owner, and leader of the Christian Church in the region. Within a few years, the home was sold to Mary Dickey, widow of a lumber mill owner. Later the house was owned by Charles S. Jackson, a former telegraph operator who became director of several manufacturing establishments.

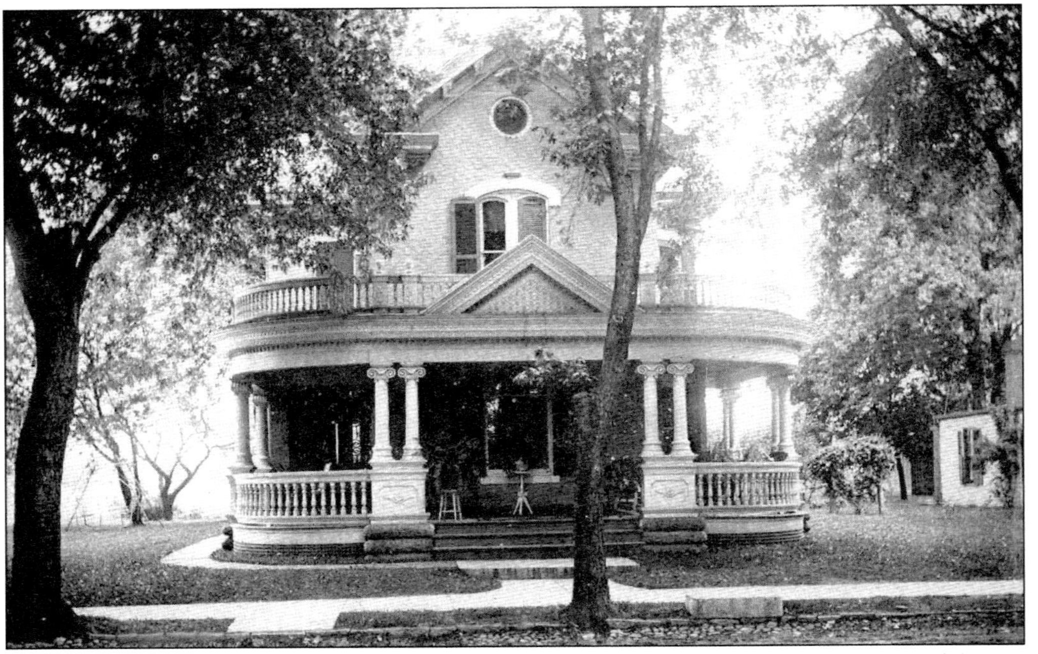

Italianate House at 742 South Main Street. This residence was built for retired farmer Daniel Brininger about 1873. After Brininger's death, the house went through two owners before being purchased by Howard Conover in 1900. Conover owned the hardware store on Main Street that bore his name. The house originally had a small verandah over its north doorway only. The unusual, heavily columned wraparound porch that appears in the photograph was added shortly before 1900.

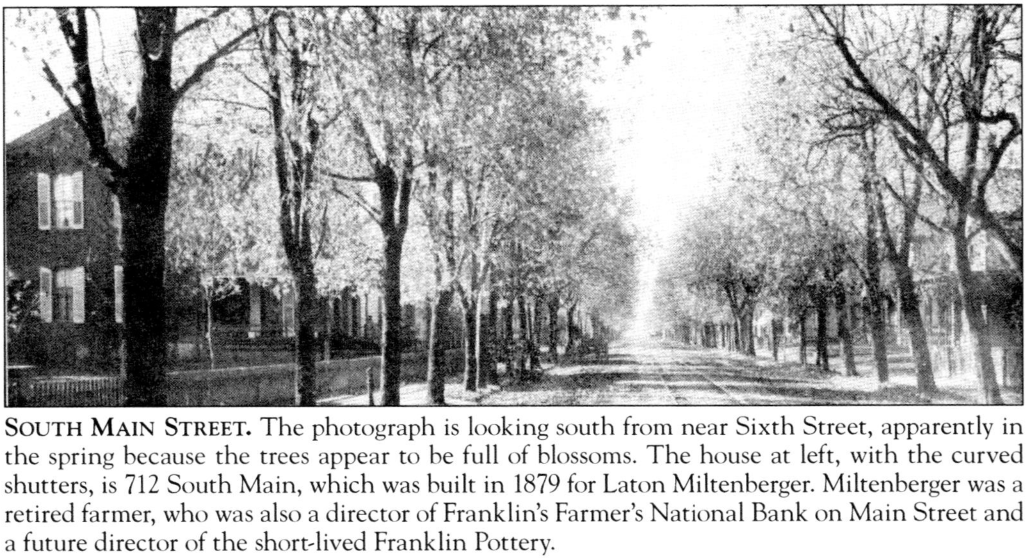

South Main Street. The photograph is looking south from near Sixth Street, apparently in the spring because the trees appear to be full of blossoms. The house at left, with the curved shutters, is 712 South Main, which was built in 1879 for Laton Miltenberger. Miltenberger was a retired farmer, who was also a director of Franklin's Farmer's National Bank on Main Street and a future director of the short-lived Franklin Pottery.

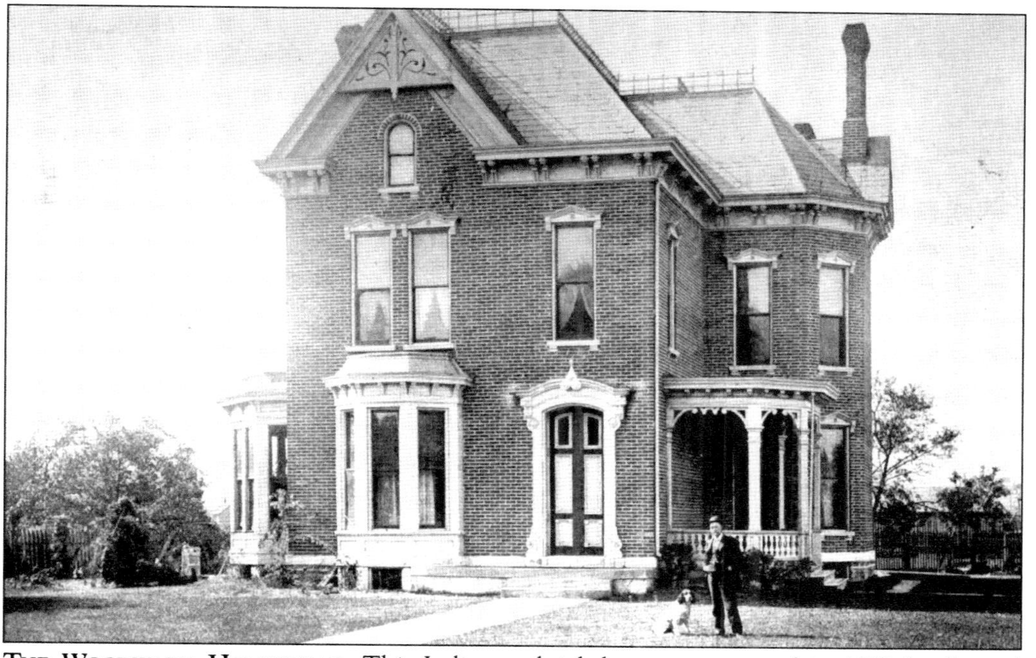

THE WOODWARD HOMESTEAD. This Italianate brick home was erected in 1882 for Samuel Beauchamp Woodward and his wife, Mary Campbell Woodward, at today's 150 East Sixth Street. After its construction, the local newspaper stated the Woodwards made a trip to Cincinnati to purchase furniture to fill it. The house was demolished in the 1950s and the site is now occupied by the Hampton Bennett School.

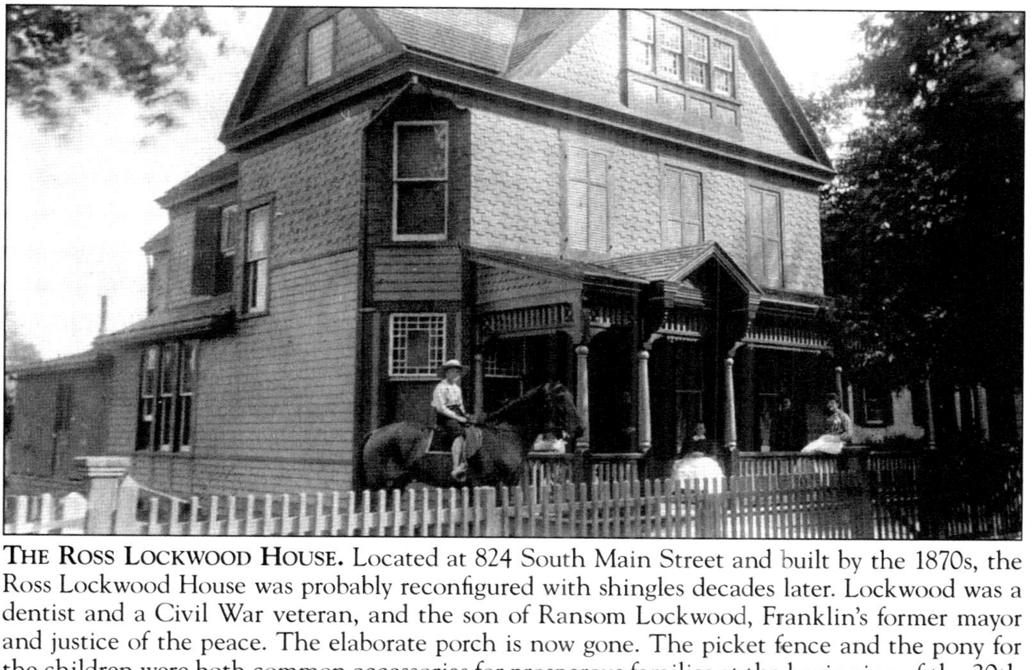

THE ROSS LOCKWOOD HOUSE. Located at 824 South Main Street and built by the 1870s, the Ross Lockwood House was probably reconfigured with shingles decades later. Lockwood was a dentist and a Civil War veteran, and the son of Ransom Lockwood, Franklin's former mayor and justice of the peace. The elaborate porch is now gone. The picket fence and the pony for the children were both common accessories for prosperous families at the beginning of the 20th century. (Courtesy of Dennie Fitzgerald.)

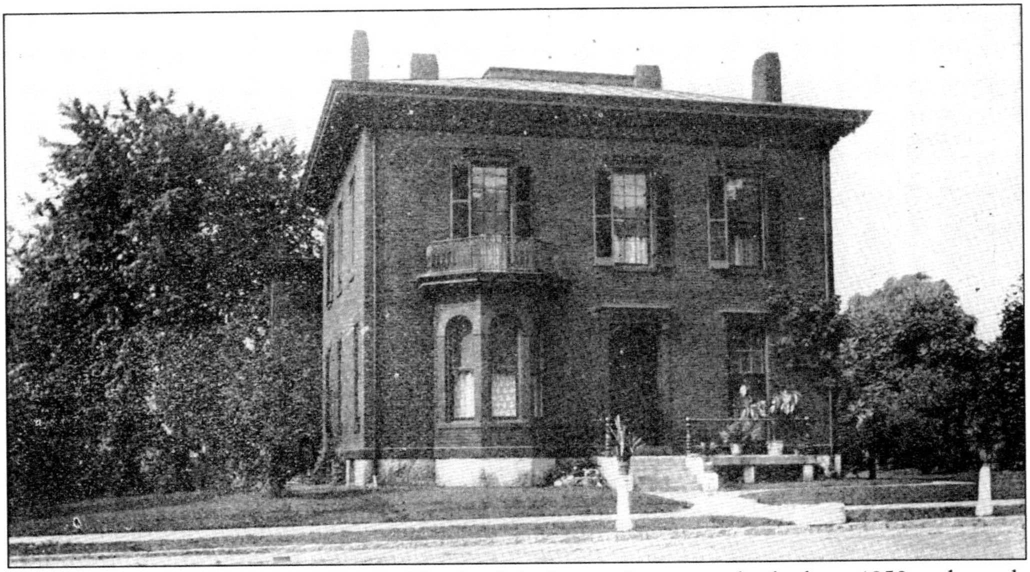

The Dr. William McAroy Home. This brick Italianate home was built about 1850 and stands on the south side of West Fourth Street, just west of Main Street. Dr. McAroy practiced for almost 40 years, much of it out of a small office building along the street west of the house. By the 1920s the house's appearance had been significantly altered by the addition of a wide Colonial-style porch and the structure's division into a duplex.

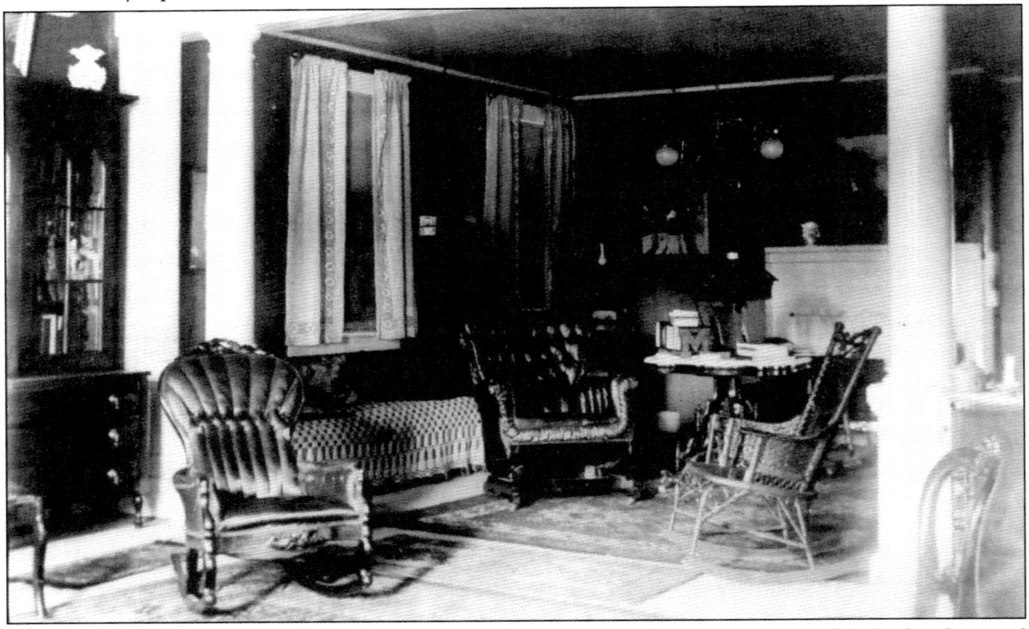

Interior of 25 West Third Street. At the time of the photograph, this Federal-period house was still owned by the Sherzer family. The first owner was Jacob Sherzer, who was a prospector during the California gold rush and a soldier in both the Mexican and Civil Wars. He owned a leather harness business on nearby Main Street. Two of Sherzer's children had the unusual distinction of earning doctoral degrees, at a time when this level of education was practically unknown.

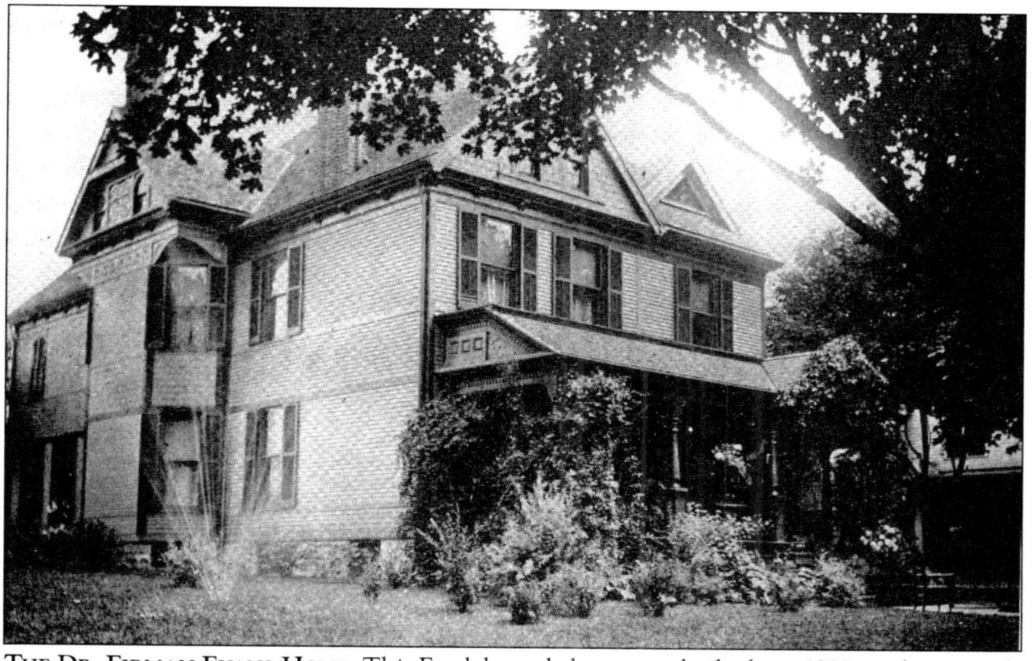

The Dr. Firman Evans Home. This Eastlake-style home was built about 1892 on the east side of River Street, between Second and Third Streets. One commentator, writing around 1940, remembered it as having the finest quality and variety of interior woodwork in the village. After Evans's death, it was the home and office of Dr. Jean Nock. In 1962, the house was demolished to create more parking for the nearby Baptist church.

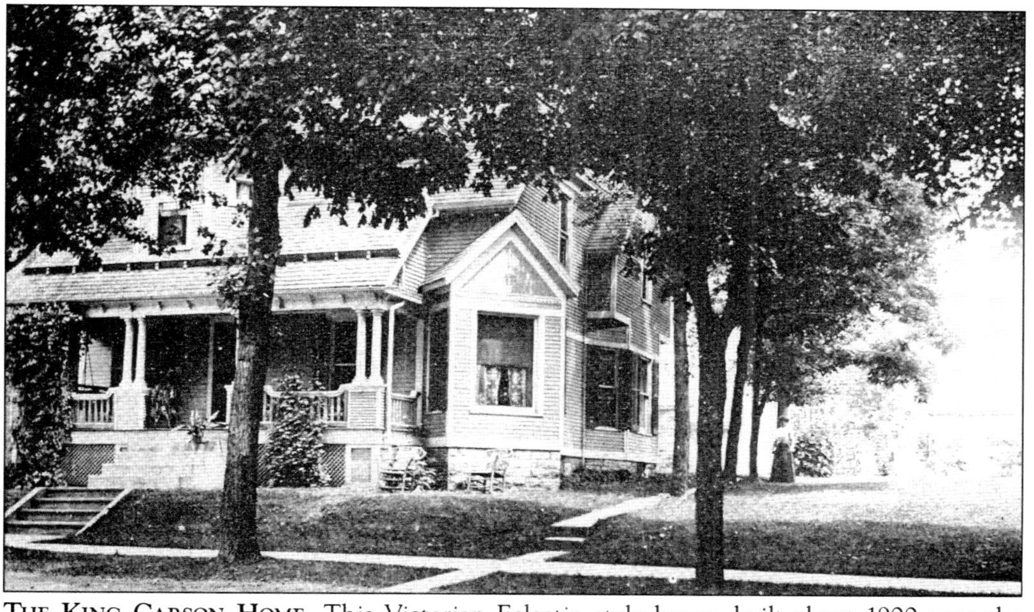

The King Carson Home. This Victorian Eclectic–style house, built about 1900 near the corner of River and Second Streets, retained its character until it was demolished around 2001 to make more room for church parking. King Carson was part owner of the legging (or spat) factory that stood a short distance away on Second Street.

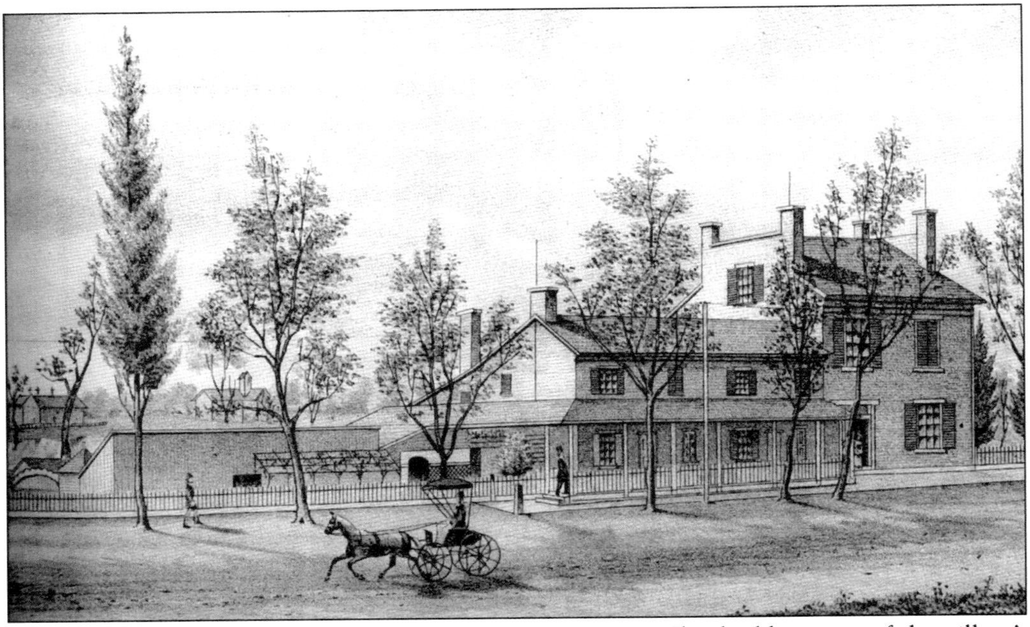

The John Noble Cumming (J. N. C.) Schenck House. This building, one of the village's first substantial residences, was constructed by 1812 and stood along the west side of River Street, half a block north of Second Street. In addition to the brick home with chimneys, there were several attached buildings and a gallery to a wharf that served flatboats traveling down the Miami River to the Ohio River to New Orleans. The old house was razed in 1972.

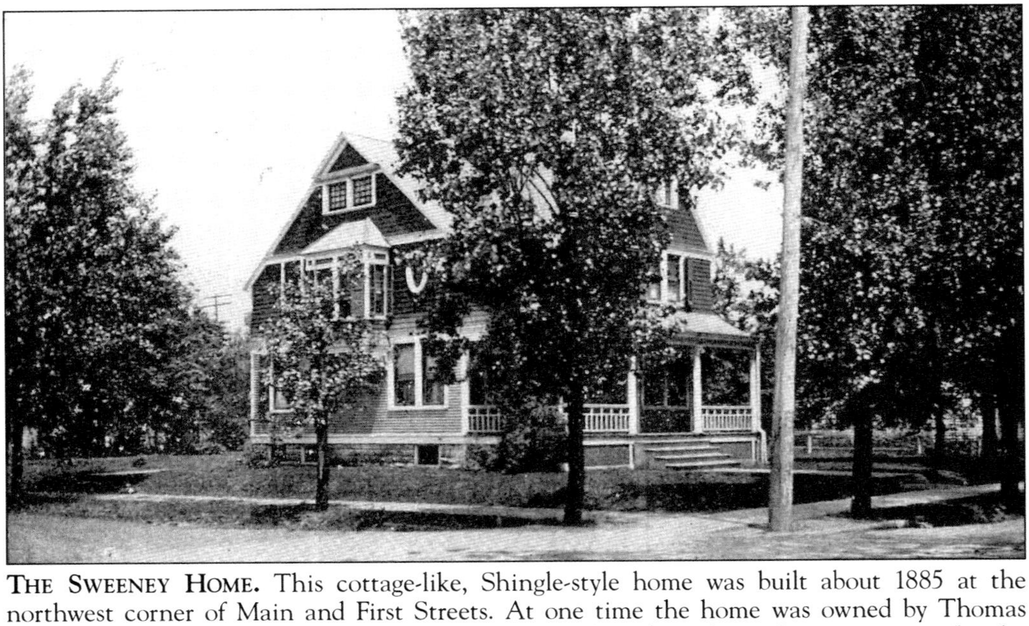

The Sweeney Home. This cottage-like, Shingle-style home was built about 1885 at the northwest corner of Main and First Streets. At one time the home was owned by Thomas Sweeney, the station agent for the Big Four Railroad, and Anthony Sweeney, agent for the Cincinnati Northern Railroad. Eventually the house was moved back on the lot to make room for a filling station and restaurant and was finally demolished to create parking for the church across the street.

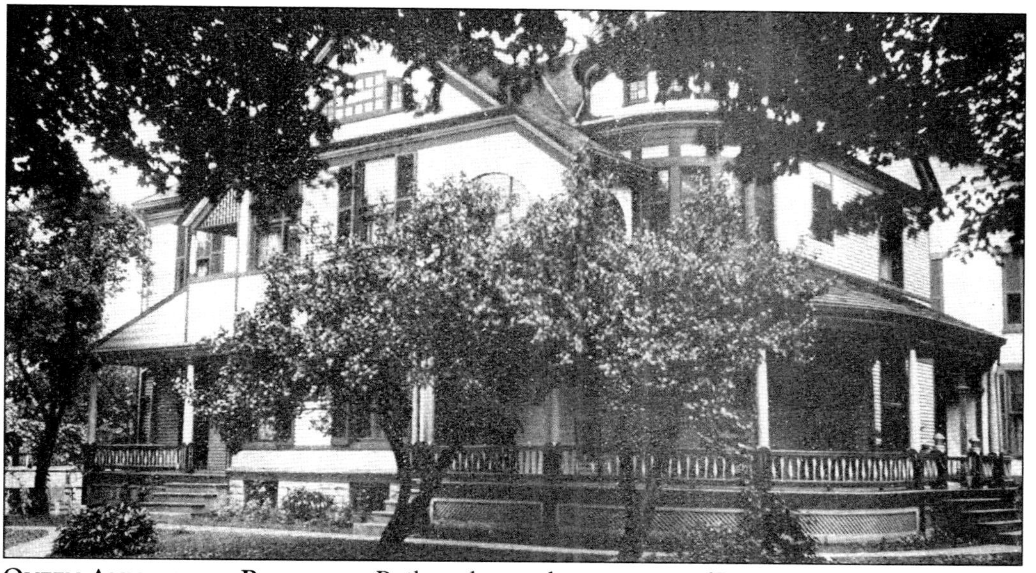

QUEEN ANNE–STYLE RESIDENCE. Built at the northwest corner of River and Jackson Streets for William A. S. Van Horne about 1885, this house was sold to the Edward Tracy family in 1908. Van Horne was an industrialist who led the construction of the hydraulic that took his name—a ditch that channeled water from the river to power nearby mills, including his own planing mill. Tracy and his descendants operated a grocery on Franklin's West Side until the 1950s.

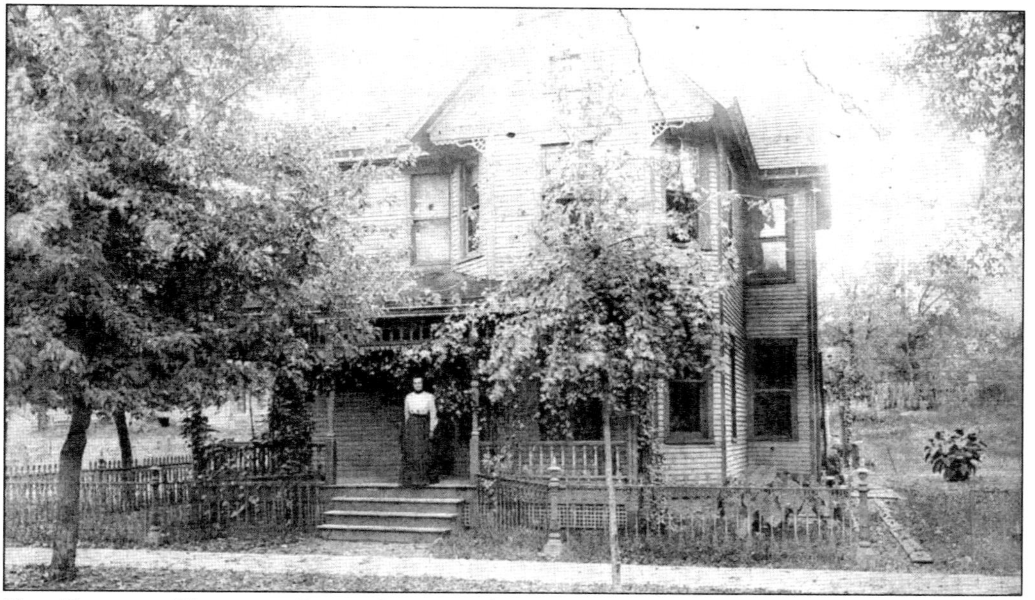

THE TRESSLER HOME ON RIVER STREET. This Queen Anne–style residence was built about 1895 for J. M. Tressler, a carpenter, and his wife, Phoebe, at the southeast corner of River and First Streets. In Phoebe's childhood home (next door to the south), lived her unmarried sister, Elizabeth Ireland, along with her other sister, Rachel, and Rachel's husband, Robert Boys, a baker. Phoebe's father, Richard Ireland, was a brickmaker who had served in the Civil War. (Courtesy of Richard Norvell.)

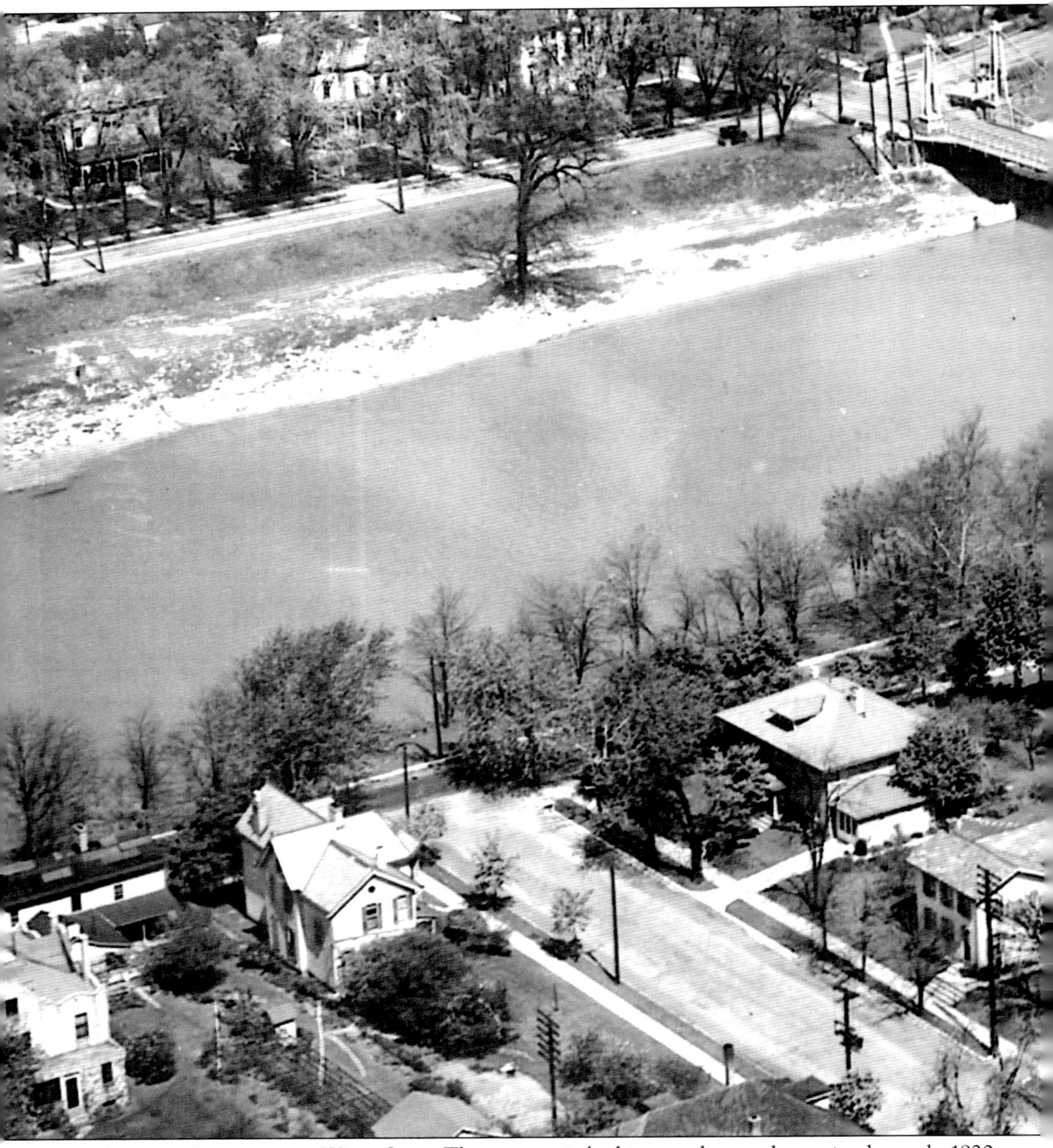

Aerial View of the West Side. The camera is looking to the northwest in the early 1920s. Miami Avenue runs north from the bridge along the west side of the river, and Oxford Road runs south. Park Avenue extends to the west from the western end of the bridge. On the west side of the river, the Croll House and farm appear at the upper right edge of the photograph. The tower of the Anderson home, at 49 Miami Avenue, is seen within the evergreens about a quarter mile to its south along Miami Avenue. The towered house at the upper left edge of the photograph is 321 Park Avenue. Diagonally to the lower left of this house is the Harding home at 302 Park Avenue. The many West Side residences visible along the river and on Park Avenue constitute the core

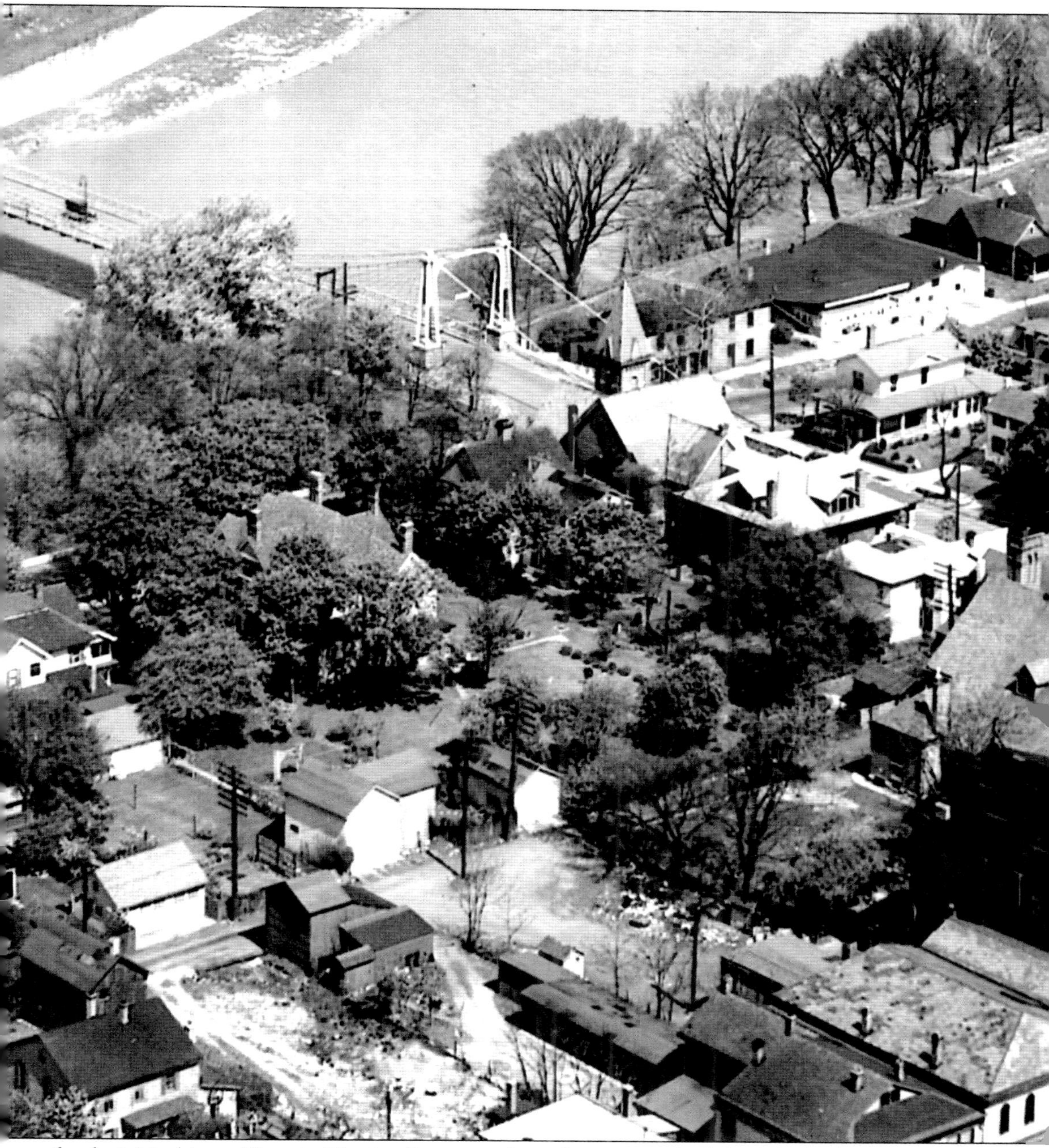

of today's Mackinaw Historic District. Running along the river to the left of the bridge are, from right to left, Nos. 205, 209, and 219 Oxford Road, which appear on later pages of this book. River Street runs along the east side of the river, and Third Street intersects River Street at the lower left. Second Street extends east from the eastern edge of the bridge. On the southeast corner of River and Second Streets is St. Paul Lutheran Church. On the southeast corner of River and Third Streets is the former Methodist parsonage, and to its south, Pat Gaynor's Alamo-shaped house. Along the north side of Third Street, the first house beyond the corner with River Street is 25 West Third Street, the home for two generations of the Sherzer family.

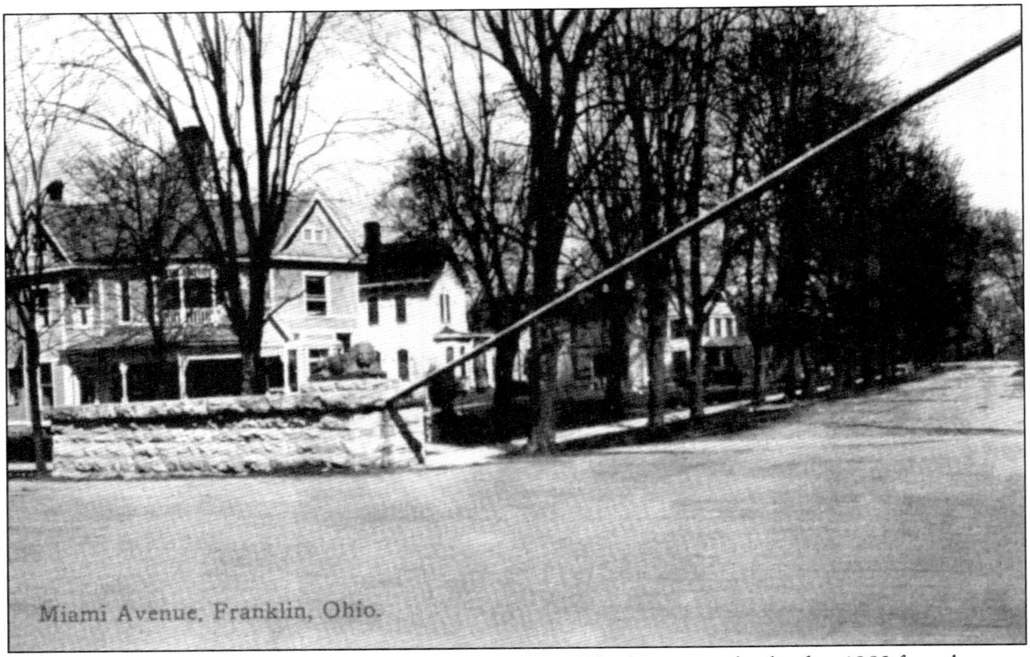

QUEEN ANNE–STYLE HOME AT 137 MIAMI AVENUE. The home was built after 1882 for salesman Charles B. Smith and his wife, Millie, who lived here with one servant until 1910. In that year the house was sold to Lewis Clifford Anderson, the manager of an electric utility company, paper company, and bank, who lived here until his death in 1936. Notice the anchorage of the suspension bridge in the foreground. (Courtesy of William Moses)

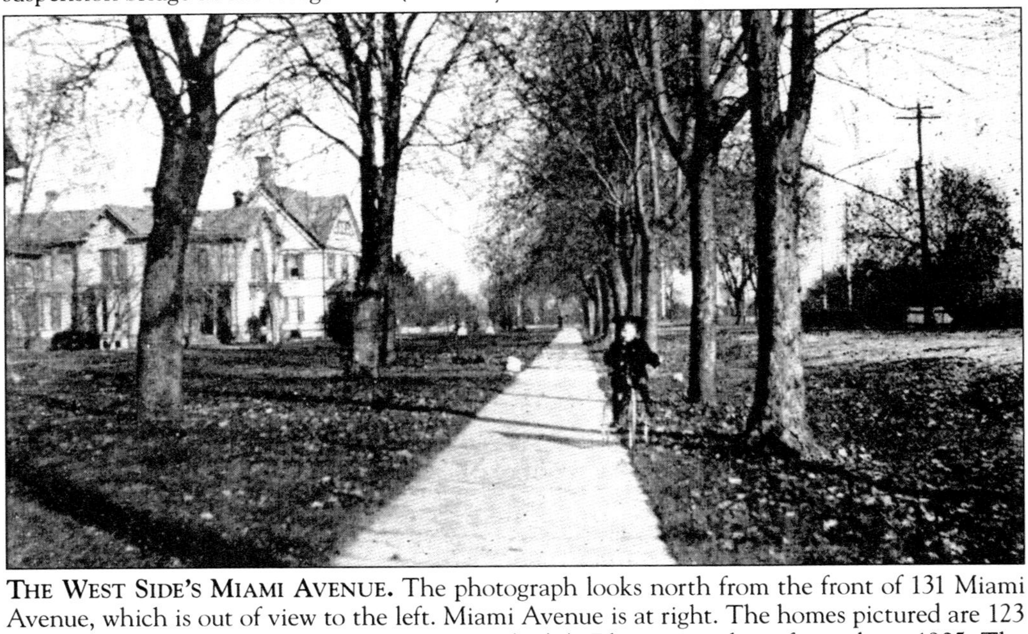

THE WEST SIDE'S MIAMI AVENUE. The photograph looks north from the front of 131 Miami Avenue, which is out of view to the left. Miami Avenue is at right. The homes pictured are 123 Miami Avenue (left) and 117 Miami Avenue (right). This image dates from about 1905. The little boy on the bike is Bob Anderson, who lived at 49 Miami Avenue. After 1920, the house at 123 Miami, originally the Baptist parsonage, was moved to Elm Street.

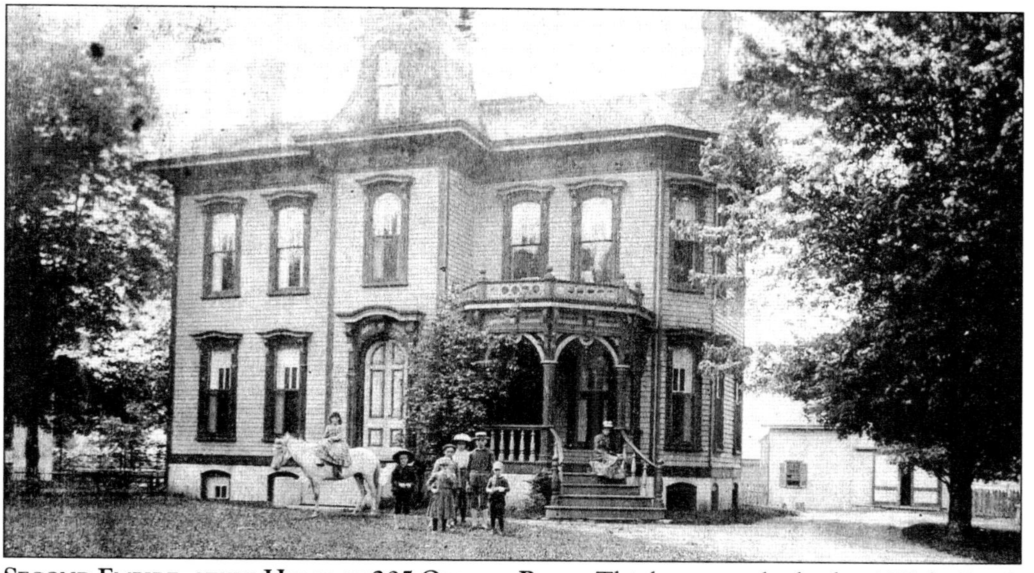

SECOND EMPIRE–STYLE HOME AT 205 OXFORD ROAD. This house was built after 1875 for Frank and Emma Douglas. Frank was an agent for the Big Four Railroad. This very early photograph shows the structure's dark clapboard and even darker trim, as well as the lack of shrubs around the house, allowing us an unobstructed view of the home's attractive foundation. The image also shows off the obligatory pony for the children of the Woolley family, who later owned the home. (Courtesy of Patty Frazee.)

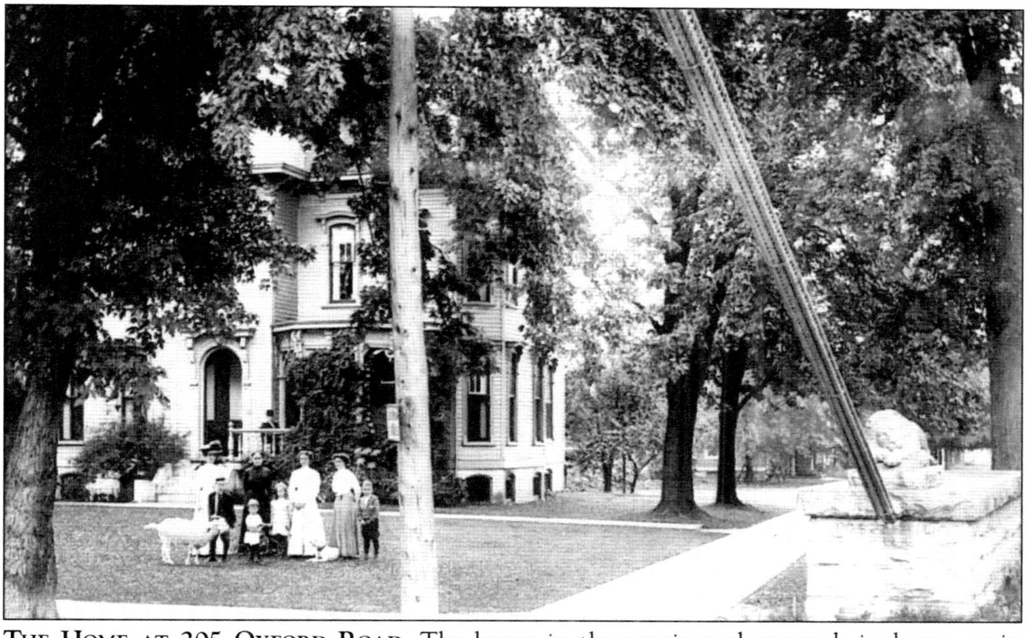

THE HOME AT 205 OXFORD ROAD. The house in the previous photograph is shown again here after it has been repainted in a more fashionably muted shade. At the time of this image, the home was occupied by the Denise family, who owned it for many years. Since the earlier photograph, the family pony has been replaced by the (probably) more practical pet goat. The southwest support of the suspension bridge is the foreground. (Courtesy of Patty Frazee.)

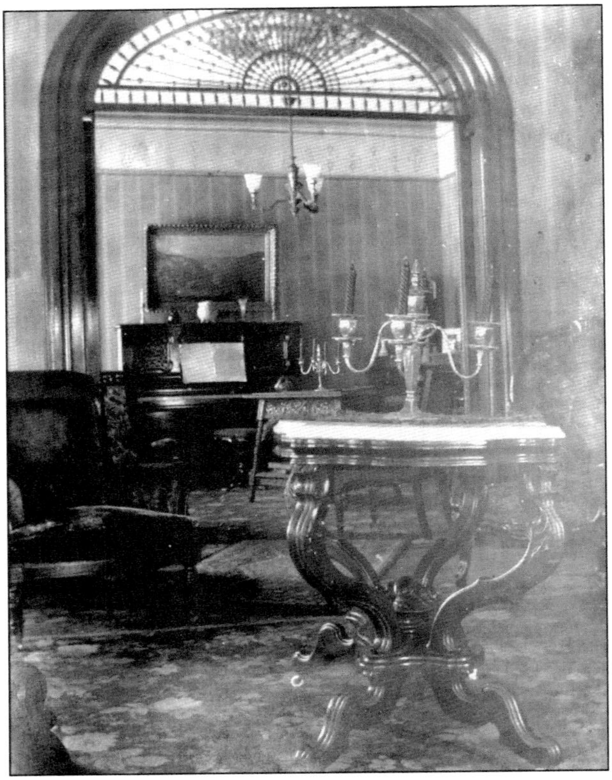

INTERIOR OF A WEST SIDE HOME. This photograph, taken about 1920, illustrates the busy pattern of the wall covering, the dark and heavy furniture, and an interesting furniture arrangement that by then was well out of fashion. This photograph appears amidst a series of exterior images of the house at 205 Oxford Road and may have been taken within that home. (Courtesy of Patty Frazee.)

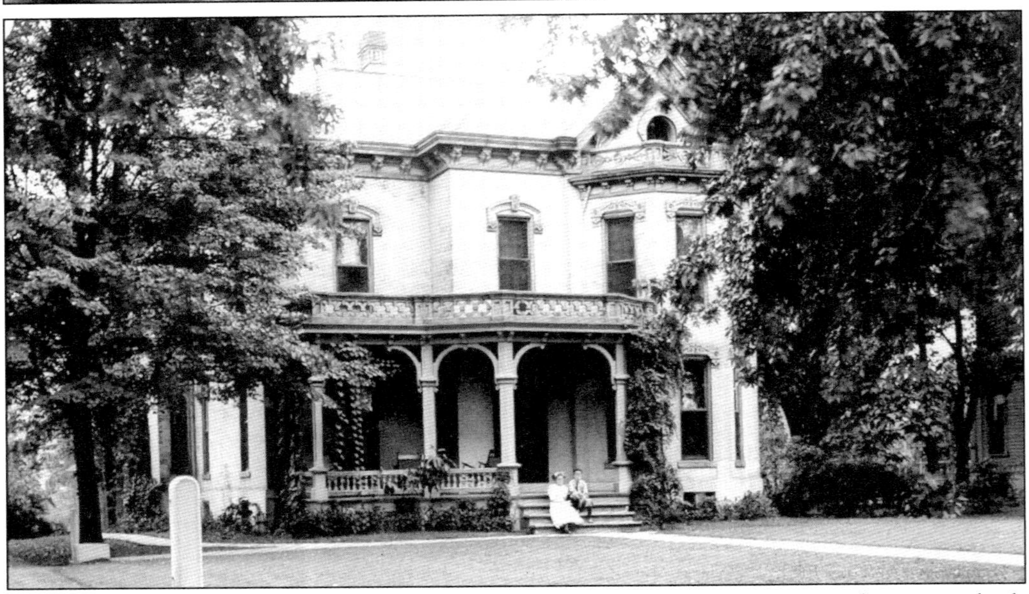

THE CHARLES HARDING HOME AT 209 OXFORD ROAD. This Italianate townhouse was built about 1876 by Mary Dickey. After passing through another owner, it was purchased in 1886 by Charles Harding, a paper mill executive and son of A. E. Harding, who built the Franklin Harding Paper Mill. Two of Charles Harding's children, Fred and Hazel, appear on the step of the house. Fred lived in the house until 1986.

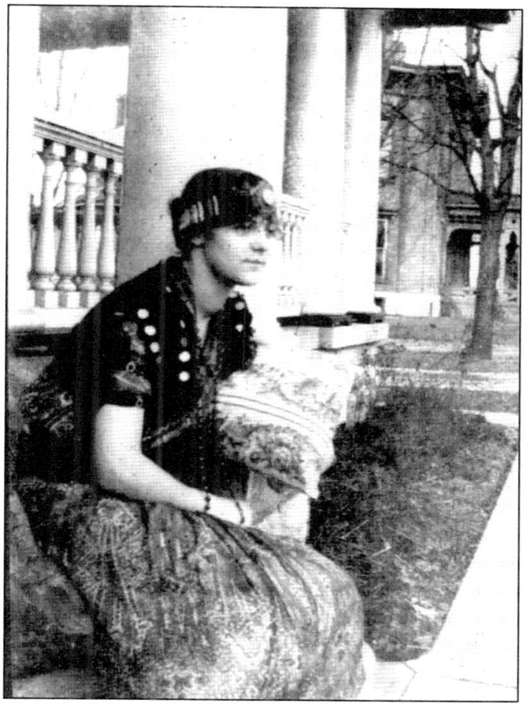

THE FRONT PORCH AT 225 OXFORD ROAD. The young woman in the foreground is sitting on the steps of the porch and is apparently dressed for a party. In the background is the Italianate house at 219 Oxford Road, a home that was built in 1876 for Ruth Schenck, a widow who endowed Franklin's first library. After her death, the house at 219 was owned by Dr. Silas Sterling Stahl, who had an office on Main Street.

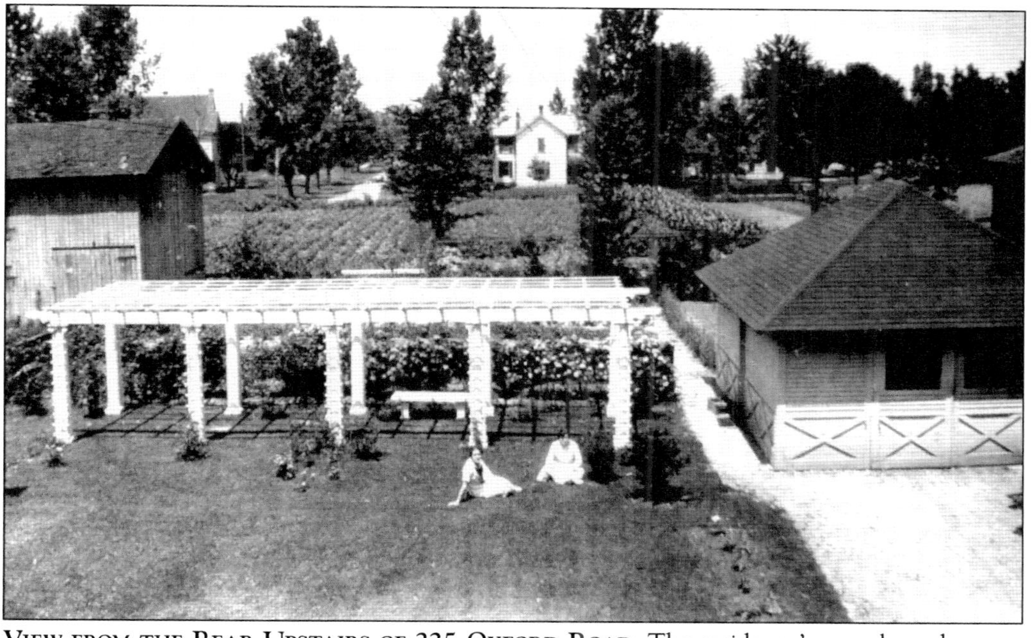

VIEW FROM THE REAR UPSTAIRS OF 225 OXFORD ROAD. The residence's pergola and garage are in the foreground. Most fashionable houses built around the beginning of the 20th century had small detached garages for the modern automobiles, just as earlier homes had detached stables. To the west is a cornfield, an indication of how rural the West Side was even in the 1920s. The house in the distance is 219 Elm Street.

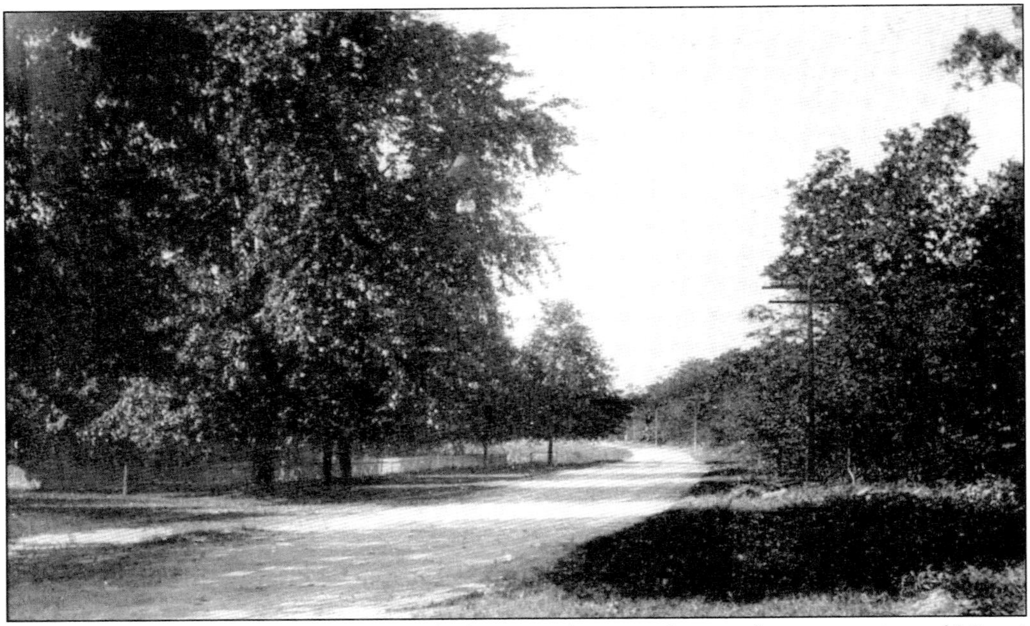

ANDERSON'S BEND. This photograph, looking north, was taken at the intersection of Miami Avenue and Lake Avenue. Anderson's Bend was so named because of the number of Andersons who owned homes nearby and the way Miami Avenue curves. L. G. Anderson's Italianate villa at 49 Miami Avenue is located in the trees behind the white picket fence at left.

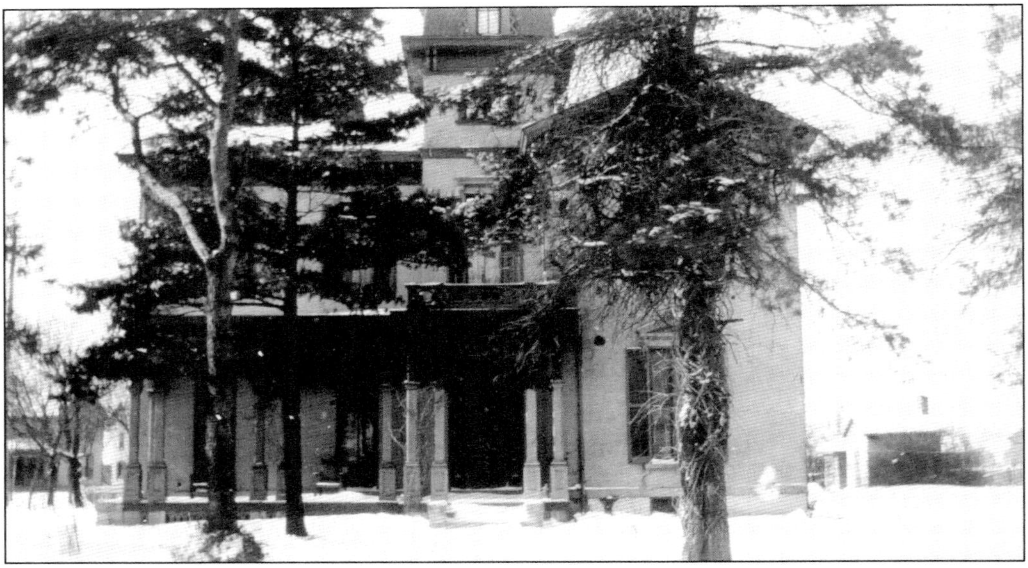

THE HOME AT 49 MIAMI AVENUE IN WINTER. Among the details of life at the beginning of the 20th century that are seen in this image are the etched glass in the front door and the easy chair kept outdoors for enjoyment on quiet afternoons when the weather warmed. The 135-year-old house and some of the evergreens still stand, although the Second Empire tower is gone and the porches have changed.

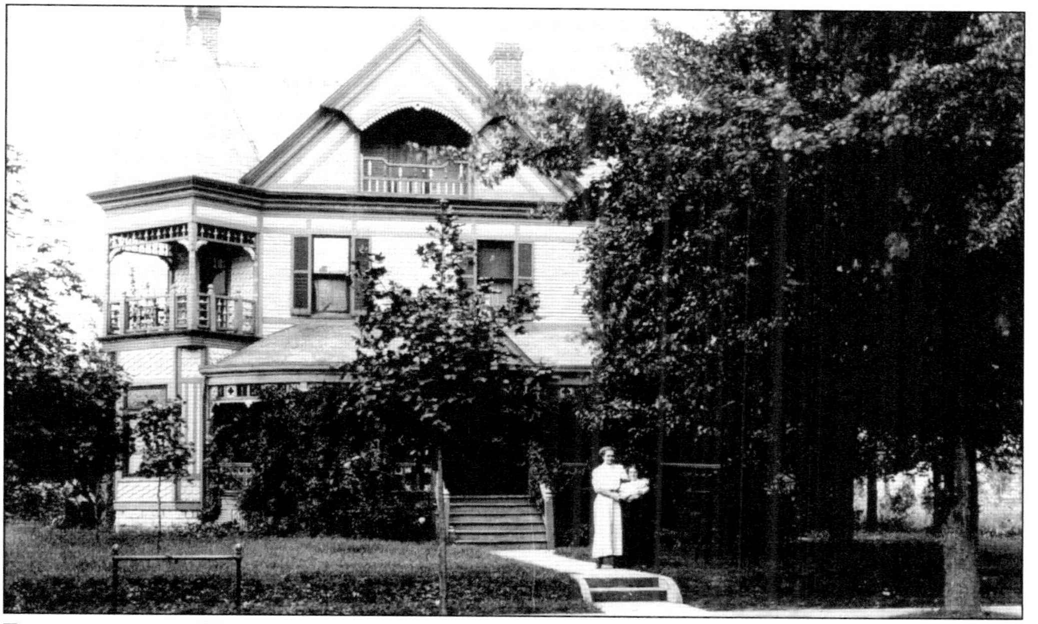

EASTLAKE-STYLE HOME AT 415 PARK AVENUE. The house was built for Perry H. Rue, a lawyer who worked on Main Street. Like many residences in this period, it was adorned with flowering vines and featured many intricate decorative details to charm the eye. Rue's son, Milton, who later owned and lived in the house, established a scholarship that has enabled many Franklin students to obtain an education at nearby Miami University. (Courtesy of William Moses.)

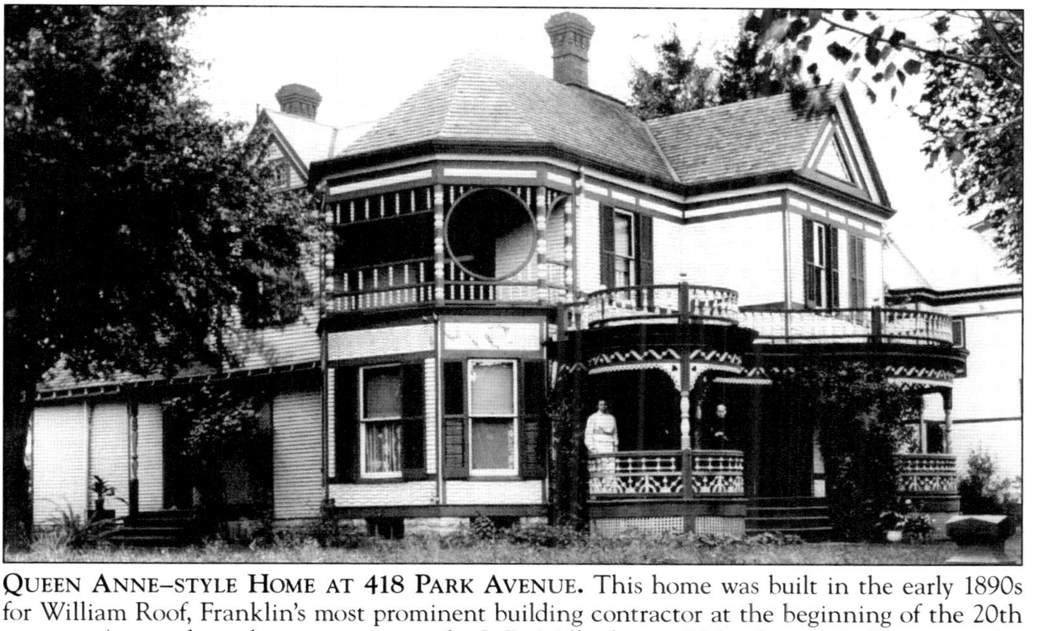

QUEEN ANNE–STYLE HOME AT 418 PARK AVENUE. This home was built in the early 1890s for William Roof, Franklin's most prominent building contractor at the beginning of the 20th century. Among his achievements were the J. D. Miller house, Valeridge, on Hill Avenue; the Conover Hardware Store; St. Mary Catholic Church on Main Street; and the Harding House at 302 Park Avenue—all of which still stand. Over the years, 418 Park's ornate porches have disappeared. (Courtesy of William Moses.)

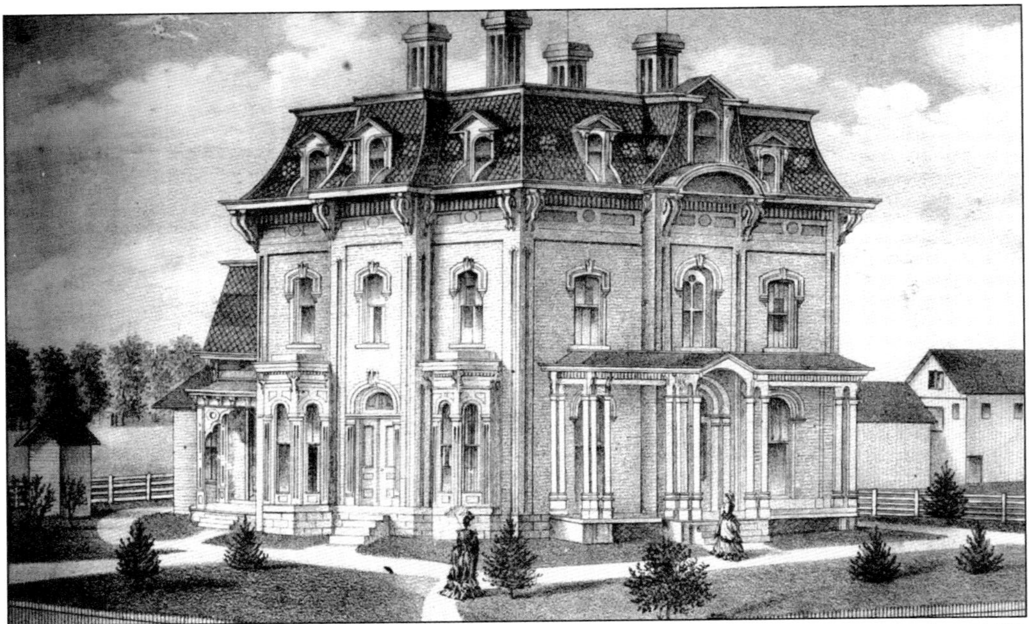

THE LEVI CROLL MANSION IN 1875. This impressive Second Empire structure was built in 1872 at 853 Dayton-Oxford Road as the centerpiece for Croll's new 194-acre farm. Croll died in 1884, and in 1895, his heirs lost almost all of their assets in the failure of the First National Bank, of which they were principal owners and where they had all of their money. The Crolls owned the home until the late 1980s.

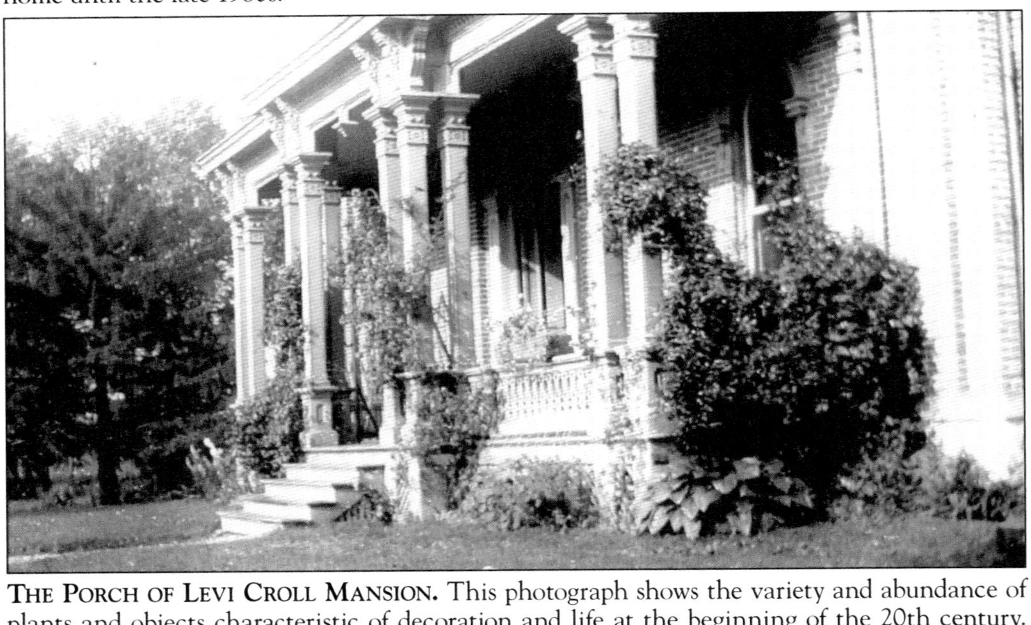

THE PORCH OF LEVI CROLL MANSION. This photograph shows the variety and abundance of plants and objects characteristic of decoration and life at the beginning of the 20th century. After Levi Croll's death, his younger son, George, supported the family by farming their land while his three sisters continued to live in the old mansion. For a short time in the 1920s, Levi Croll's grandson Frank operated a funeral home here, a purpose for which the house was well suited. (Courtesy of Bob Croll.)

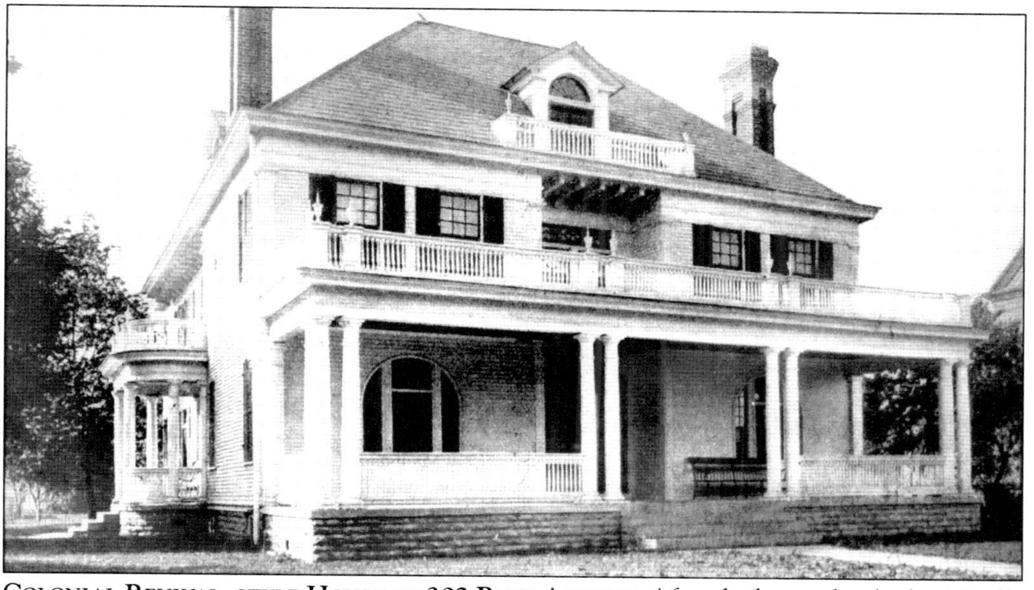

Colonial Revival–style House at 302 Park Avenue. After the house that had originally stood at 302 Park Avenue was moved to 321 Park, Clarence and Lilly Harding built this home. Clarence Harding was a member of a prosperous paper manufacturing family. The building is now the Harding Museum and houses the Franklin Area Historical Society. Clarence and Lilly's sons had distinguished careers in the army and the law.

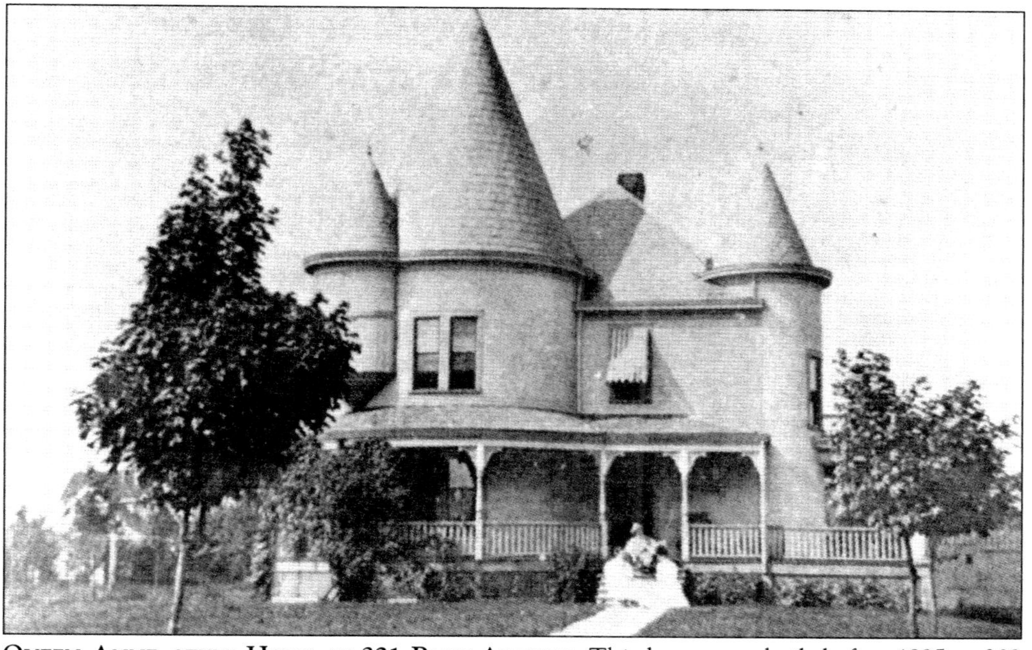

Queen Anne–style Home at 321 Park Avenue. This house was built before 1895 at 302 Park Avenue by James Thompson, and was moved to 321 Park after the lot at 302 Park was purchased. After the structure had been moved to 321 Park, it was owned by Joseph Weis, a chemist at a paper mill. Weis, his wife, their family, and two servants were living here in 1900. In 1906, the home was sold to Walter Siegfried, a dentist who practiced in downtown Franklin.

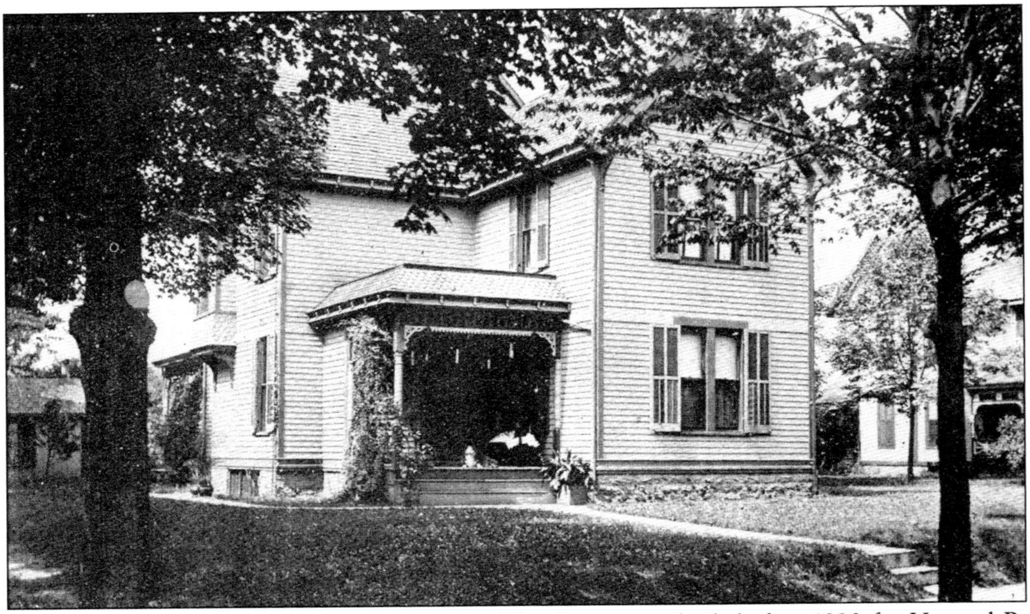

ITALIANATE HOME AT 302 LAKE AVENUE. This house was built before 1890 for Howard B. Anderson, third son of L. G. Anderson, who lived on the other side of Lake Avenue. Howard spent his life working in the family grain and lumber business, located along the canal at Fourth Street in Franklin. His daughters Gertrude and Barbara lived in this home until the 1960s. Like most West Side houses, this one still stands, although its porch has been changed.

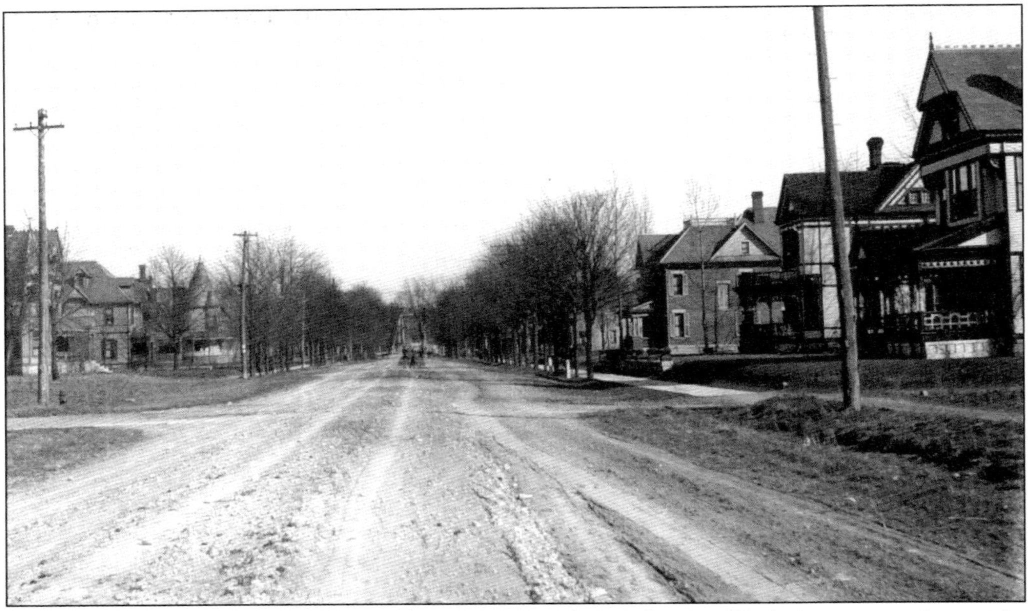

PARK AVENUE FROM THE WEST. The homes seen on the south side of Park Avenue are, from right to left, Nos. 420 (porch only visible), 418, and 414. The residence at 420 Park was subsequently razed to make room for an apartment complex. The houses pictured on the north side of Park Avenue are, from left to right, Nos. 415, 403, and 321 (with the turret). The rest of these fine Queen Anne–style homes still stand.

Three

At Work

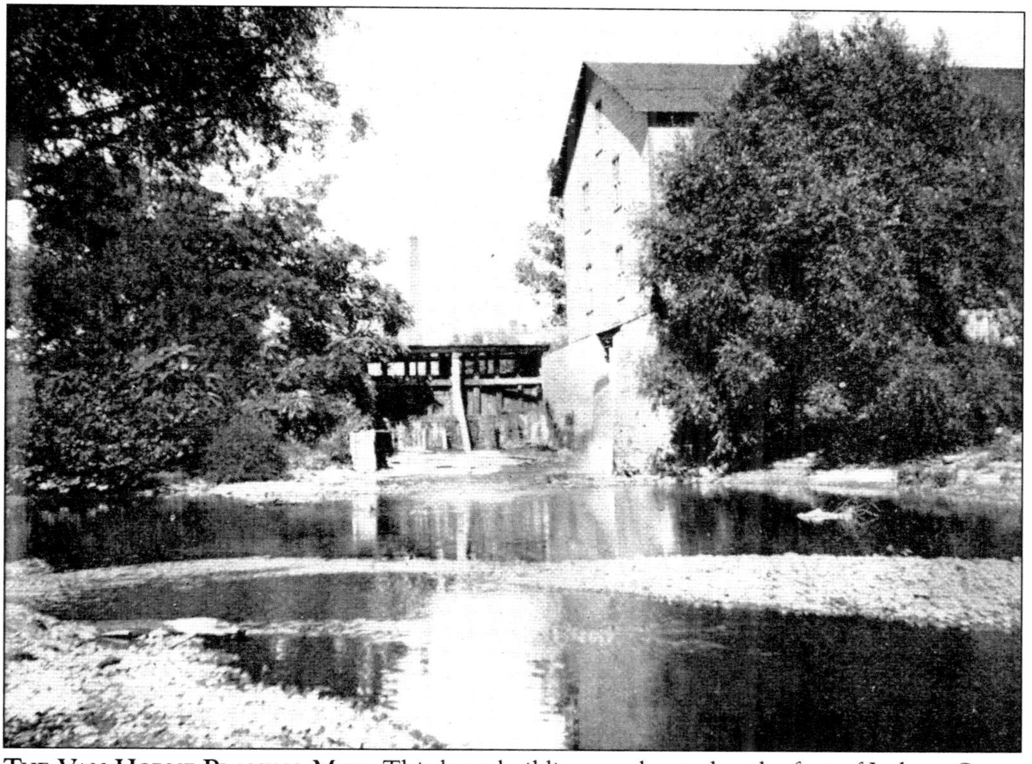

The Van Horne Planing Mill. This large building was located at the foot of Jackson Street in north Franklin and was constructed around 1880. It was powered by water from the millrace at the south end of the Van Horne Hydraulic diverted from the Great Miami River by the Chautauqua Dam. The fire insurance plat for 1882 states the mill manufactured sashes, blinds, and door frames. Next door to it stood a gristmill. Both buildings had disappeared by 1920.

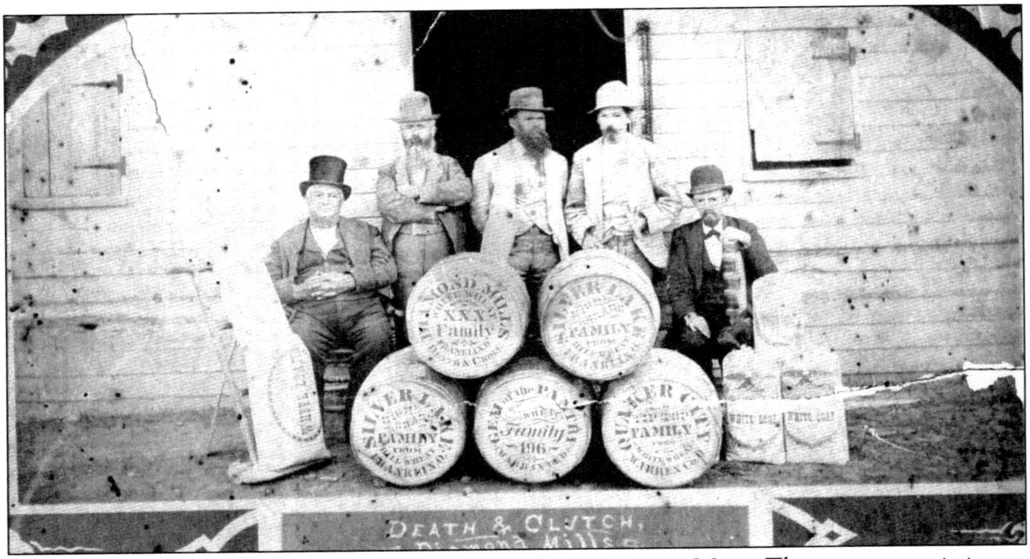

OWNERS AND EMPLOYEES OF THE DEATH AND CROLL FLOUR MILL. The stout man sitting at left with folded hands is Hugh Death. The bearded man in the light suit with crossed arms is Levi Croll. The other three men are almost certainly three of the company's four employees. By 1870, Croll had sold his share of the company to Daniel Clutch (whose name appears on the image), making Croll a very rich man.

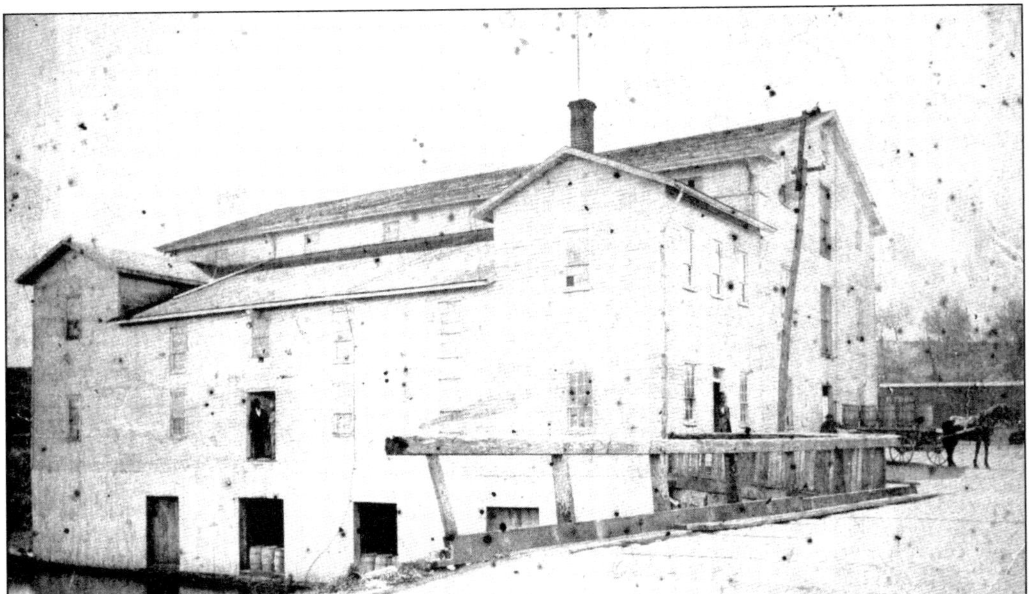

THE DEATH AND CROLL FLOUR MILL. This view from the northwest was photographed about 1869. Standing to the east side of today's Dixie Highway (which is at right in the photograph), the Death and Croll mill was powered by water diverted from the Miami-Erie Canal. The 1870 census shows the mill employed 4 workers and processed 84,000 bushels of wheat and corn into 22,000 barrels of flour and 4,000 barrels of cornmeal. The buildings were later converted into a paper mill.

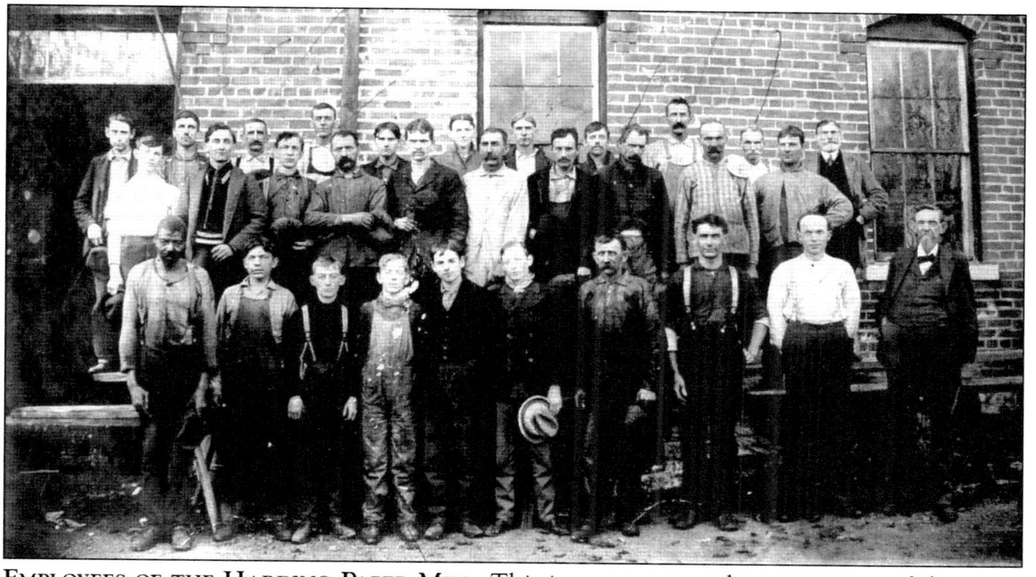

EMPLOYEES OF THE HARDING PAPER MILL. This image captures the appearance of the many and varied men who performed the hot, dirty, and malodorous industrial work at local mills. The bearded man in the suit in the front row at right is Harry Engle, one of the mill's management staff and a member of the Harding family. The bearded, professorial-looking man in the rear row may be Joseph Weis, a chemist, who lived at 321 Park Avenue.

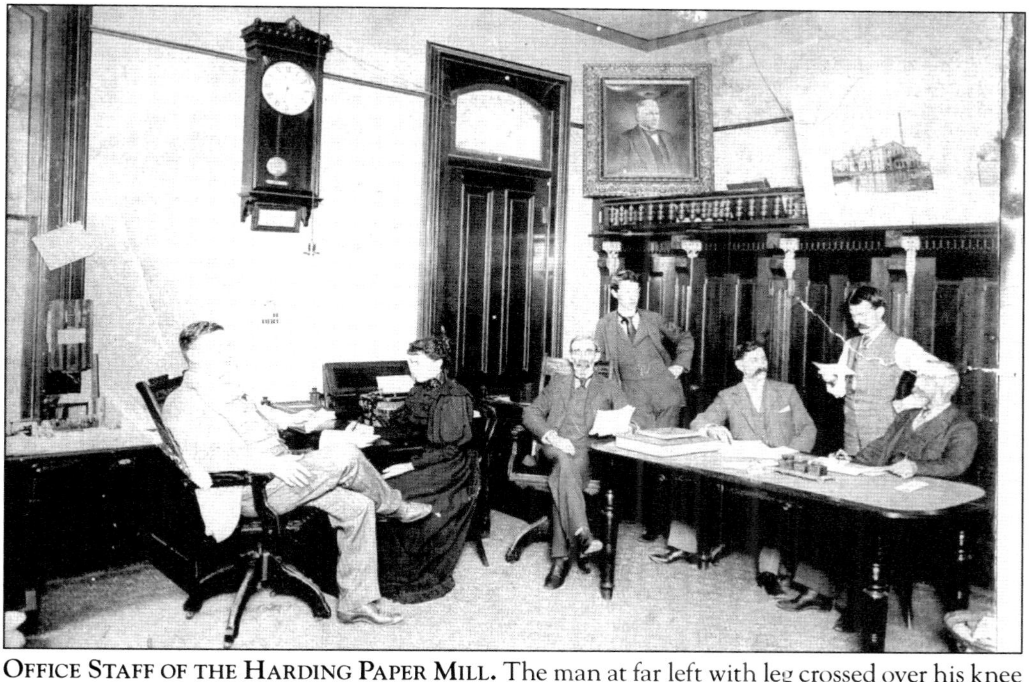

OFFICE STAFF OF THE HARDING PAPER MILL. The man at far left with leg crossed over his knee is Clarence "Larry" Harding, the father of Edwin Forrest and Justin Harding. The grey-bearded Harry Engle stares at the camera. The clean-shaven man with hand on hip is Thomas Albert Dwight "Tad" Jones, later a first-team All-American football player at Yale. The gentleman with Vandyke beard, sitting at the table at right, is Elias Folk.

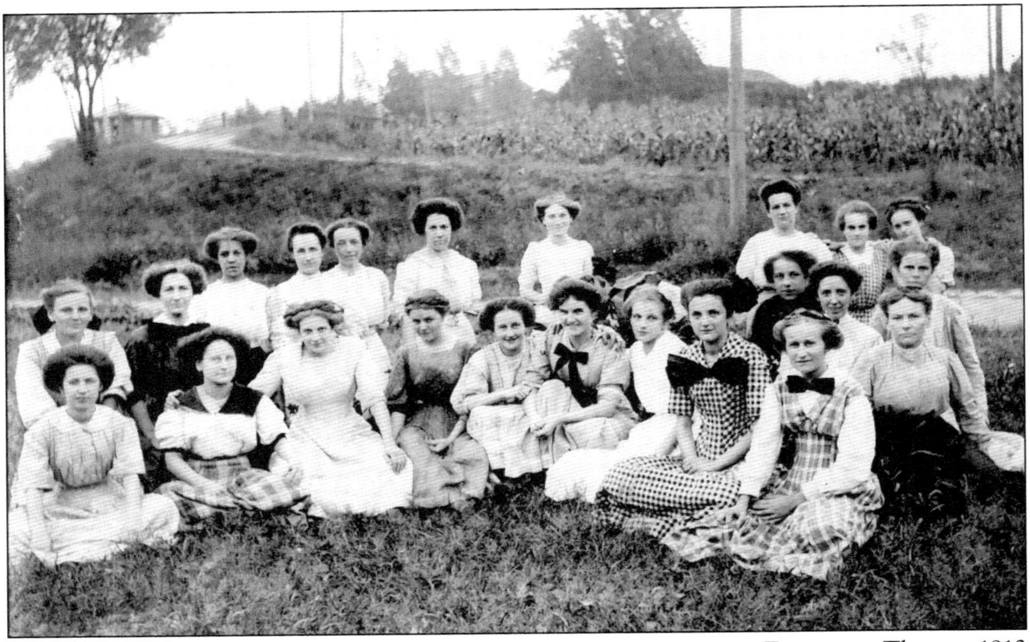

EMPLOYEES OF THE BROWN, CARSON, AND SCHEIBLE LEGGING FACTORY. This *c.* 1913 photograph, looking northeast, was taken on the east side of the canal, near the intersection with Van Horne Avenue. Leggings, or spats, as they were better known, were rapidly going out of style, and must have been highly combustible, too, because an earlier factory on Second Street burned in 1909, almost taking the whole north side of Franklin with it.

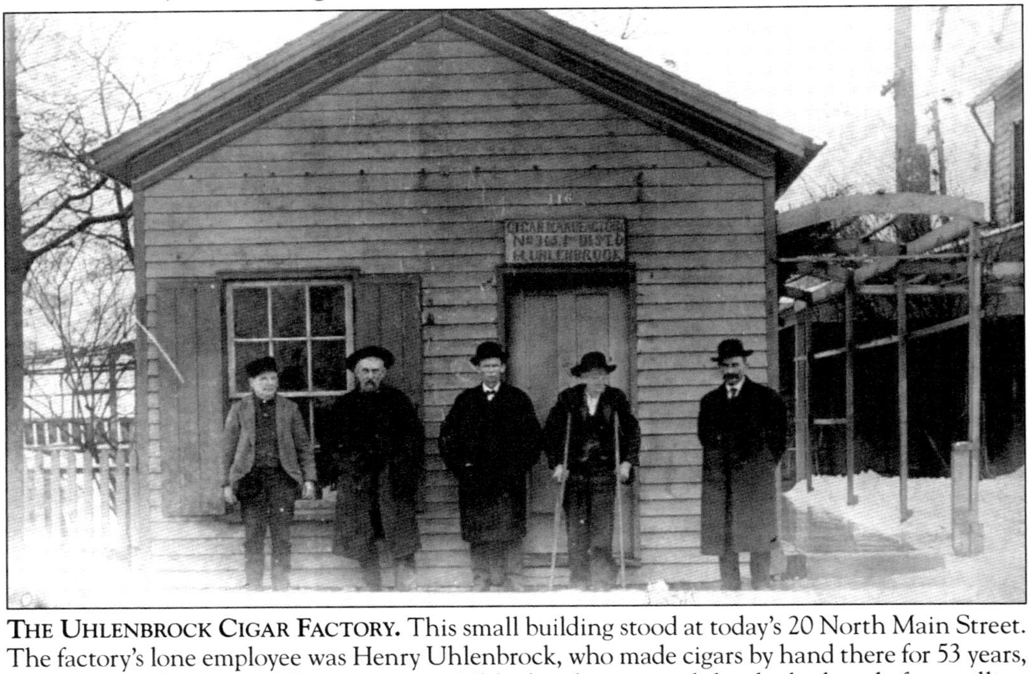

THE UHLENBROCK CIGAR FACTORY. This small building stood at today's 20 North Main Street. The factory's lone employee was Henry Uhlenbrock, who made cigars by hand there for 53 years, beginning in the 1890s. After retirement, Uhlenbrock estimated that he had made four million cigars during his career. In the warm months, vines grew on the arbor that appears at right.

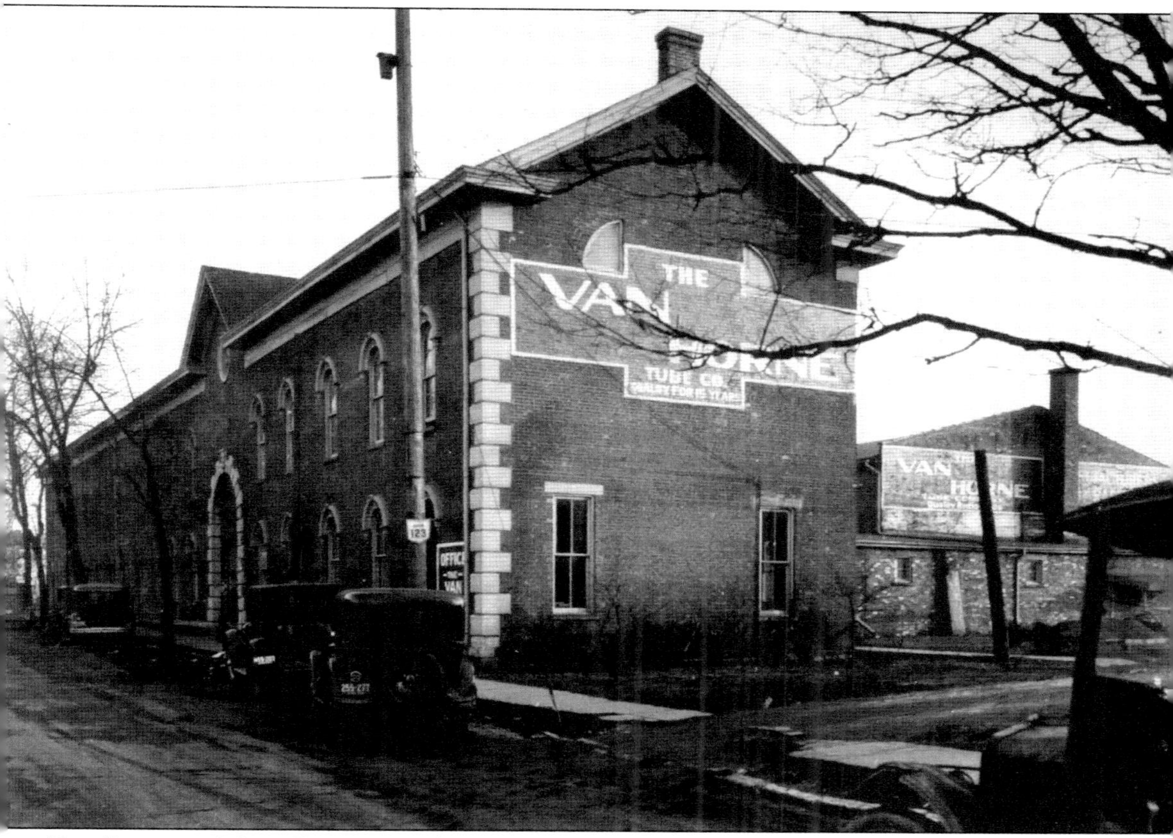

The Burrows Malt Building. This was located on the south side of Sixth Street, near the intersection with the canal, and was the site of many of the village's early industries. Prior to the construction of this building, the area near this corner was home to a pork packing house. In 1850, the village's packing houses slaughtered more than 6,000 hogs, generating 2,500 barrels of pork and a quarter of a million pounds of lard. Amazingly this gory work was performed by only about four (probably extremely hardened) men. This business was replaced by the malt house, built at great expense, which operated in the 1860s and 1870s. The census of 1870 shows that the malt house employed 10 workers and processed 64,000 bushels of barley. In 1881 the buildings were occupied by the very short-lived Franklin Pottery, which contained two 50-foot-tall kilns and employed 100 men. That business failed within a year, and subsequently, two paper companies operated here. Between 1914 and the onset of the Depression, the buildings were occupied by the electric tube company shown in this photograph.

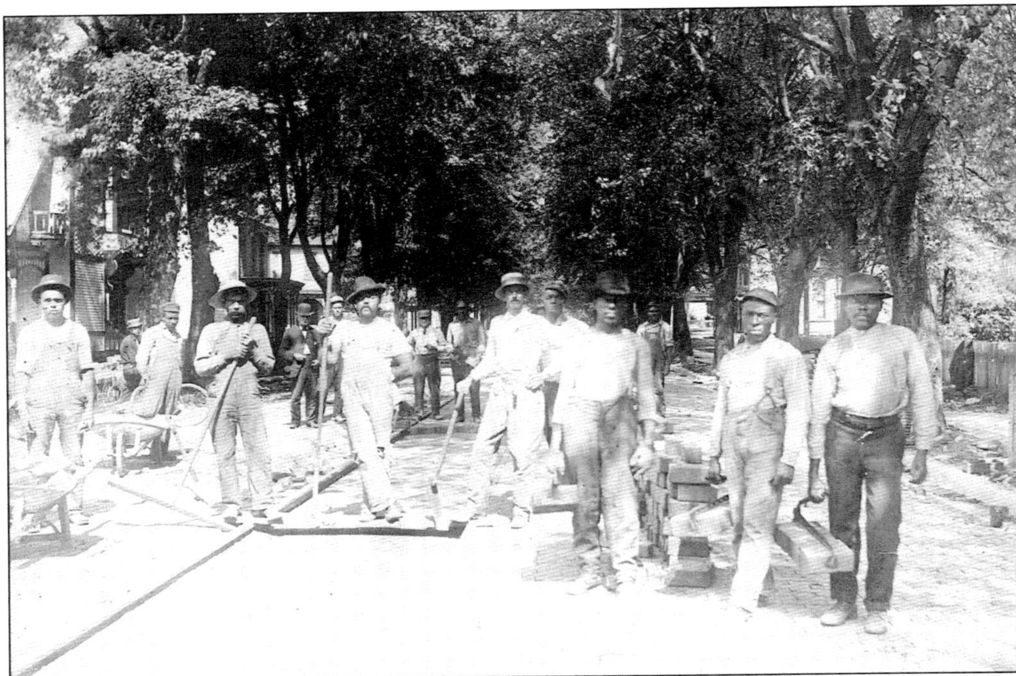

PAVING CREW ON SOUTH MAIN STREET. This view is looking north. The unusual window decoration at left identifies that address as 765 South Main. Chestnut trees form a canopy over the street and white picket fences front many of the residences. The man wearing the cap in the middle distance (near center), whose face is visible over the shoulder of the man holding the shovel, is Vernon Willis. (Courtesy Weesie Polley.)

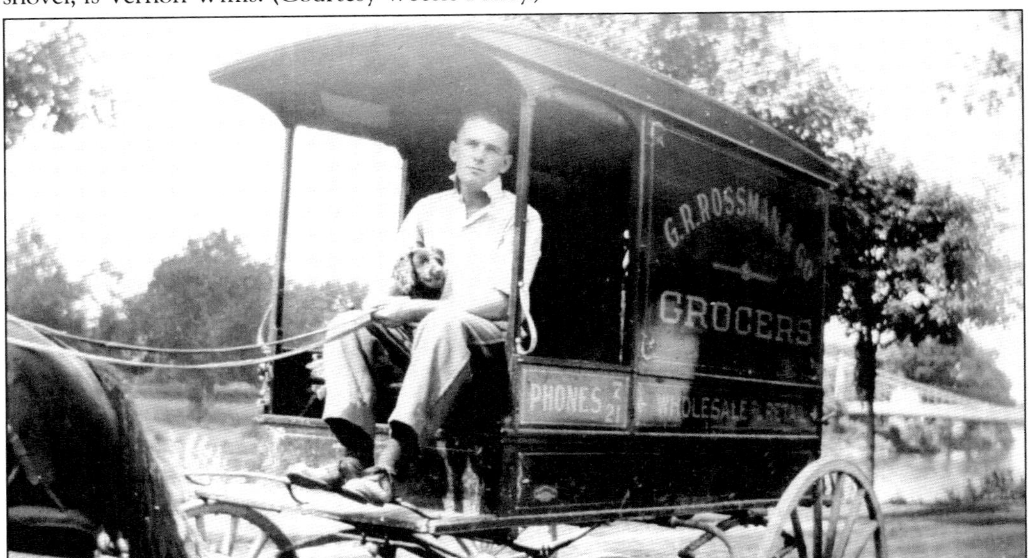

THE ROSSMAN GROCERY DELIVERY WAGON. The view is looking northwest from River Street. Though the small downtown groceries offered very limited variety, they could provide their customers with the convenience of local delivery. The Rossman Grocery operated on the corner of Main and Second Streets from 1881 to 1949.

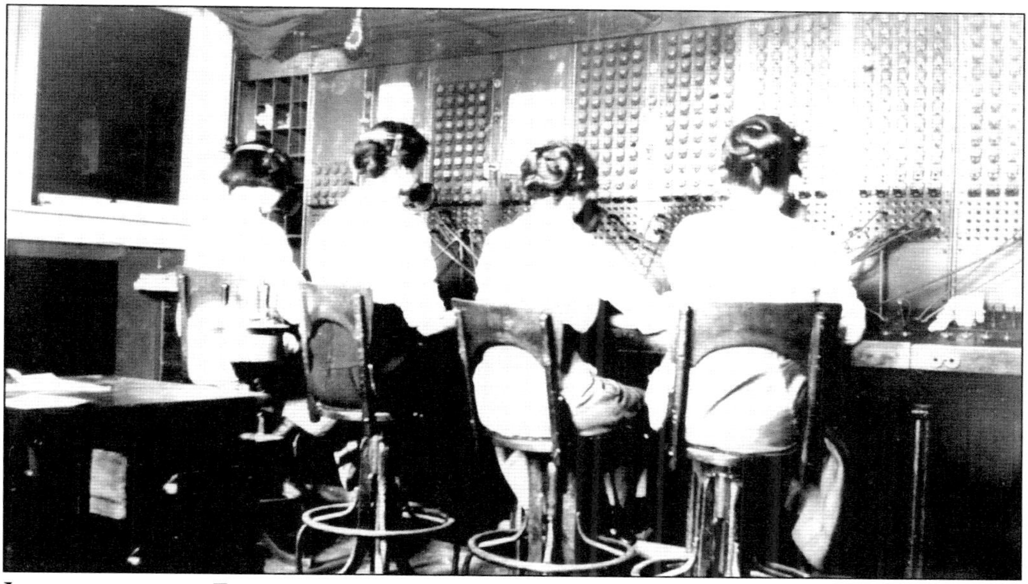

Interior of the Franklin Telephone Exchange. These young ladies are hard at work connecting their customers. When this photograph was taken in about 1910, the village's telephone exchange was housed in a former Thirkield home, located to the rear of the department store, on the north side of East Fourth Street. The telephone book for that year shows the community had about 650 phone numbers.

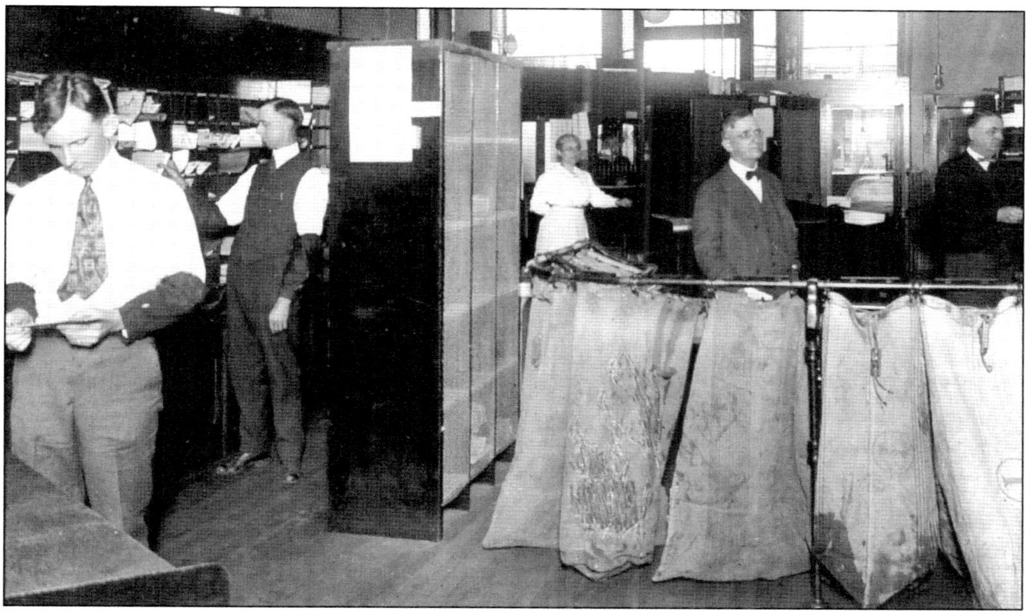

Interior of the Franklin Post Office. Smartly dressed employees sort the mail in very cramped conditions about 1910. When this photograph was taken, the village's post office was probably located in the brick building just north of Conover's.

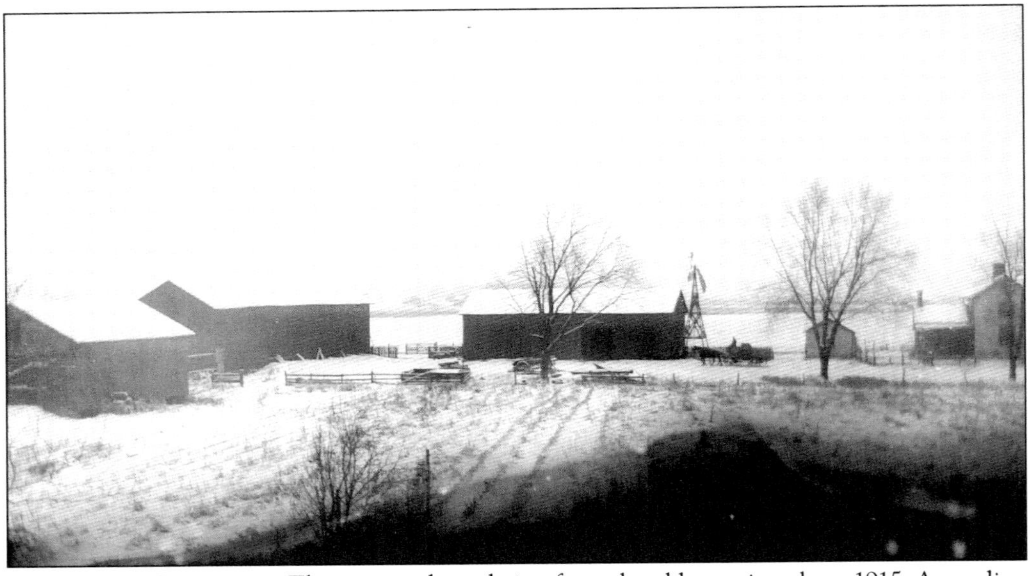

CROLL FARM BUILDINGS. This is a northward view from the old mansion about 1915. According to records from the late 1800s, the Croll farm produced corn and hay, and raised hogs, pigs, sheep, lambs, cows, heifers, and calves, as well as horses (each of whom was listed by name). The records also list a great many pieces of farm equipment on the premises. Later the Crolls raised tobacco and chickens and operated a dairy that served the local market. (Courtesy of Bob Croll.)

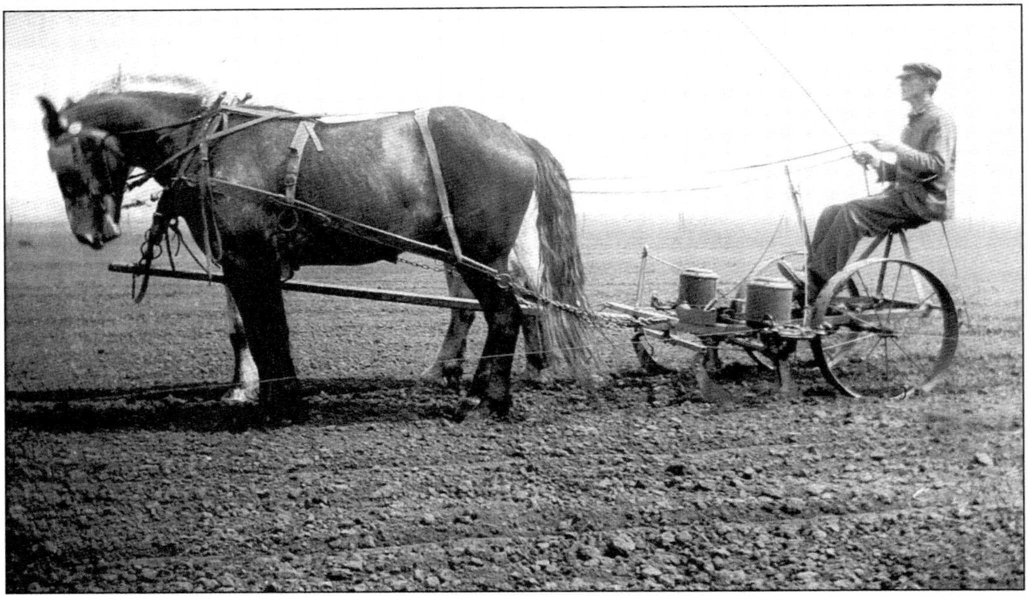

GEORGE CROLL ON THE CORN PLANTER. The two cans on the planter contained the corn seed. When their bank deposits were embezzled and the family bank collapsed, the Crolls were especially hard hit financially. With their fortune lost, there was no recourse except for George Croll to make a living by farming, which he did successfully. Croll was known locally for the perfect geometry of his corn rows and fields, in which he took great pride. (Courtesy of Bob Croll.)

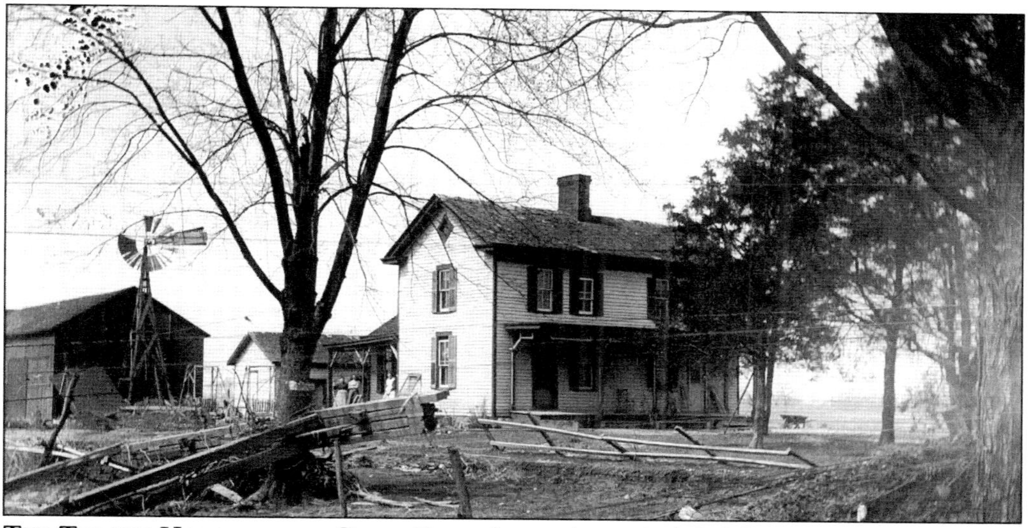

The Tenant House of the Croll Farm. Located at today's 813 Dayton-Oxford Road, this very old two-story log cabin, covered by weatherboarding, was where Levi Croll lived during the years when his mansion was under construction in the early 1870s. The photograph shows female members of the Croll family hard at work. Visible in the background is a windmill used to power the pump on the farm's well. (Courtesy of Bob Croll.)

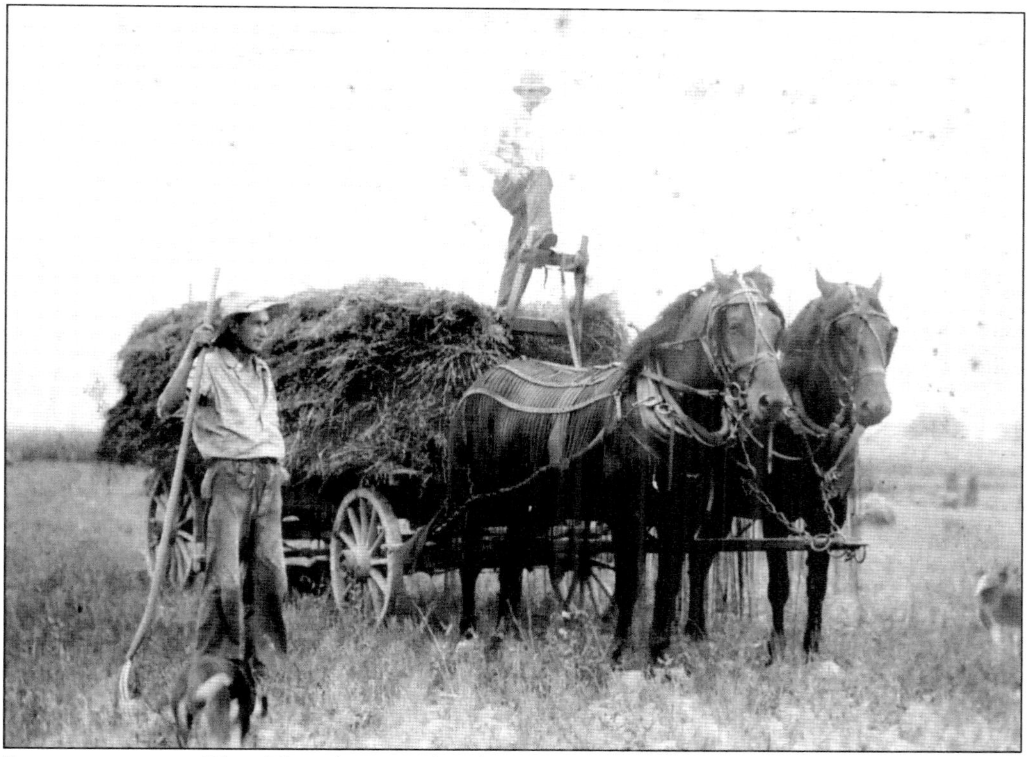

Bringing in the Hay. This photograph, taken in 1913, shows Demosthenes Weer standing on the wagon. The Weers (or Wehrs) worked a family farm in the hills northeast of Franklin, on the north side of the Pennyroyal Road.

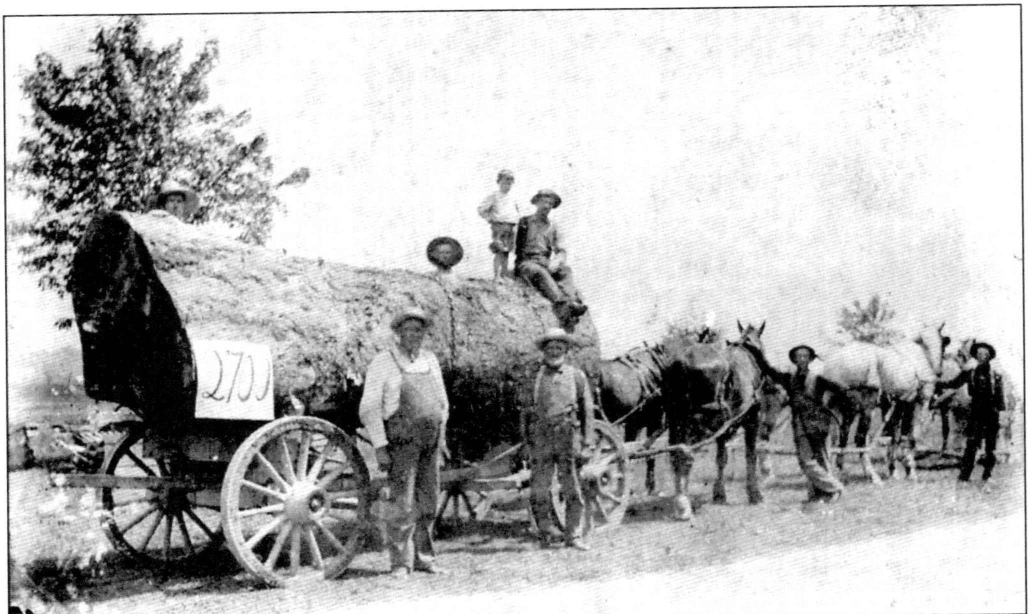

HANKINSON'S LUMBER WORKERS. James V. Hendrickson operated a wholesale lumber company on Forest Avenue in the very early 1900s. By one account, the enchanting walnut grove at the end of Lake Avenue that had contained the original Franklin Fairgrounds was cut down by Hendrickson. Perhaps this huge section of tree trunk is from one of the ancient walnuts that had earlier formed the canopy over the village's original fairgrounds.

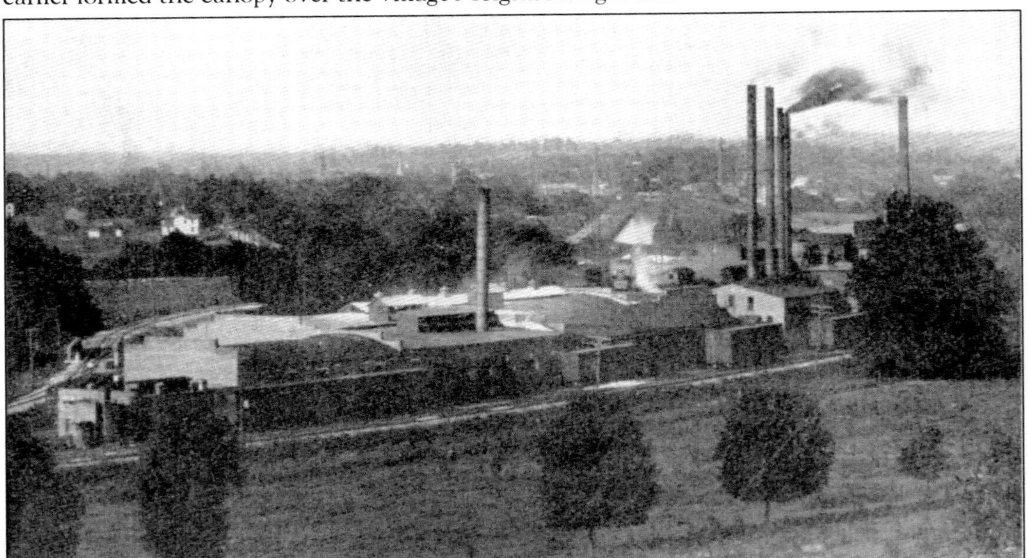

THE SMOKESTACKS OF FRANKLIN. In the early 20th century, when smokestacks bespoke a community's prosperity, Franklin must have been seen as indeed blessed. This view, looking north from Woodhill Cemetery about 1910, shows the stacks of south Franklin. Closest are those of Patent Vulcanite, which manufactured roofing materials on the site of the Death and Croll Flour Mill. The smokestacks of three paper mills around Sixth Street are in the distance. The gleaming ribbon in the center distance is the old Miami-Erie Canal.

Four

SCHOOL DAYS

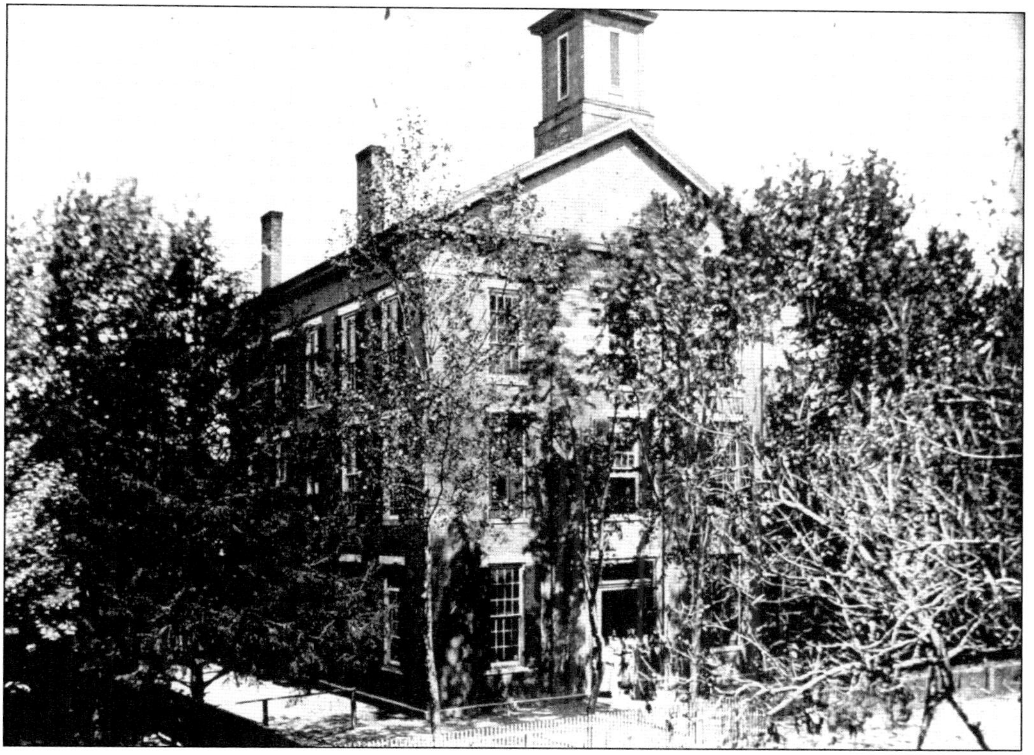

FRANKLIN'S OLD CENTRAL SCHOOL. This steepled, T-shaped structure, with base facing Main Street, was built in 1848. First known as the Union School, it was originally 2 stories high and contained 10 rooms. Later a third floor was added and paid for by the Odd Fellows and Free Masons. After these organizations constructed their own halls, the third floor became the school laboratories. The building housed classes until 1931, when a new school was completed on Second Street. The old school was then demolished and the new post office was built on its site in 1935.

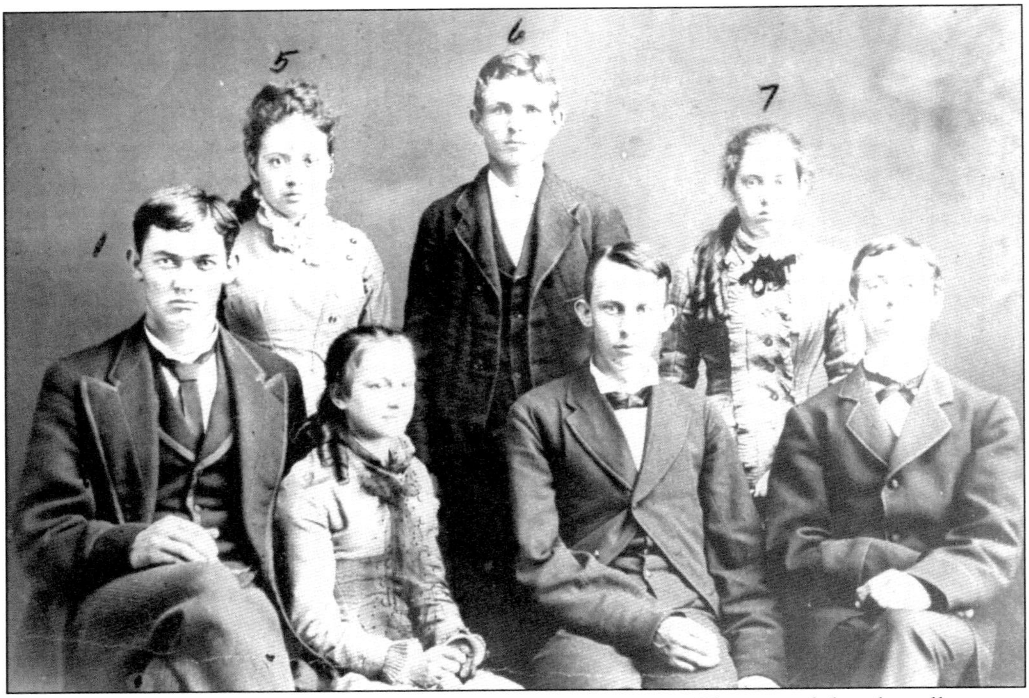

THE FRANKLIN HIGH SCHOOL GRADUATING CLASS OF 1878. The size of the class illustrates the degree to which completing one's education was seen as having value in late-19th-century Franklin. Student No. 1 is Perry H. Rue, later a successful lawyer and village mayor. Student No. 6 is Henry Meeker, who later owned an insurance company. Sitting in right front is Edwin S. Eldridge, later a successful traveling salesman.

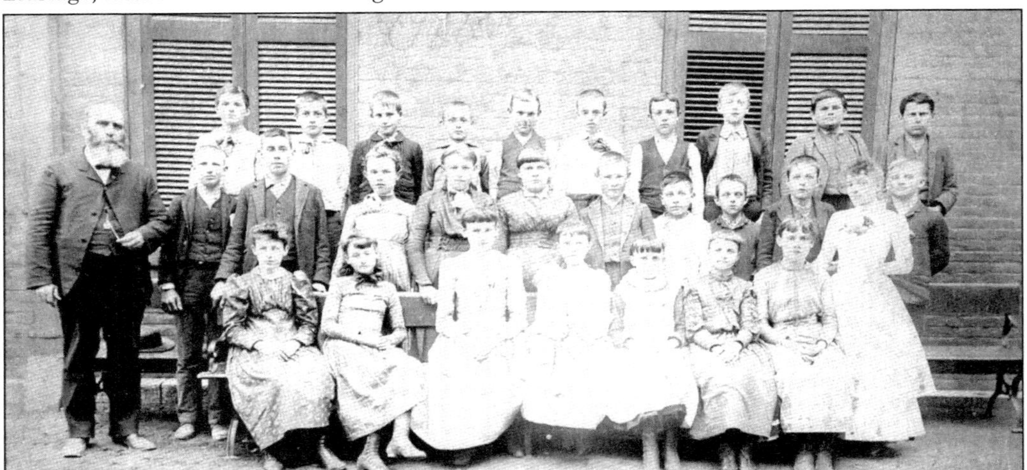

EARLY CLASS AT ELEMENTARY SCHOOL. The slightly shabby man at left is the superintendent of Franklin Schools, Hampton Bennett. A Civil War veteran, Bennett was first principal of the Union School in 1866, and was superintendent of schools until 1894. In addition to his other duties, Bennett was a farmer and rang the bell that summoned students to their labors. Bennett was subsequently dismissed by the school board because it objected to his plans for a four-year high school curriculum.

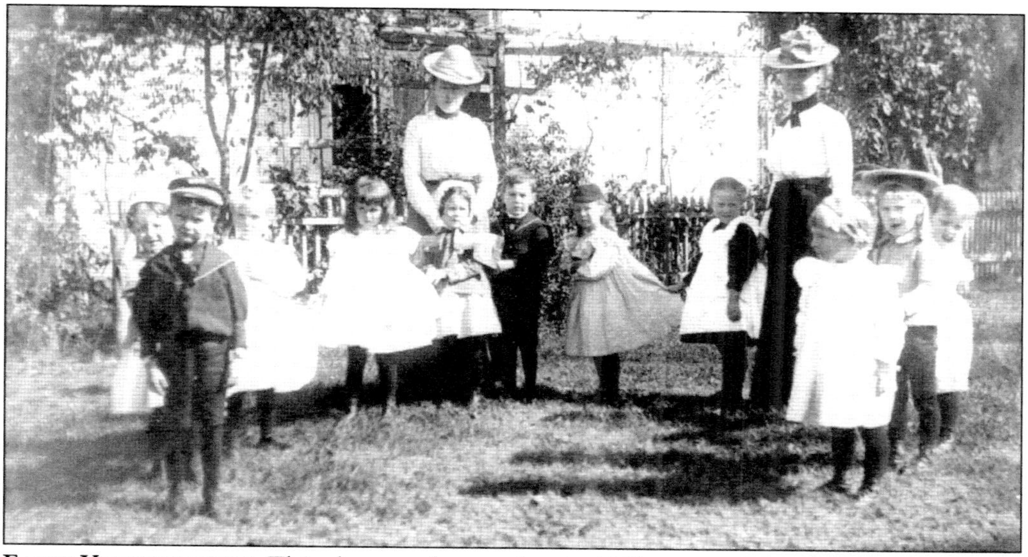

EARLY KINDERGARTEN. This photograph was taken in 1901 in a yard near the southeast corner of Main and Fourth Streets. The manly little chap in the sailor suit is Bob Anderson, later manager of the family lumber company located in downtown Franklin.

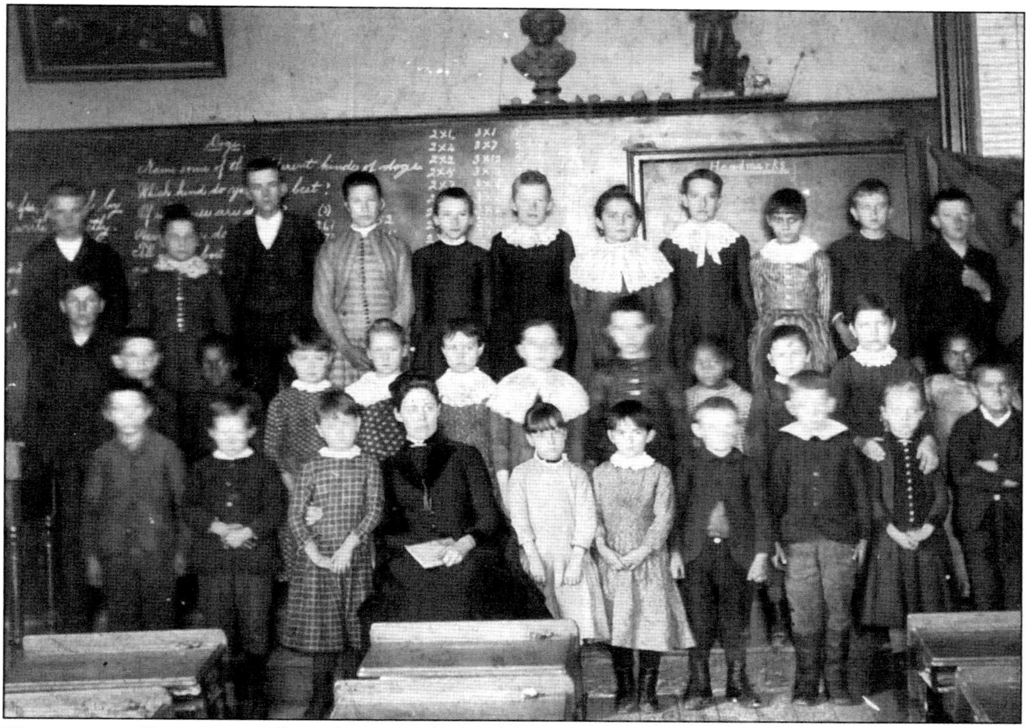

CLASSROOM INTERIOR. This photograph would appear to have been taken in the 1880s, most likely in the Central School. The children are dressed in their disparate best for the occasion. The bust of Shakespeare, probably donated to the school, sits on the shelf to inspire any budding geniuses. Another unidentified statue and painting also decorate the classroom, for the enlightenment of the young.

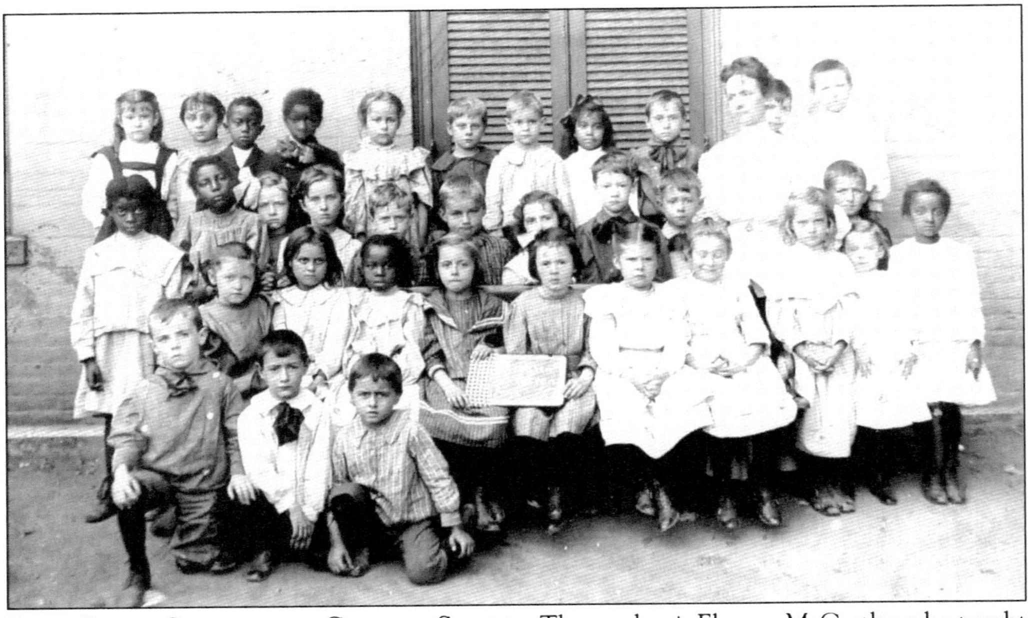

First-Grade Class at the Central School. The teacher is Eleanor McCarthy, who taught from before 1910 until the 1920s. At the time of this photograph, she still lived at home with her family on the 300 block of Lake Avenue. McCarthy's father was a plumber, and her younger sister, Irene, who was also a school teacher, lived at home as well.

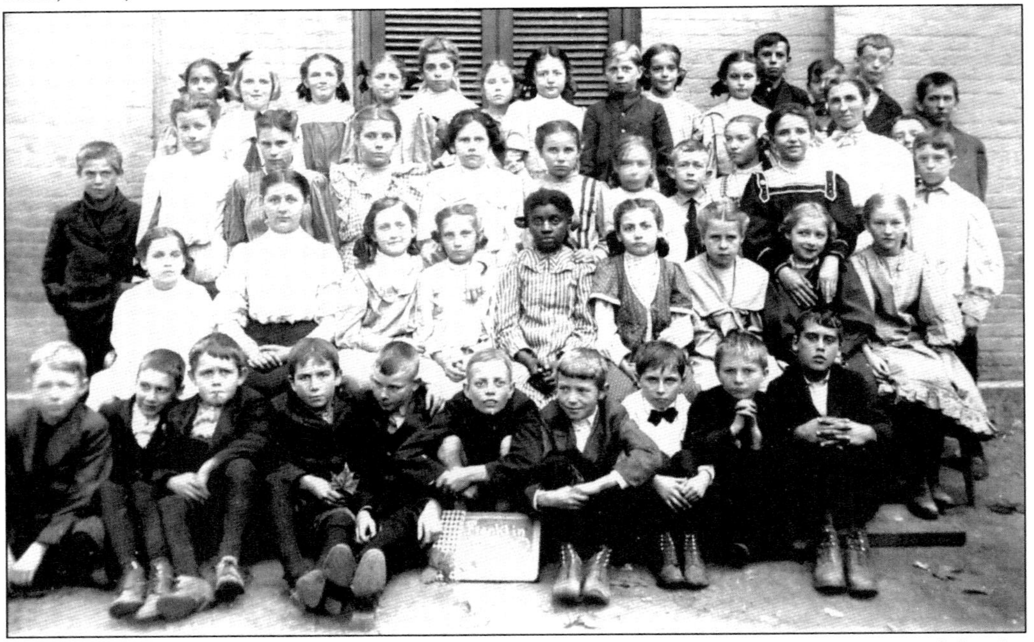

Central School Fourth-Grade Class. The exterior of the school is background for the photograph. The teacher is Minnie Roudebush. All of the students in the photograph have been identified. Among these is Mary Jane Anderson, in the rear row just to the right of the door frame. She graduated from Oberlin College, and spent over 30 years as a teacher in Pennsylvania, New Jersey, Ohio, and Maryland, before returning to Franklin.

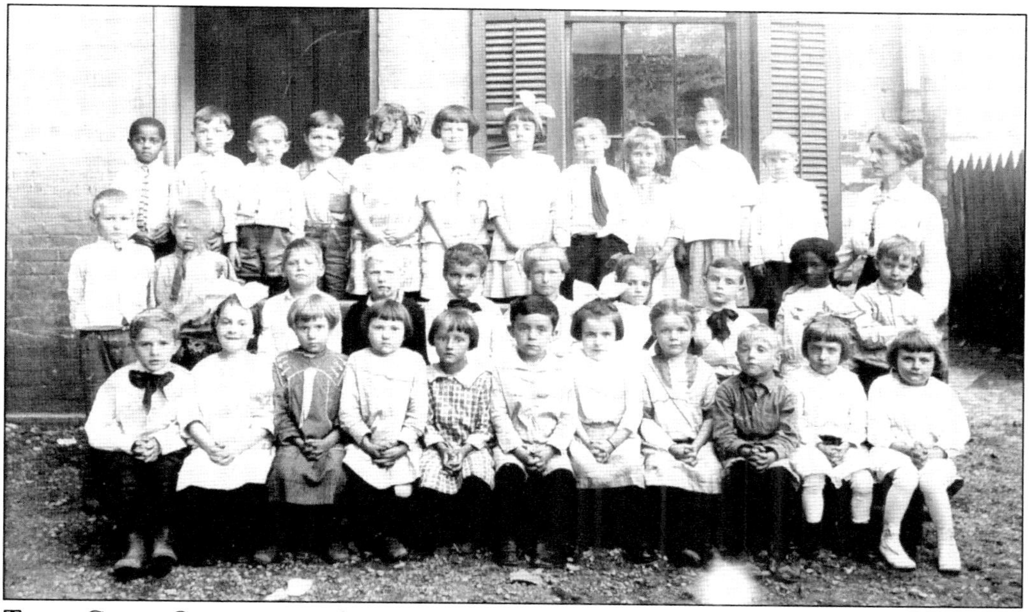

THIRD-GRADE CLASS AT THE CENTRAL SCHOOL. The teacher at right is Alice O'Donnell. She was the daughter of John O'Donnell, superintendent of the Franklin Board and Paper Company, and lived in a Queen Anne house located at 305 Elm Street. Alice O'Donnell taught after 1910 until 1915. She joined the Sisters of Charity and was then known as Sister Martha Marie. She passed away in 1962.

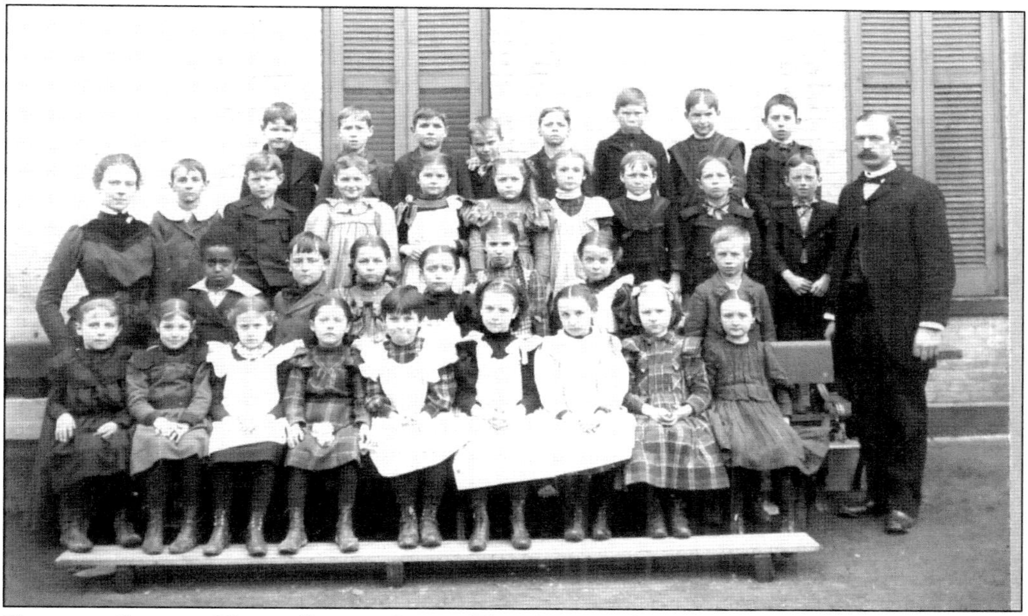

CENTRAL SCHOOL THIRD-GRADE CLASS. The photograph was taken in 1899. The teacher at left is Nancy "Nan" Carpenter, whose father was a Civil War veteran and whose mother was the daughter of the owner of Thirkield Department Store. Nan lived at home in the Queen Anne–style house located at 230 Park Avenue. The serious-looking fellow at right is F. Gillum Cromer, who was superintendent of Franklin Schools from 1894 to 1901.

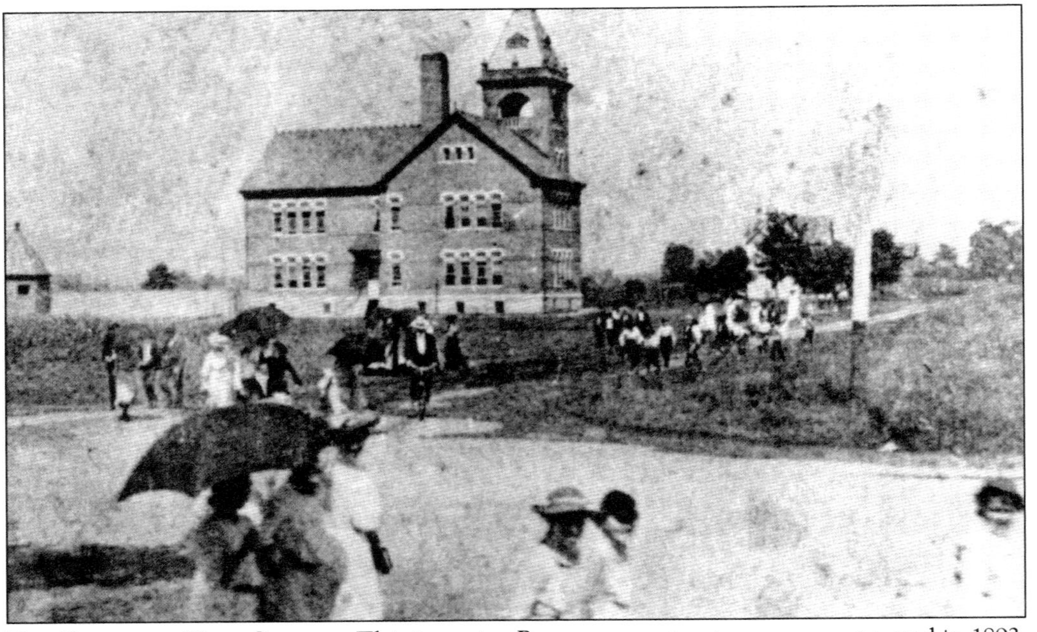

THE FRANKLIN HIGH SCHOOL. This imposing Romanesque structure was constructed in 1893. The camera view is from the west and shows the rear of the school. The sentry box–type structure at left is one of the two octagonal outhouses. The event being captured in the photograph is unknown. In 1921, a new high school was built on East Sixth Street and this building became the West Elementary School, remaining in use until it was destroyed by fire in 1958.

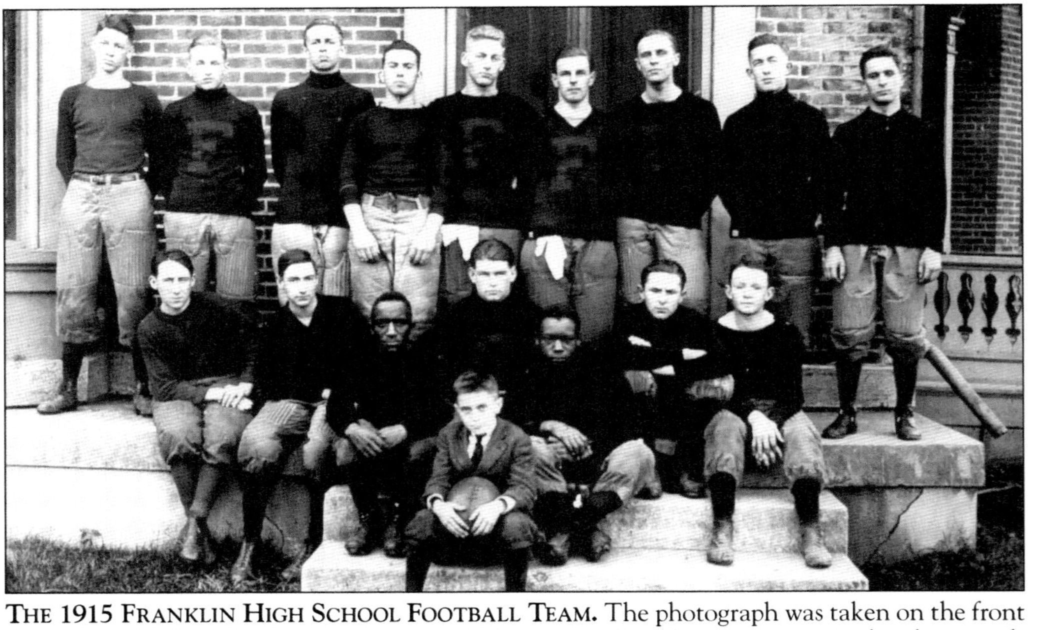

THE 1915 FRANKLIN HIGH SCHOOL FOOTBALL TEAM. The photograph was taken on the front doorstep of the Woodward home on East Sixth Street. All of the young men in the photograph have been identified. Among those pictured is Fred Harding, standing in the middle of the rear row, who lived at 209 Oxford Road. Sitting in front of Harding is Buss Gaynor, one of the sons of lawyer Pat Gaynor, who lived on River Street.

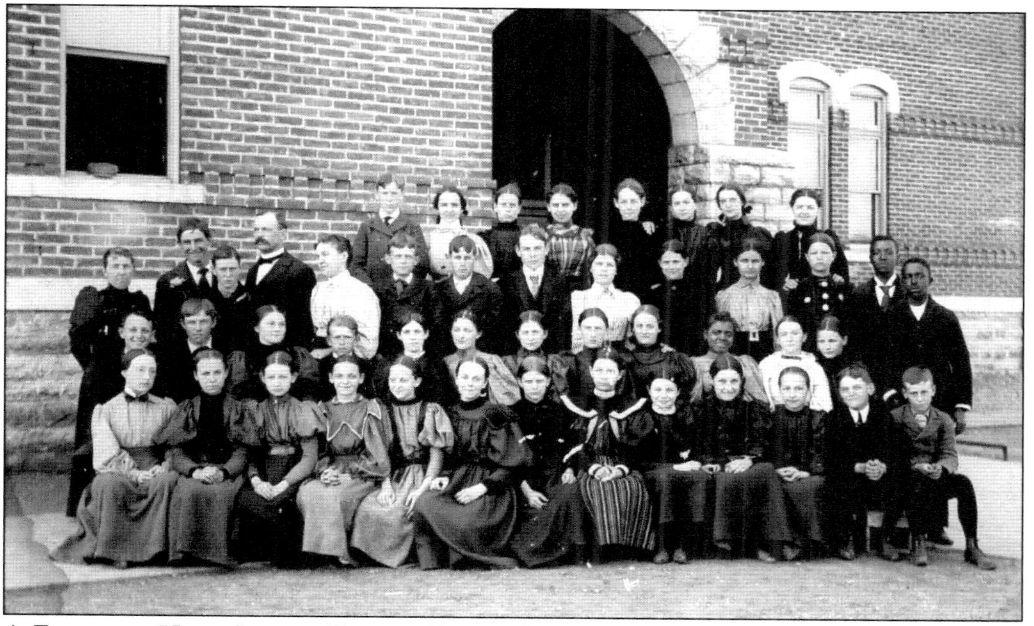

A FRANKLIN HIGH SCHOOL EIGHTH-GRADE CLASS. The photograph was taken in the late 1890s in front of the entrance to the high school. The teacher is Lena Shirley. The gentleman in the black suit is F. Gillum Cromer, superintendent of Franklin Schools until 1901. After that, Cromer became president of the Miami Valley Chautauqua, a post which offered him a wider stage upon which to impose his predilection for sober thought and deed.

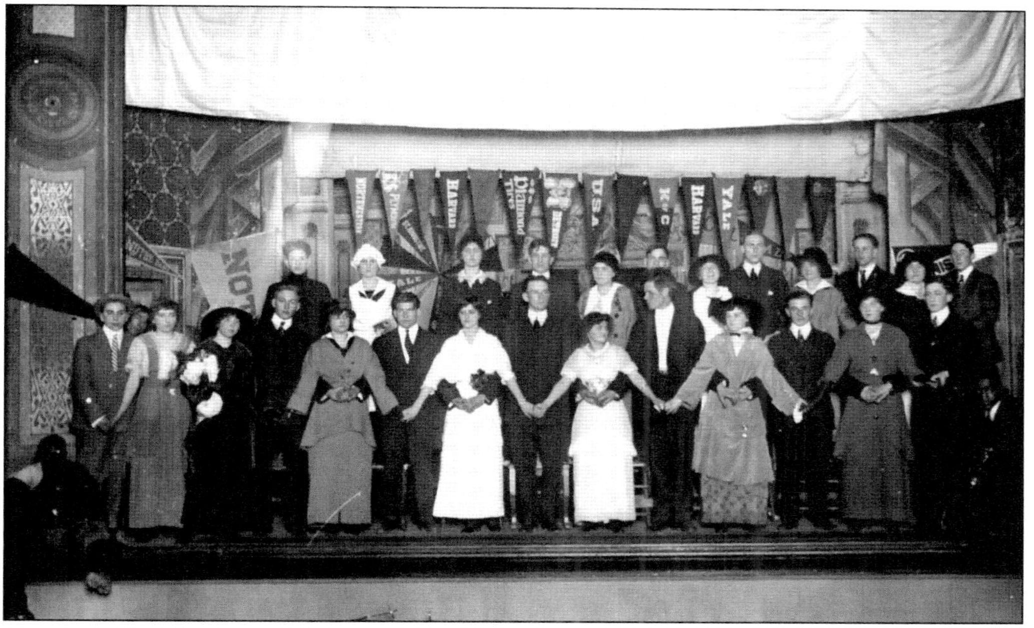

A PERFORMANCE OF *END OF THE RAINBOW*. This high school production occurred on January 6–7, 1915, probably in the old city building on Fourth Street. The level of effort and participation of this performance indicates how far the community's notions of what constituted a useful education had evolved since the days of Hampton Bennett.

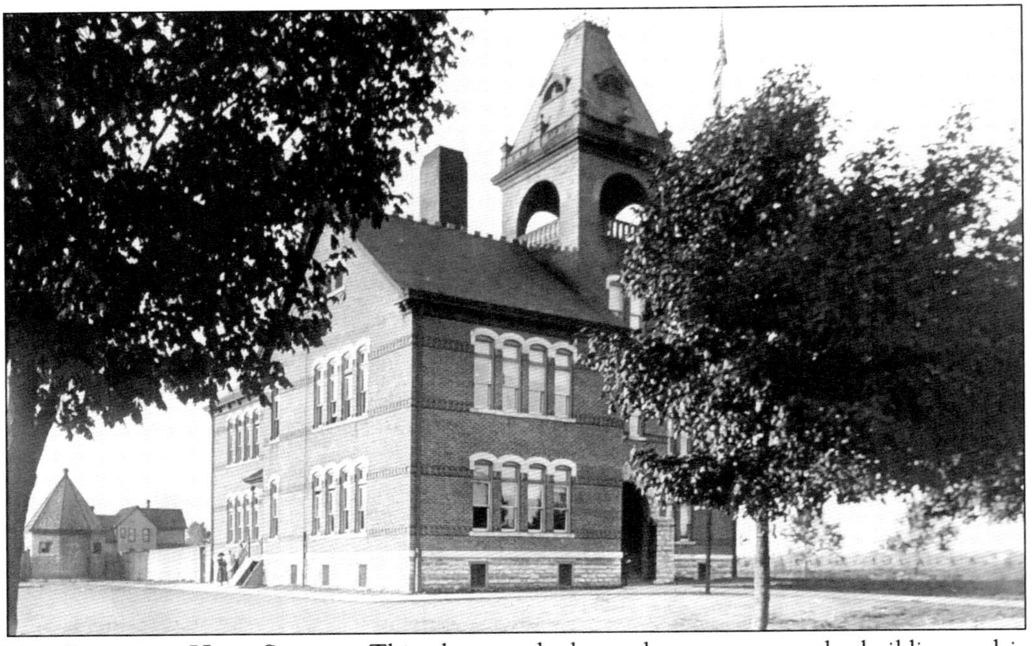

THE FRANKLIN HIGH SCHOOL. This photograph shows the entrance to the building and is looking west from Pine Street. One of the two octagonal outdoor toilets sits discreetly at left.

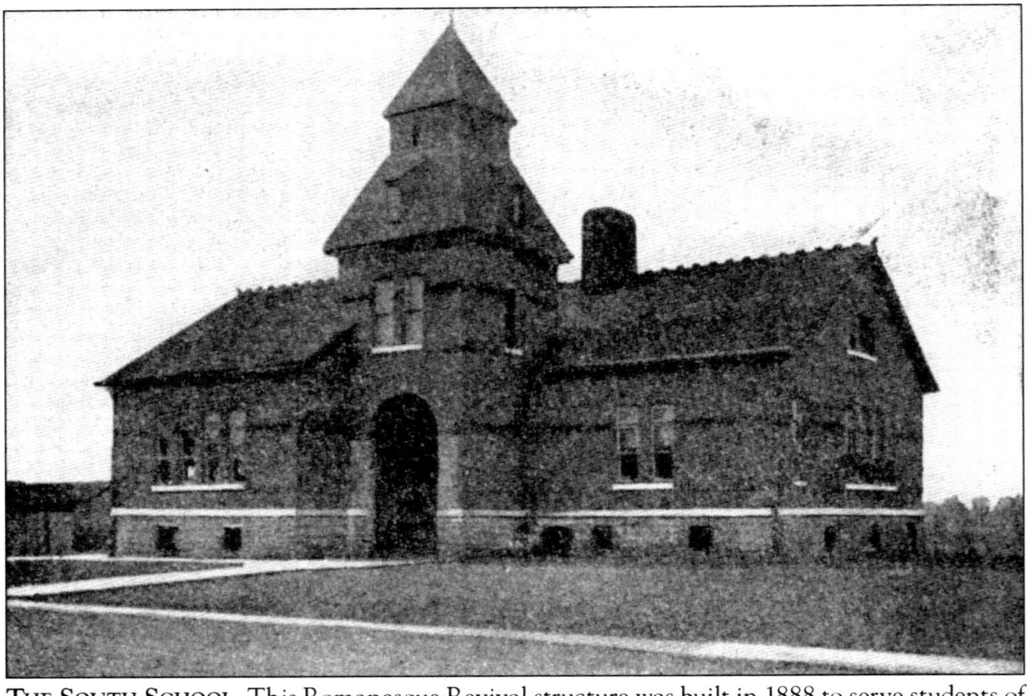

THE SOUTH SCHOOL. This Romanesque Revival structure was built in 1888 to serve students of grades one through six who lived in the south end of town. It stood at the southwest corner of Main and Eighth Streets and was razed in 1965.

Five

LIFE AND LEISURE

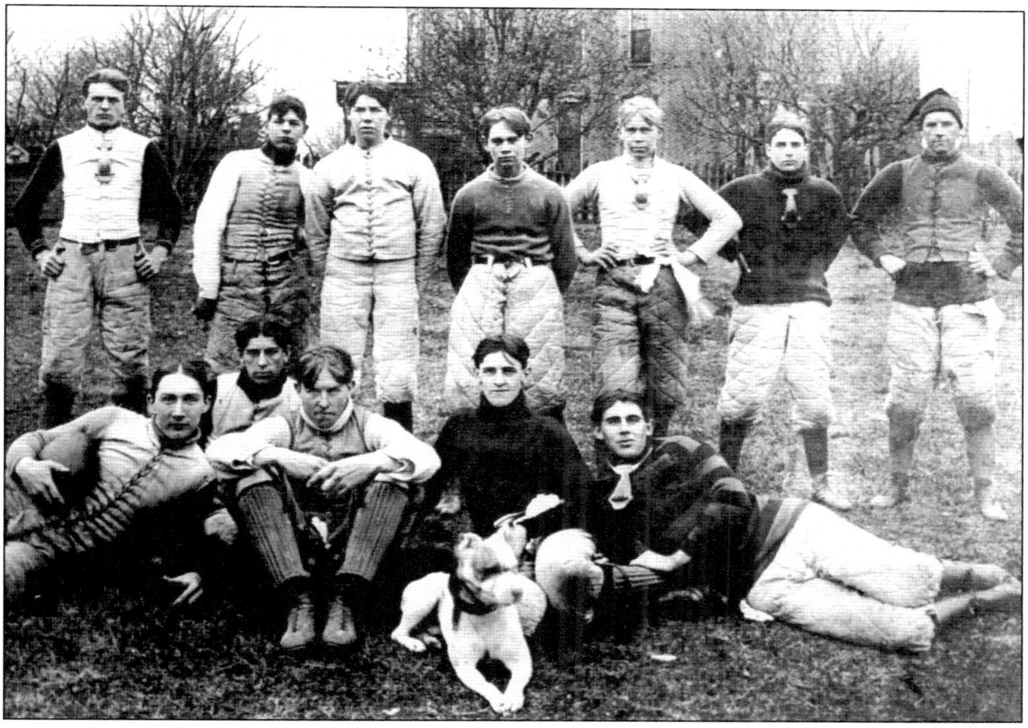

FRANKLIN'S HEROES OF THE GRIDIRON. The view looks west from just south of today's Route 123. In the background is the Woodward homestead that stood where the Hampton Bennett School is located today. The blond young man standing third from right, with hand on hips, is Carl Harding, son of paper mill manager Charles Harding. The Hardings lived in an Italianate home that still stands at 209 Oxford Road. Judging from Harding's age, the photograph would have been taken about 1905, when Theodore Roosevelt was in the White House, and the country was just beginning its love affair with team sports.

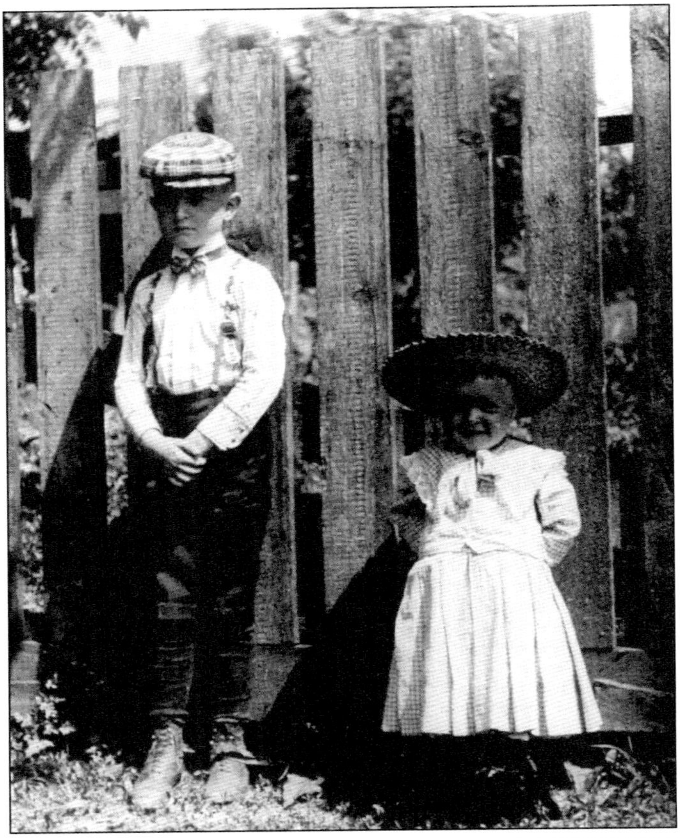

The Neal Brothers at Play. The dignified Walter Neal stands at left with his less formally attired younger brother, Ross. The two are posing about 1900 in their grandmother's back yard. She lived at what was then 11 Allen Avenue, located on the east side and north end of that street. They were visiting their grandmother from their home in Dayton, where their father worked as an inspector for the electric railroad.

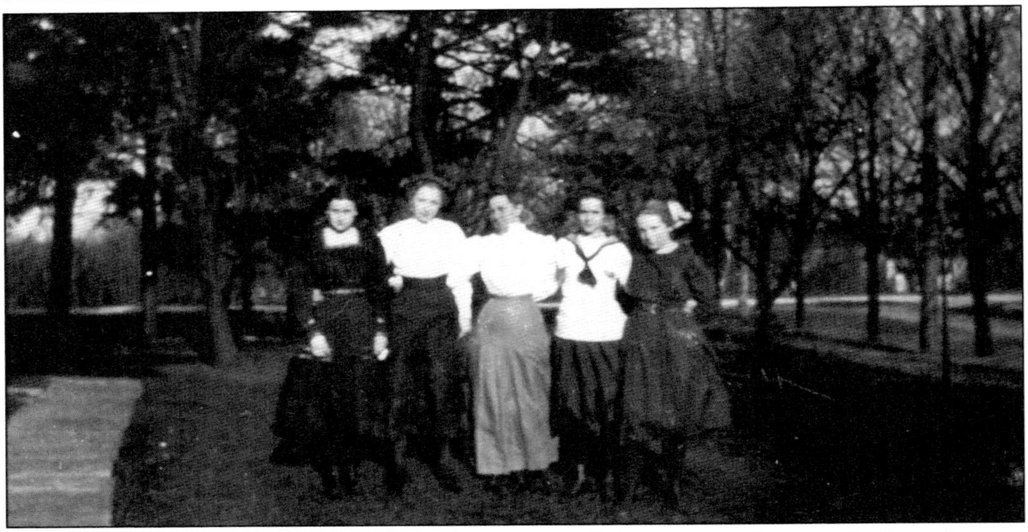

Young Women Stop by for a Visit. These young ladies are standing on the front lawn at 49 Miami Avenue about 1913. The identities of all of these interestingly dressed individuals are not known, but they are probably friends of teenage Mary Jane Anderson, who lived in the home at that time. The photograph is looking east, toward north Franklin. Behind the lawn is today's Miami Avenue, with the Great Miami River on the other side.

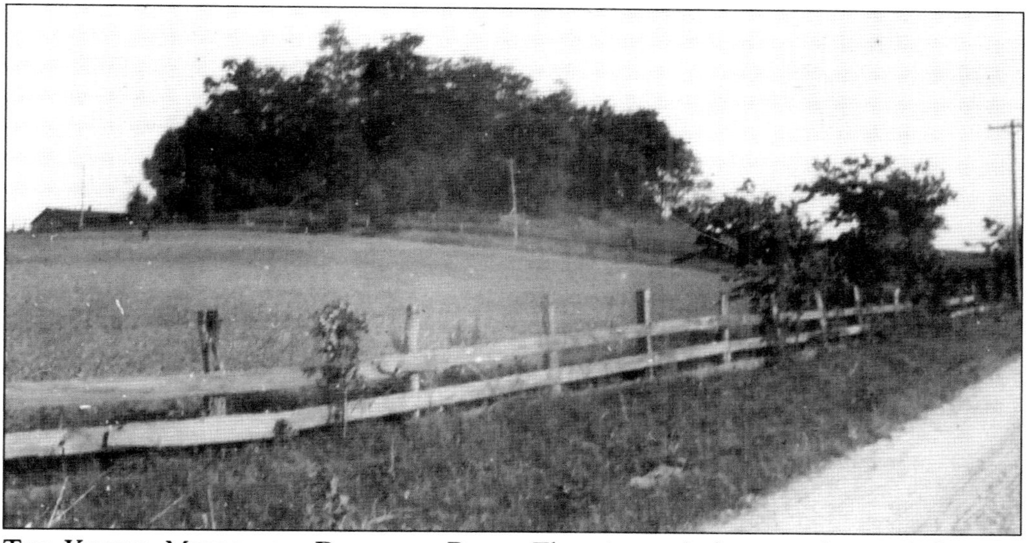

THE KINDER MOUND ON DEARDOFF ROAD. The view is looking southeast. A frequent destination for local hiking trips, especially for schoolchildren, was this burial mound. It was built by the Native American Adena Culture, which flourished in the river valleys of southern Ohio from 800 BC to 100 AD.

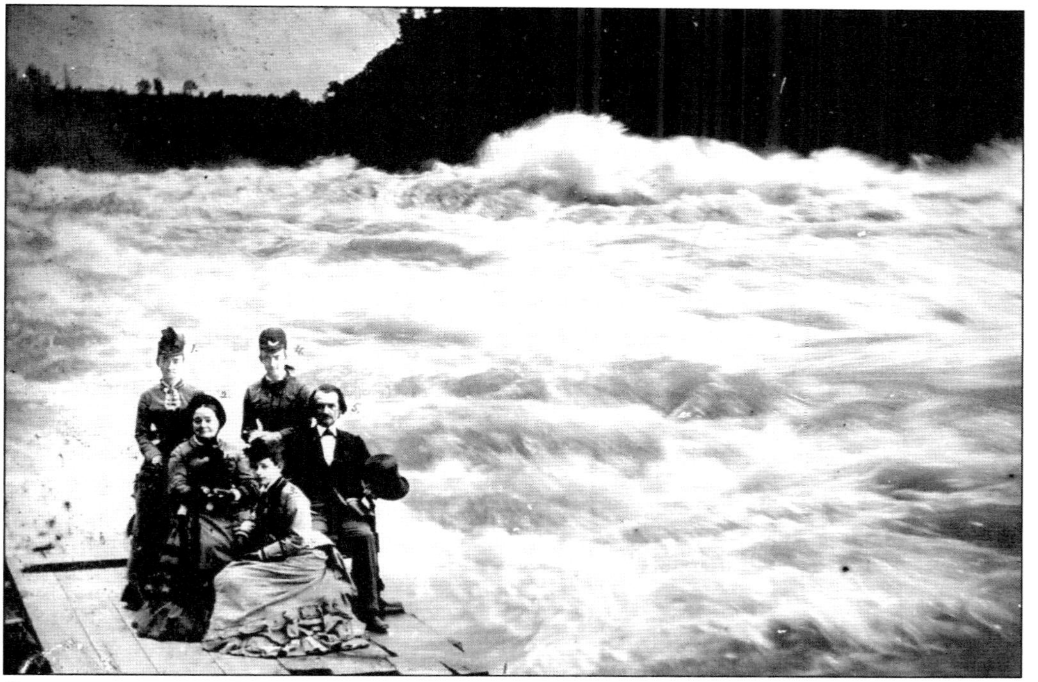

COMMEMORATING A VISIT TO NIAGARA FALLS. This image, a bit of trick photography, shows young Lilly Woodward of Franklin, with her cousins the Campbells of Hamilton, on August 17, 1876. Lilly sits in the foreground. The dignified gentleman seated is Lilly's uncle, Edwin D. Campbell, a former member of the House of Representatives. The other ladies are his wife and daughters. Their studio image is cleverly superimposed over a raft, and this combination over a view of the falls.

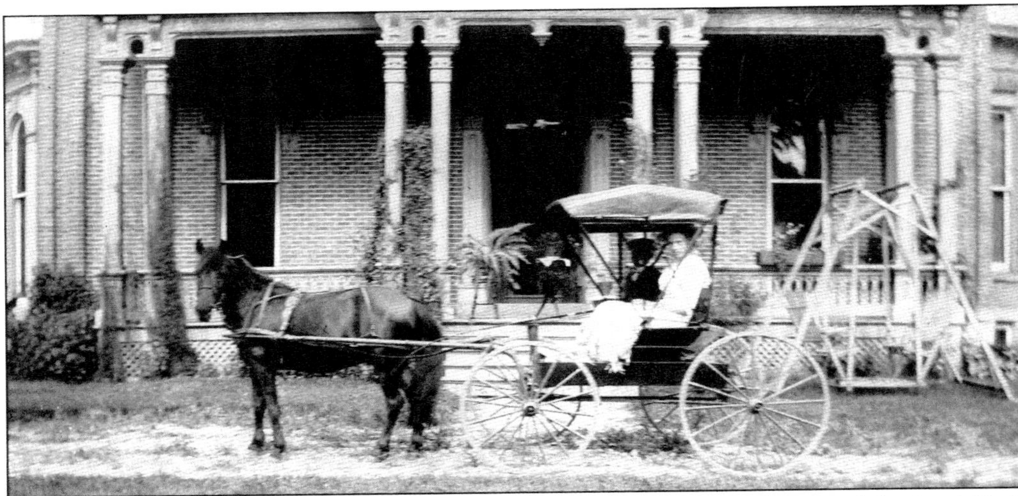

MARY CROLL IN THE FAMILY BUGGY. The photograph was taken in front of the Levi Croll mansion about 1915. One of Mary's brothers, either Carl or Frank, sits with her in the conveyance, which is drawn by their horse Teddy. Mary was the daughter of George Croll, who farmed the property. George was the youngest son of Levi, who built the residence. Mary would one day open a flower shop on the property that would operate until the 1980s. (Courtesy of Bob Croll.)

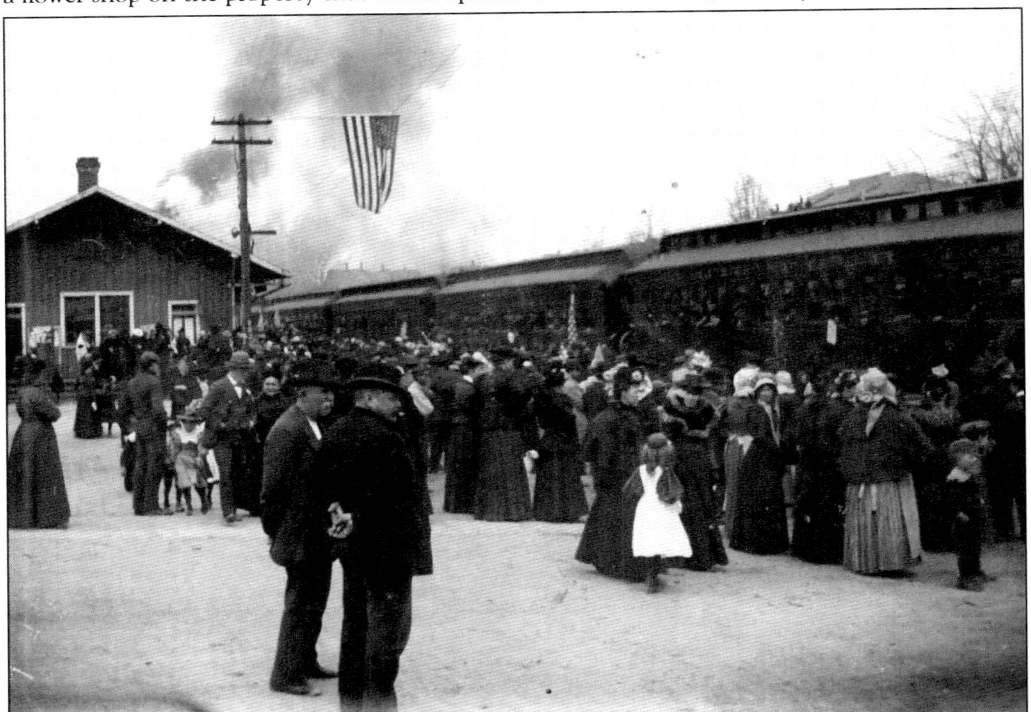

THE FIRST OHIO VOLUNTEER INFANTRY IN FRANKLIN. This is one of three photographs taken of the regiment at the Big Four (Cincinnati, Cleveland, Columbus, and Indianapolis) Railroad Station on Fourth Street, looking north, about 1898. The regiment is either departing for or returning from service in the Spanish-American War or Philippine Insurrection. Two Franklin men served in the First Ohio Cavalry during the war, and died as a result of their service.

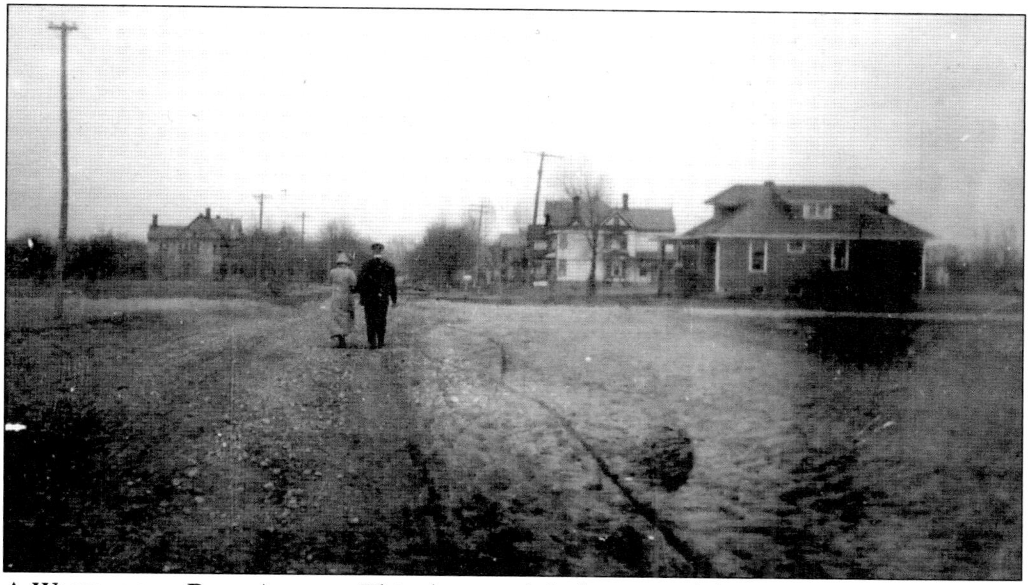

A Walk along Park Avenue. This photograph looks east and shows the western edge of the village at that time. The bungalow-type home near right is now 508 Park Avenue. The large white house to its left is 420 Park Avenue (which no longer stands). The couple taking the walk appear to be Justin and May Harding, who lived at 302 Park Avenue.

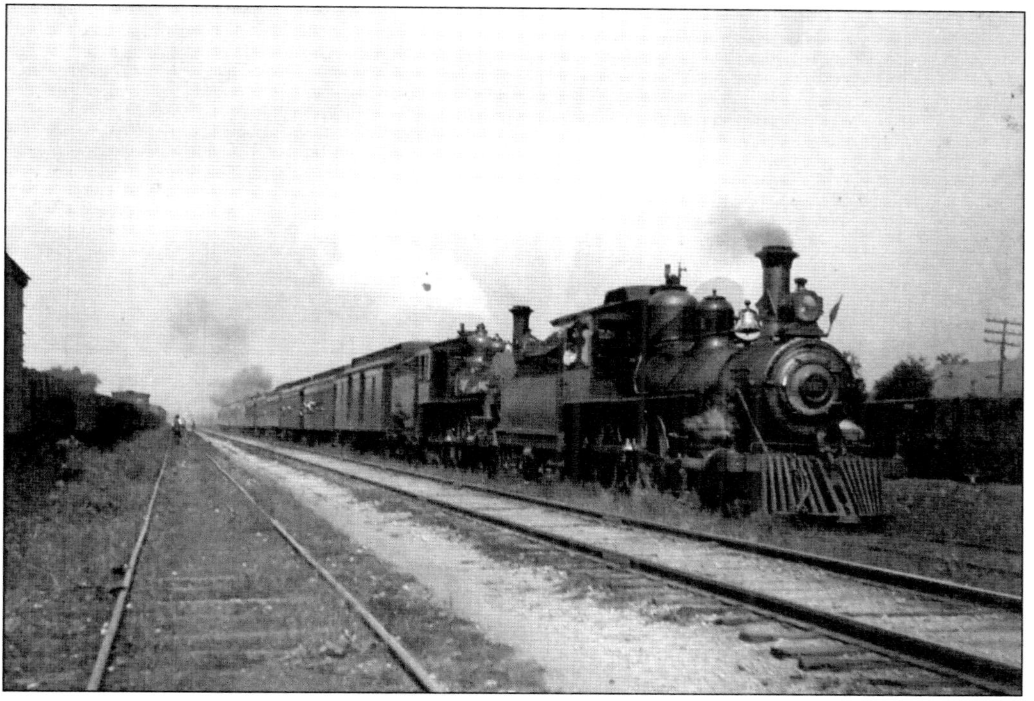

Doubleheader Steam Engines on Franklin's West Side. Visible are three sets of tracks, an indication of the level of rail activity at the time. Note the employee dismounting from the cab of one of the moving engines. The locomotives were turned around in the Y-shaped roundhouse for their return to Jackson, Michigan. (Courtesy of Tom Foley.)

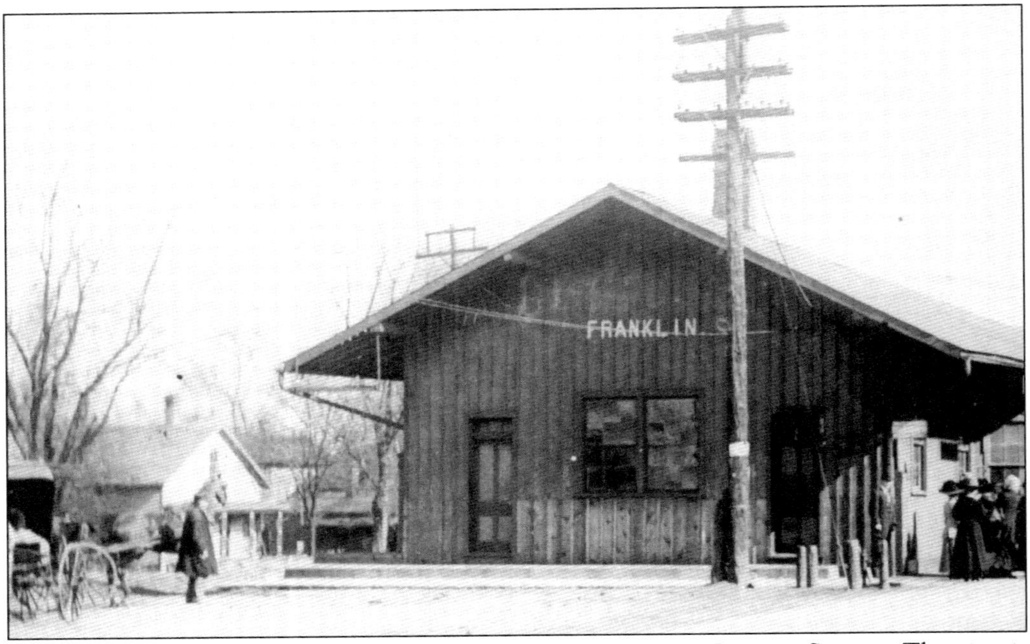

THE BIG FOUR (NEW YORK CENTRAL) RAILROAD STATION AT FOURTH STREET. The view is north from Fourth Street. Passengers are waiting for the arriving train. The houses at left are on the west side of the Miami-Erie Canal that is situated between them and the station building. During the 19th century, there were two passenger stations in downtown Franklin. (Courtesy of Tom Foley.)

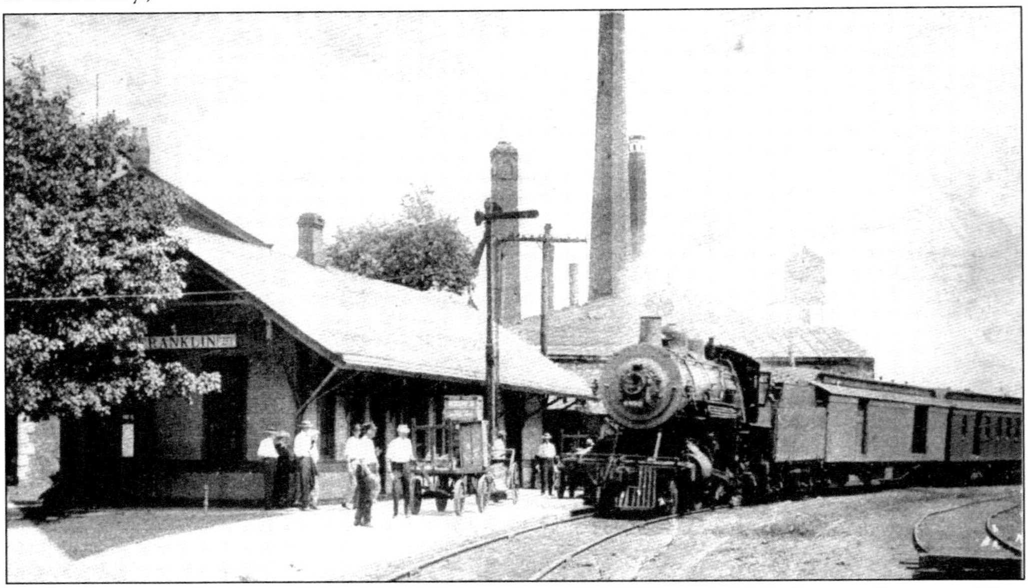

THE COMBINED BIG FOUR/CINCINNATI NORTHERN STATION ON SIXTH STREET. This photograph of a steam engine pulling into the station is looking southeast before 1918. Franklin's passenger stations were combined here after the construction of the Carlisle cutoff in 1911, which led to the removal of the tracks east of the river, north of Franklin. Note the water tower and smokestacks of Franklin's south end paper factories in the distance. (Courtesy of Tom Foley.)

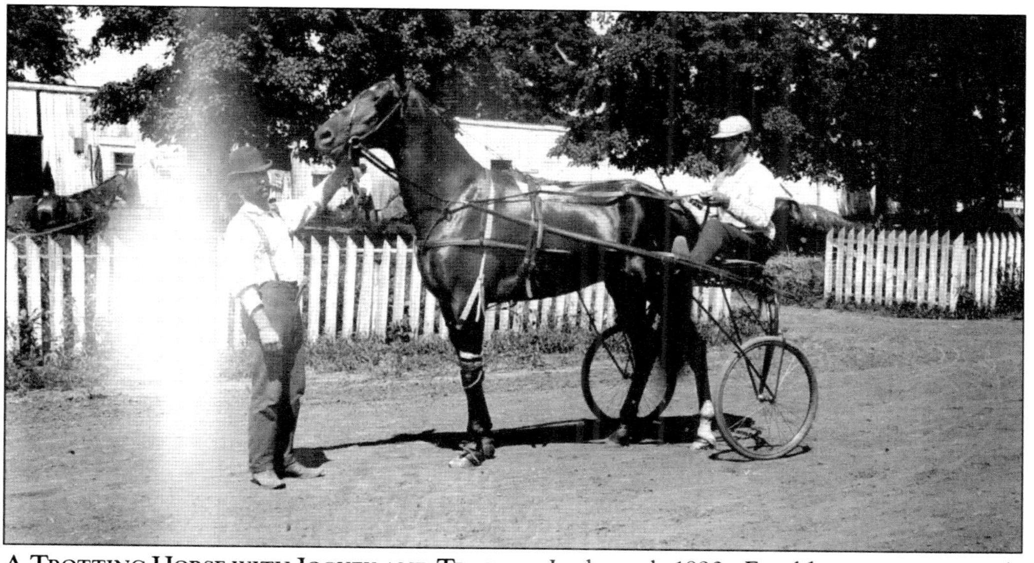

A TROTTING HORSE WITH JOCKEY AND TRAINER. In the early 1890s, Franklin went temporarily mad over racing trotting horses. The stimulus for this insanity was the string of successes had by Nightingale, a filly owned by two highly respected locals, Derrick Anderson and Charles Harding. The community returned to reality when the horse was finally defeated. It has been suggested that this may be a photograph of that very animal.

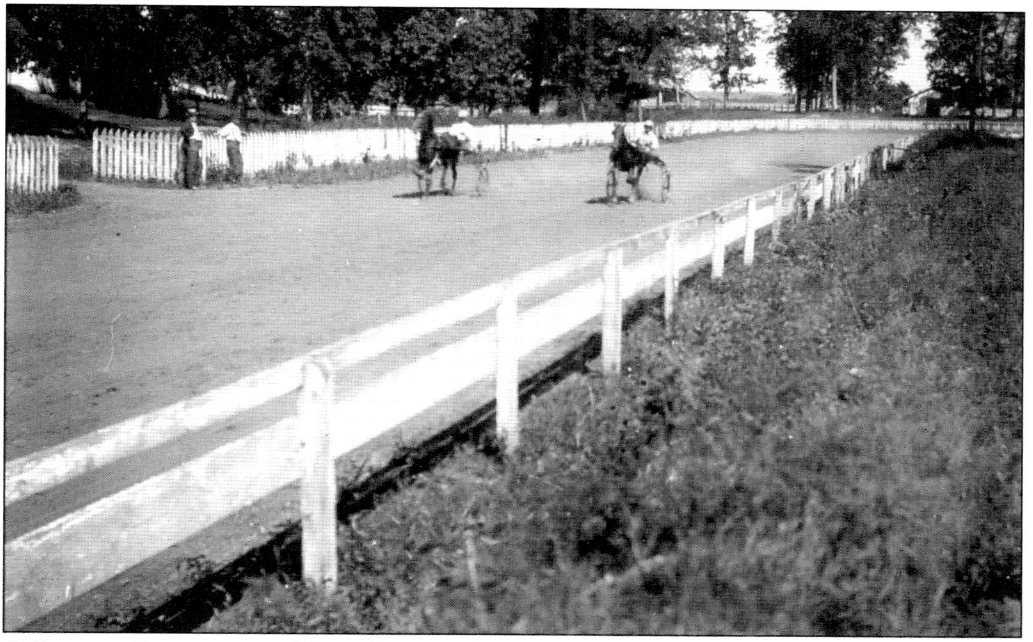

A PAIR OF TROTTERS AT THEIR PACES. The site of this photograph is unknown, but it does not seem to be the racetrack at the Franklin Fairgrounds. After Nightingale's winning streak in 1892, many locals were convinced of the horse's invincibility and placed huge wagers on her success. Predictably, the trotter was finally defeated and many citizens suffered losses they could not afford. It was even speculated that the horse's defeat led to the failure of the village's only bank.

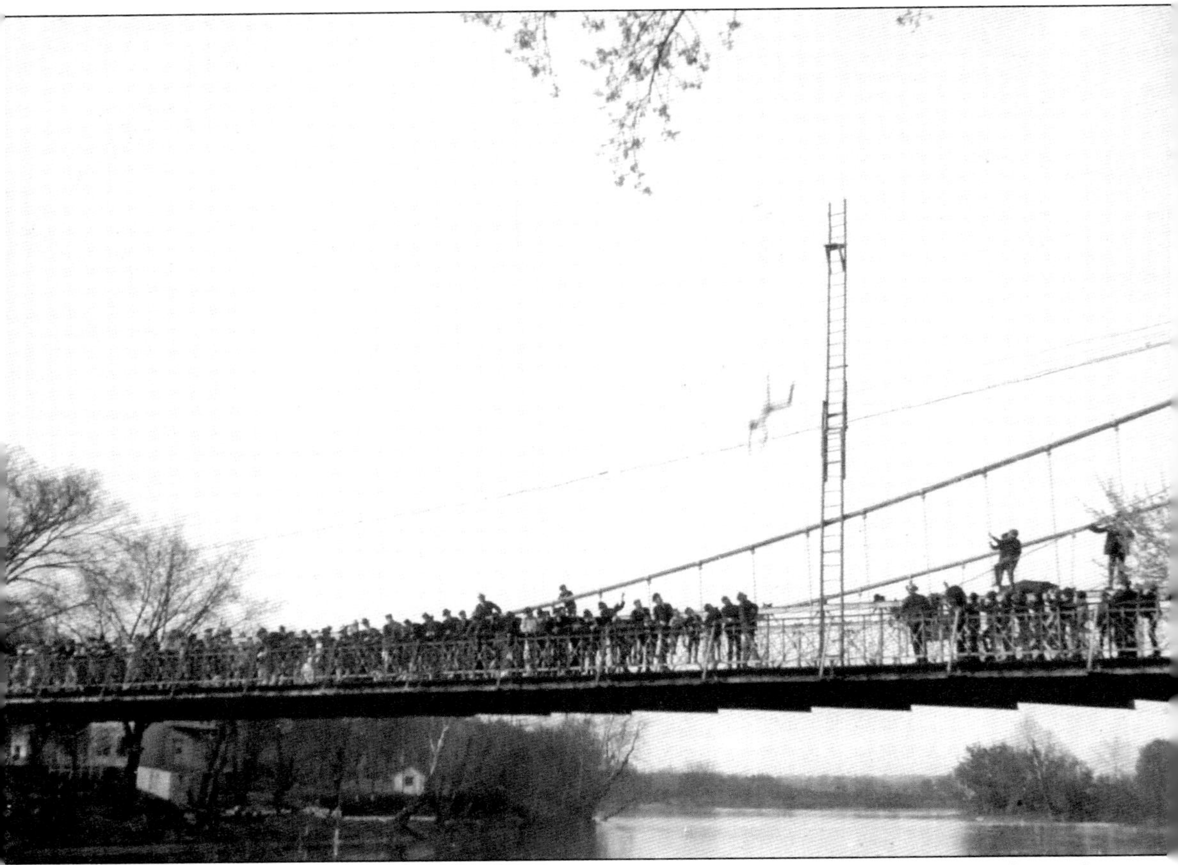

DIVING FROM THE FRANKLIN SUSPENSION BRIDGE. The young men observing the diving from the ladder appear to be similarly attired and so may be members of the National Guard. The photograph, looking north, was taken prior to 1913. At left is the gently sloping west bank of the Great Miami River as it appeared prior to the construction of the levee. Note the shed in the distance that is located almost on the river bank and was vulnerable to being carried away at the first high water.

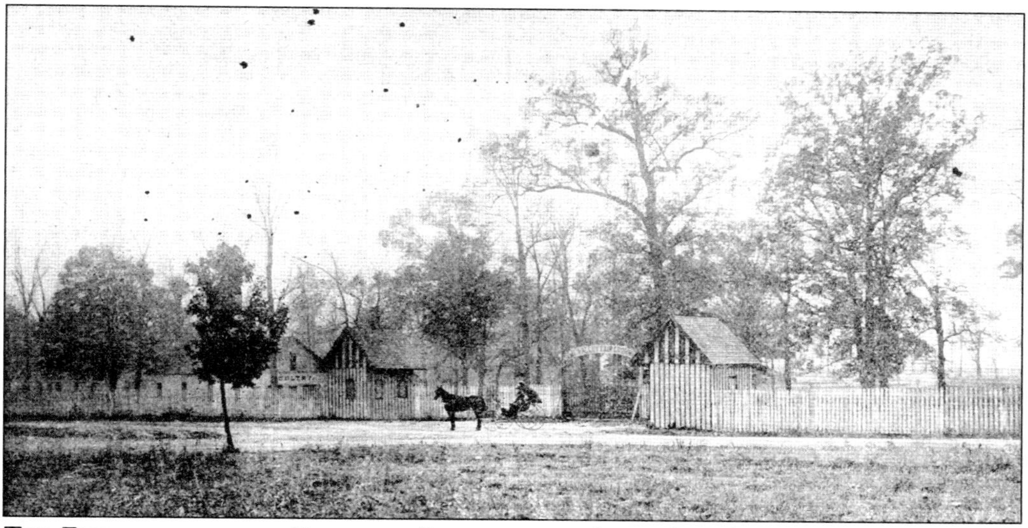

THE ENTRANCE TO THE FRANKLIN FAIRGROUNDS. Located at the corner of Lake Avenue and Walnut Street, the fairgrounds were developed in the grove of walnut trees located on the L. G. Anderson farm. The site was the original home of the Miami Valley Chautauqua, which operated there from 1895 to 1900. The fairgrounds contained a variety of wooden structures, including a racetrack, dining hall, and art hall, which became derelict after the Chautauqua moved to its new home along the river.

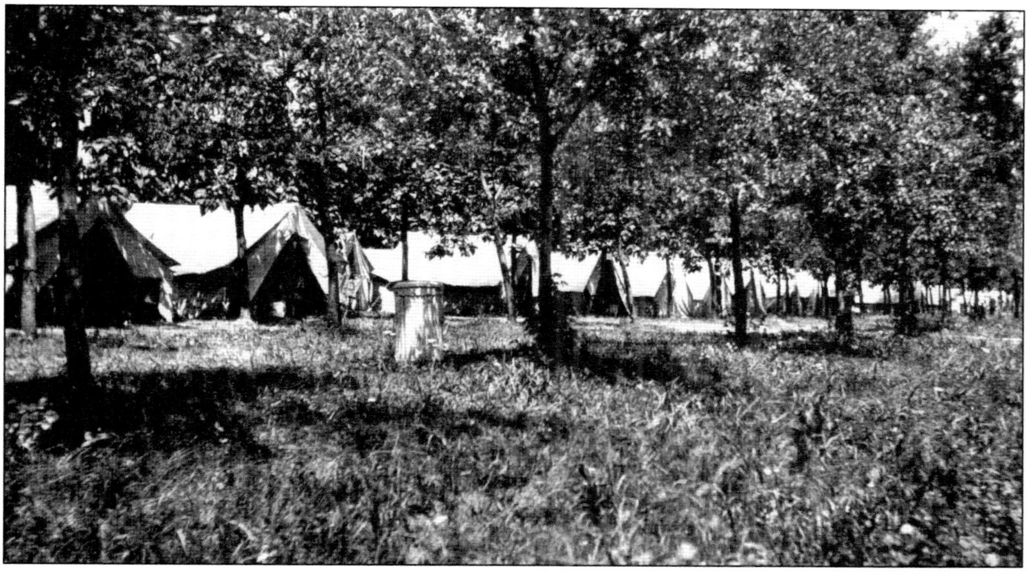

THE TENT CITY AT CHAUTAUQUA. After its relocation in 1901 to a site along the river, the scene of the Chautauqua now resembled that of its namesake along a lake in New York. Twelve hundred trees of 40 varieties were planted to create a new grove. The typical Chautauqua season lasted for two weeks in July and August. In 1906, the tent population reached its peak of 600. These tents were located on Sunset Avenue, on the western edge of the community.

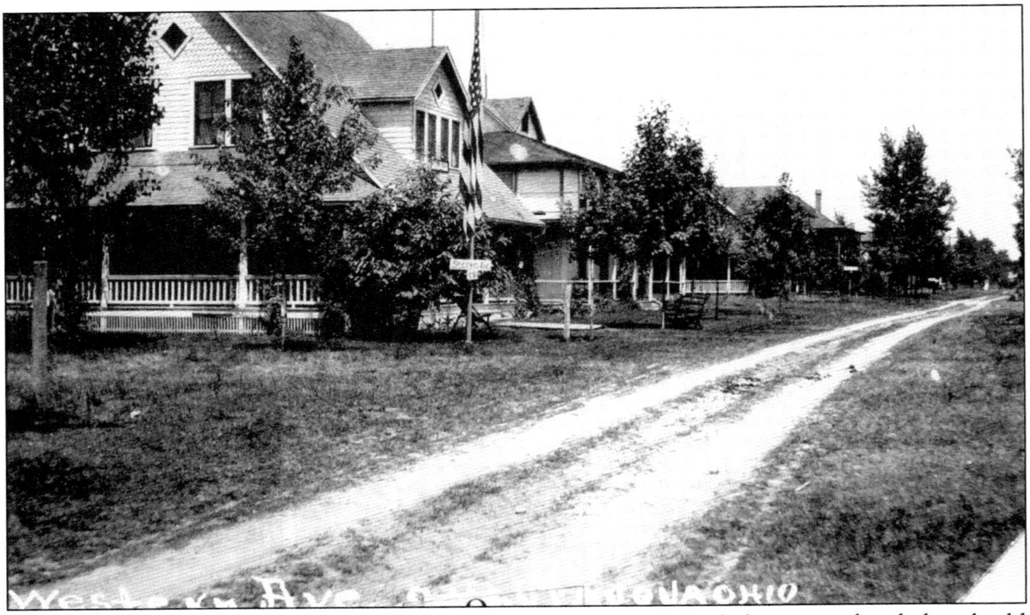

CHAUTAUQUA COTTAGES. Eventually the frequent and well-heeled visitors decided to build comfortable cottages, and by 1908, sixty had been constructed. The cottages acquired whimsical names, such as Quaint Marinuka, Rustic Rest, Bon Air, Good Luck, Hermosa Villa, and Swastika (a good luck symbol before it acquired later connotations). This photograph was taken at the intersection of Western Avenue and First Street and looks west on First Street.

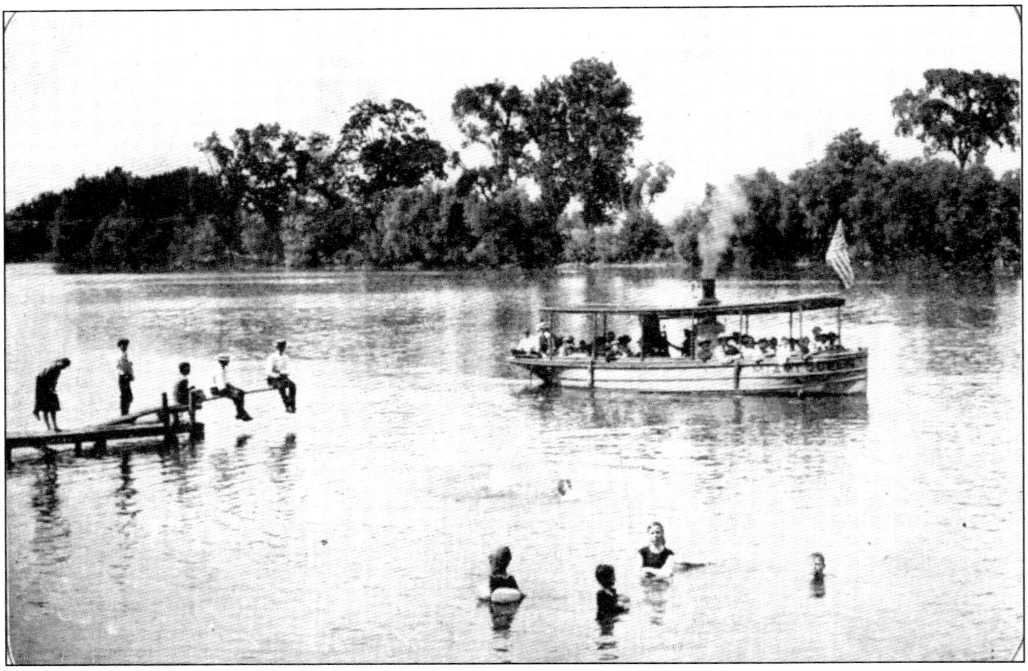

ON THE GREAT MIAMI RIVER AT CHAUTAUQUA. One of the attractions of the Chautauqua season was the opportunity for time on and along the river. Typically this included a short, chugging journey in this small steamer, the *Miami Queen*.

THE BANDSTAND AT THE MIAMI VALLEY CHAUTAUQUA. Visitors spending a few days in the bosom of Mother Nature were not necessarily deprived of the finer things, such as good music. From this natural podium, guests could be serenaded with waltzes, marches, or popular songs. (Courtesy of William Moses.)

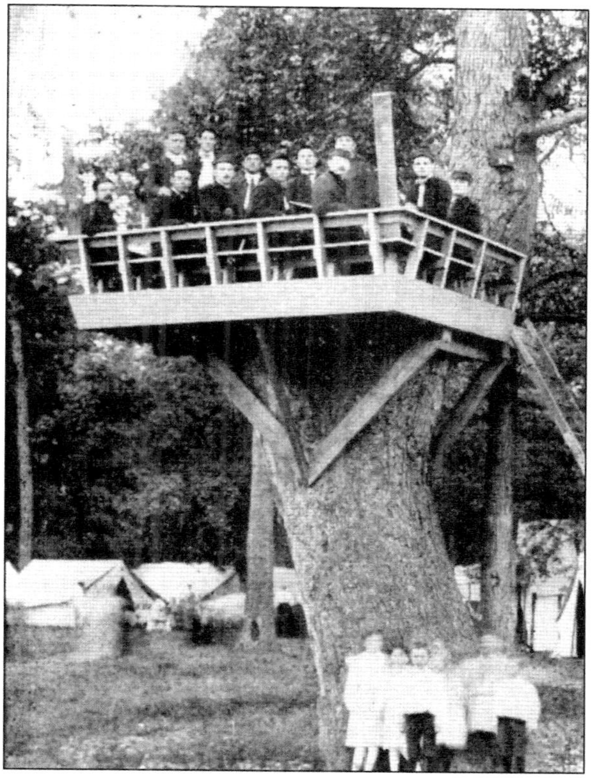

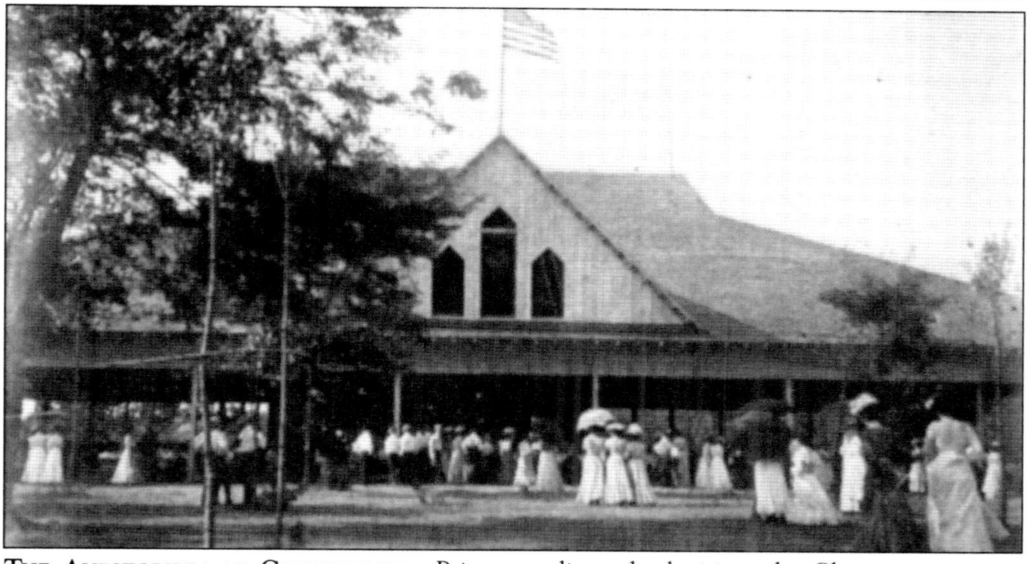

THE AUDITORIUM AT CHAUTAUQUA. Prior to radio and television, the Chautauqua season provided local residents the opportunity to hear speakers of national reputation in their own backyard. And the auditorium was where these events were held. Most renowned among the early speakers was orator William Jennings Bryan, the Democratic candidate for the presidency in 1896, 1900, and 1908. Eleanor Roosevelt also spoke here in the 1940, although the local Republicans did not appreciate her visit.

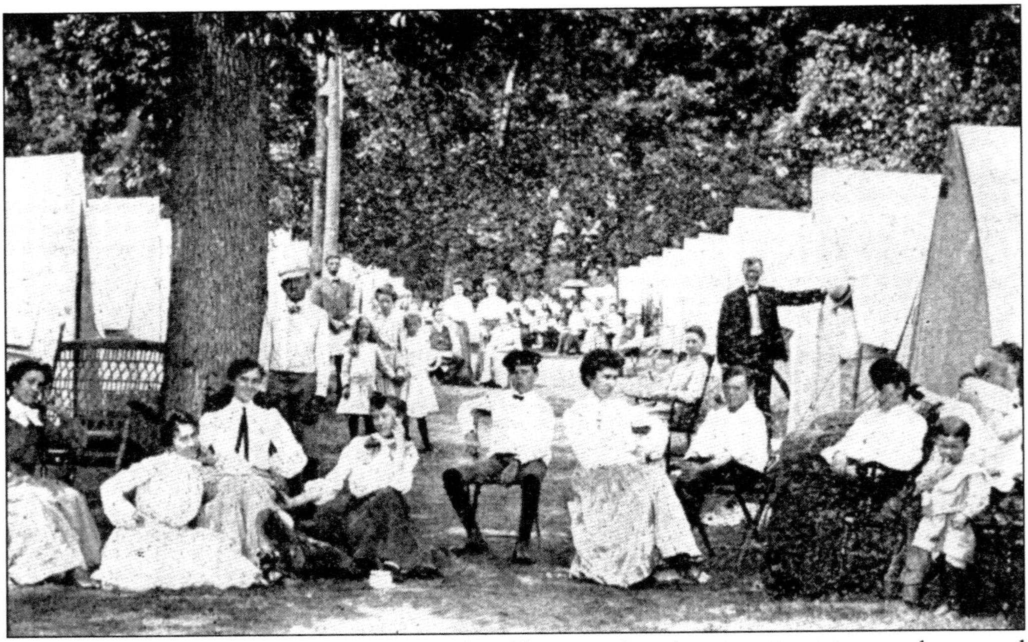

AMONG THE CAMPERS AT CHAUTAUQUA. In addition to the education, inspiring speakers, good music, abundant food, river scenes and sounds, time at Chautauqua offered the opportunity for many hours of leisurely conversation with friends and neighbors under the trees. (Courtesy of William Moses.)

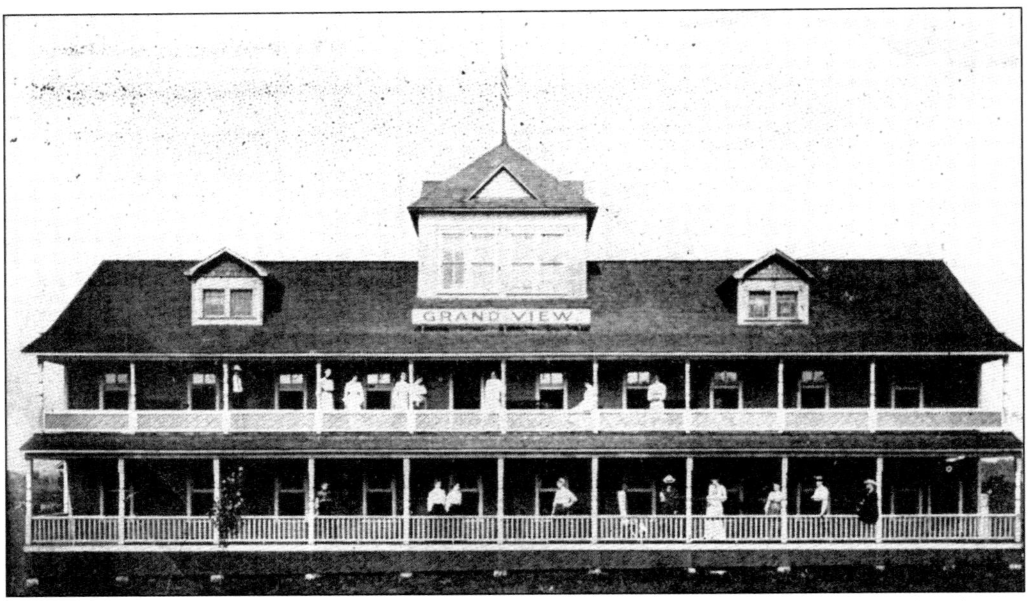

THE GRAND VIEW HOTEL AT CHAUTAUQUA. For those who did not appreciate the charms of sleeping in tents with the field mice, snakes, and insects, the comforts of civilization were readily at hand. This hotel was one of several built at the site, and closely resembled the resort accommodations available at the original Chautauqua in New York. This hotel contained 54 guest rooms. It was later a victim of arson. (Courtesy of William Moses.)

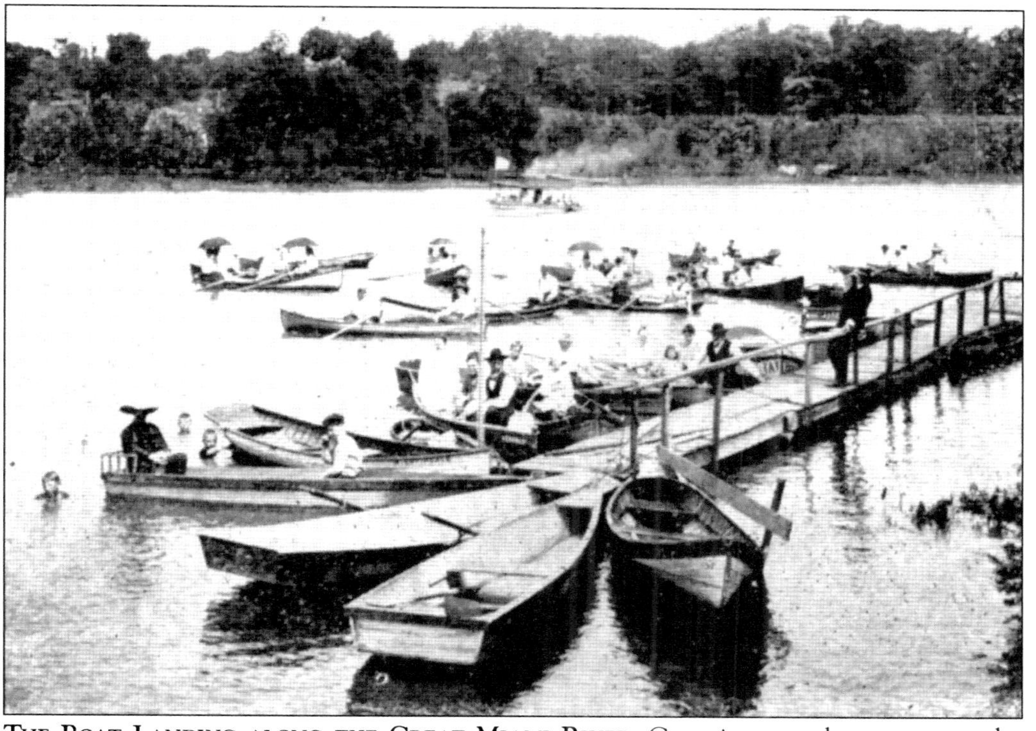

THE BOAT LANDING ALONG THE GREAT MIAMI RIVER. Canoeing was also a very popular activity, but potentially dangerous. Newspapers from this period describe drownings that occurred when canoes overturned and the occupants, attired in suits or flowing dresses, quickly sank. (Courtesy of William Moses.)

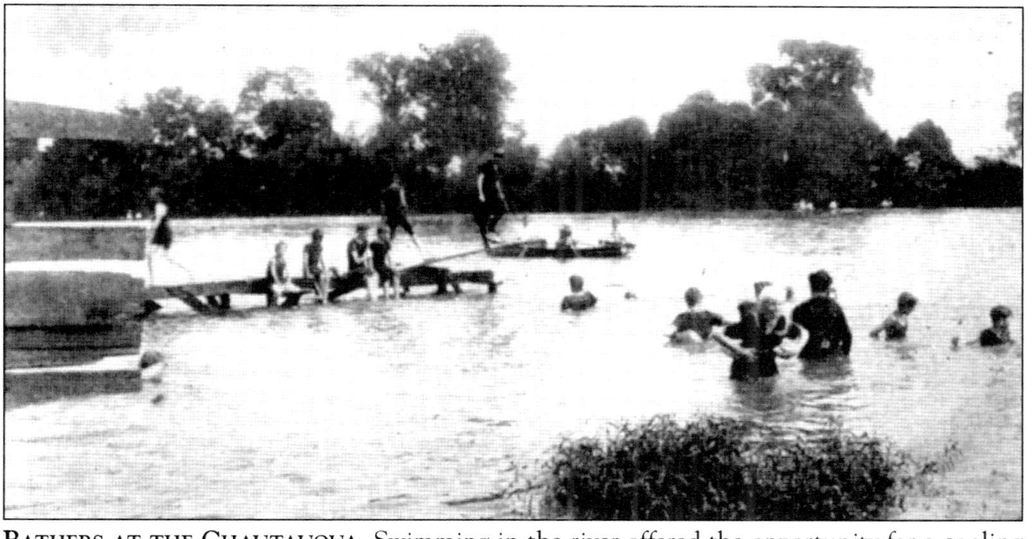

BATHERS AT THE CHAUTAUQUA. Swimming in the river offered the opportunity for a cooling escape from the July and August heat. It also offered the excitement of the latest and most-revealing bathing costumes in a time when men and especially woman customarily were hidden under layers of voluminous clothing. The management of the Chautauqua was, however, ever on guard to protect the morals of its young visitors. (Courtesy of William Moses.)

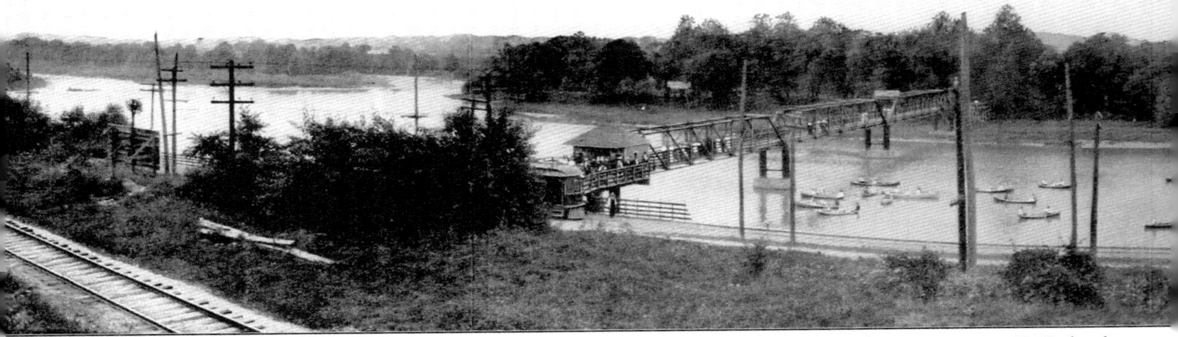

THE MIAMI VALLEY CHAUTAUQUA. This panoramic photograph taken prior to 1913 looks west from the hills along the east side of the Great Miami River. The line across the river at far left is the spillway over the Chautauqua Dam. The three-span iron footbridge at left was built to facilitate the arrival of visitors via the traction cars from other cities. This bridge was

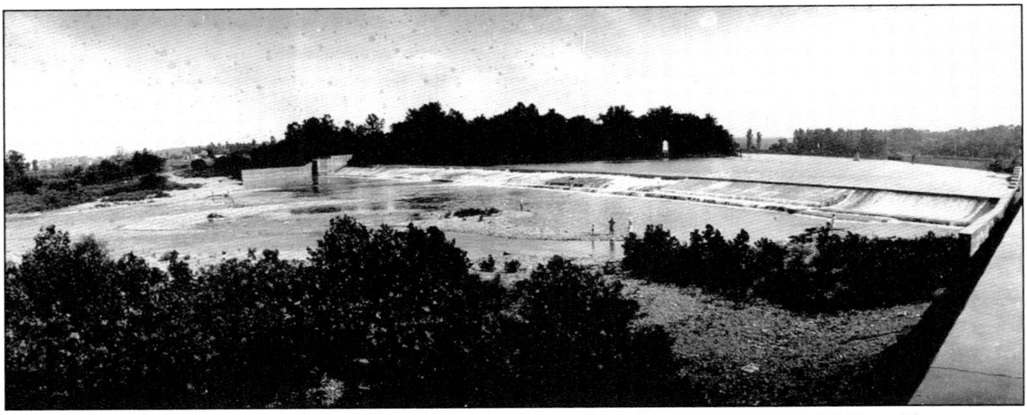

THE CHAUTAUQUA DAM. The photograph looks north. The Great Miami Valley Chautauqua site was in the woods on the west side of the river, in the left distance. In the right center foreground is the wall of the Van Horne Hydraulic that channeled water from the river to power the early industries in the north end of Franklin.

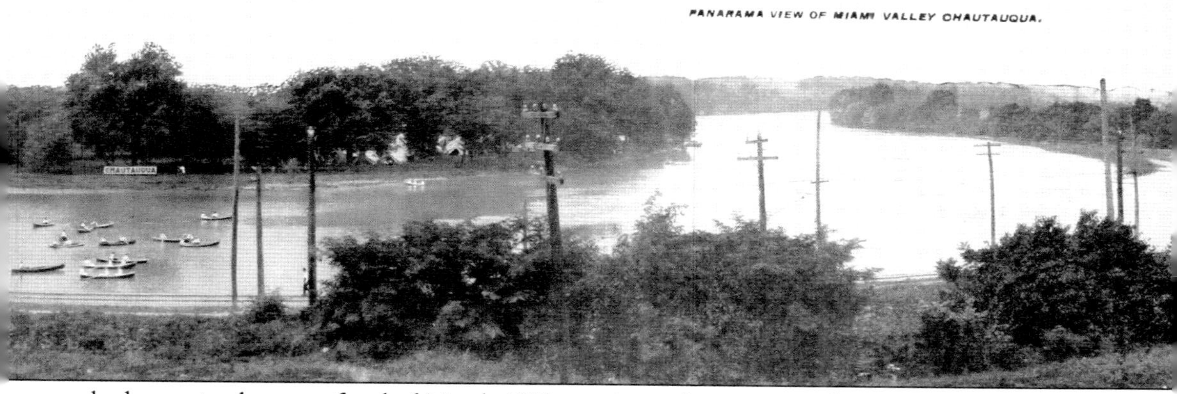

washed away in the great flood of March 1913, requiring the erection of a temporary pontoon bridge. In the right distance, some tents of the encampment are visible in the bend on the opposite shore. Most of the cottages, however, would have been further back in the trees in the center distance.

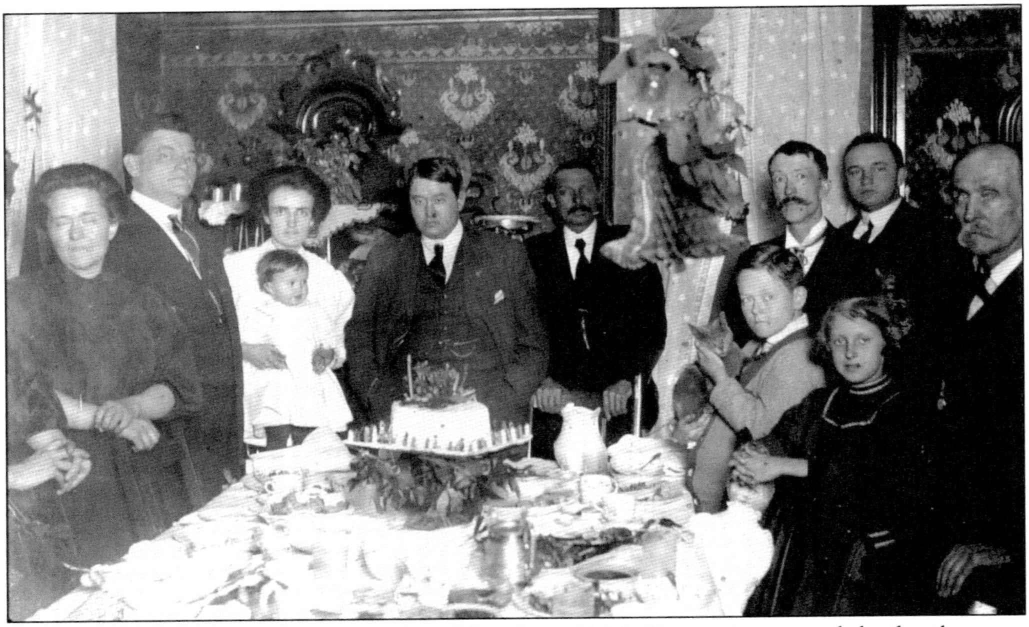

CHRISTMAS DINNER AT GRANDMOTHER NEAL'S IN 1908. Dinner is over and the family seems about ready to cut into the holiday cake at the Neal home on Allen Street. The walls are covered with very elaborate and probably colorful wallpaper. The manner of dress of the family members reflects the changing times, with the older generation of men still wearing large moustaches and butterfly collars, while the younger men are clean shaven.

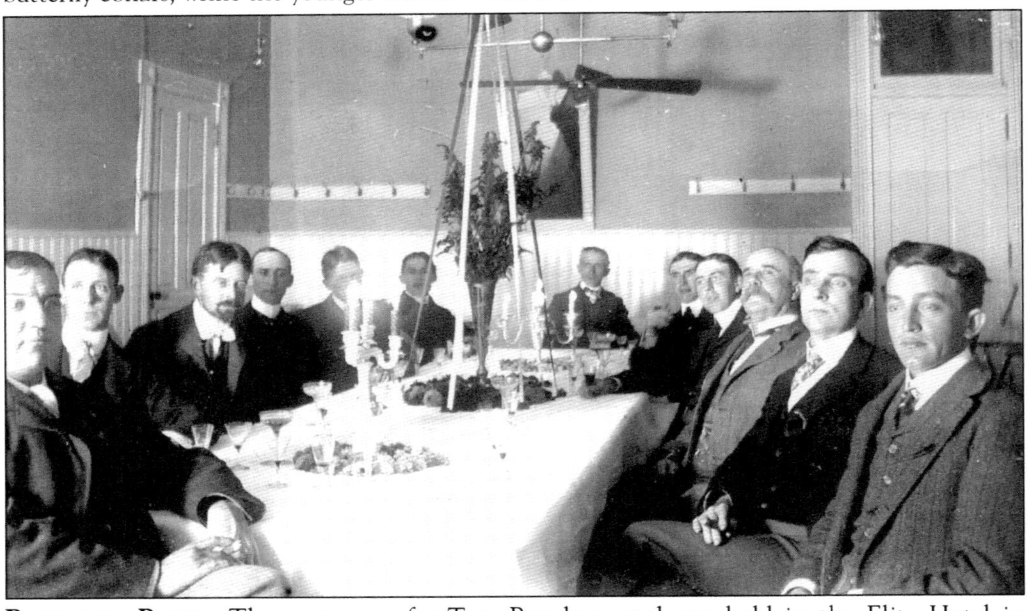

BACHELOR PARTY. The party was for Tom Barnhart and was held in the Elite Hotel in 1901. Under the ceiling fan and gaslights, the groom and the guests are enjoying unknown beverages and cigars. Tom sits at the head of the table in the distance. Jim Governey, the hotel's proprietor, sits third from right, in the light suit. Howard Conover, owner of the local hardware store, sits at left.

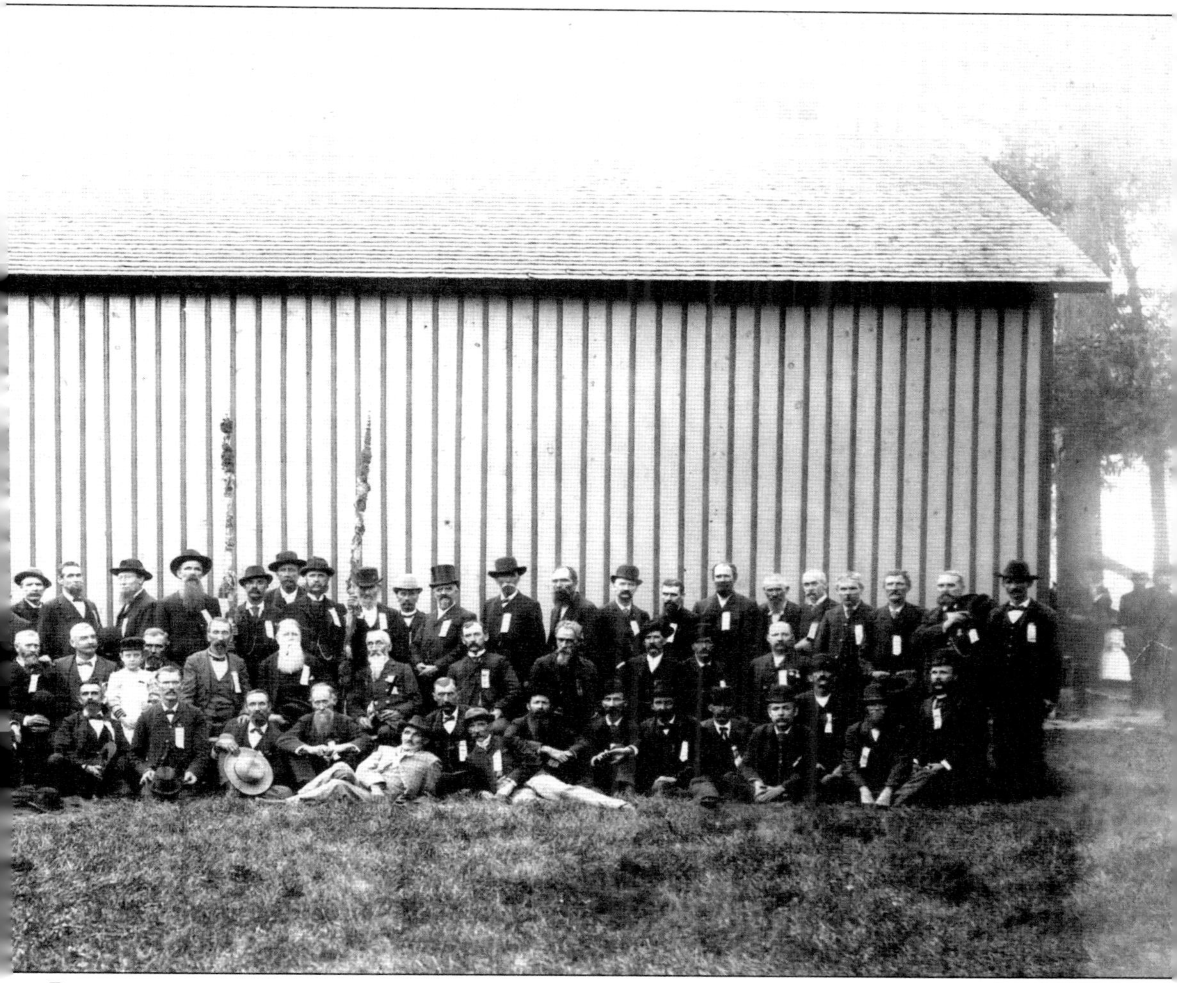

REUNION OF THE 75TH OHIO VOLUNTEER INFANTRY. The view was photographed at the Franklin Fairgrounds in 1896 or 1897, in front of its Art Hall. Behind the men stand their old regimental colors, borrowed from the state house in Columbus. The man with the broad white beard seated between the colors is Nathanial McLean, the regiment's first colonel and the son of Supreme Court justice John McLean. To his left, in the light suit, sits Andrew L. Harris, the regiment's second colonel and future Ohio governor (in 1906). The unit's lieutenant colonel, with the white, pointed beard, is Ben Morgan, who sits to McLean's right. The 75th Ohio fought in the Shenandoah Valley in 1862. In 1863, it served with the Army of the Potomac, and was heavily engaged at Gettysburg. Later the regiment served as mounted infantry in Florida. Company F of the 75th Ohio was recruited in Franklin by Morgan, and at least 32 men from the township served in that company. Of these 32 men, 4 died during the war, another 7 were wounded in action, and 11 were captured. Overall at least 28 Franklin men died as a result of their service (most of disease), and among those were some of the 31 men wounded in action during the conflict. (Courtesy of Jackie Lane.)

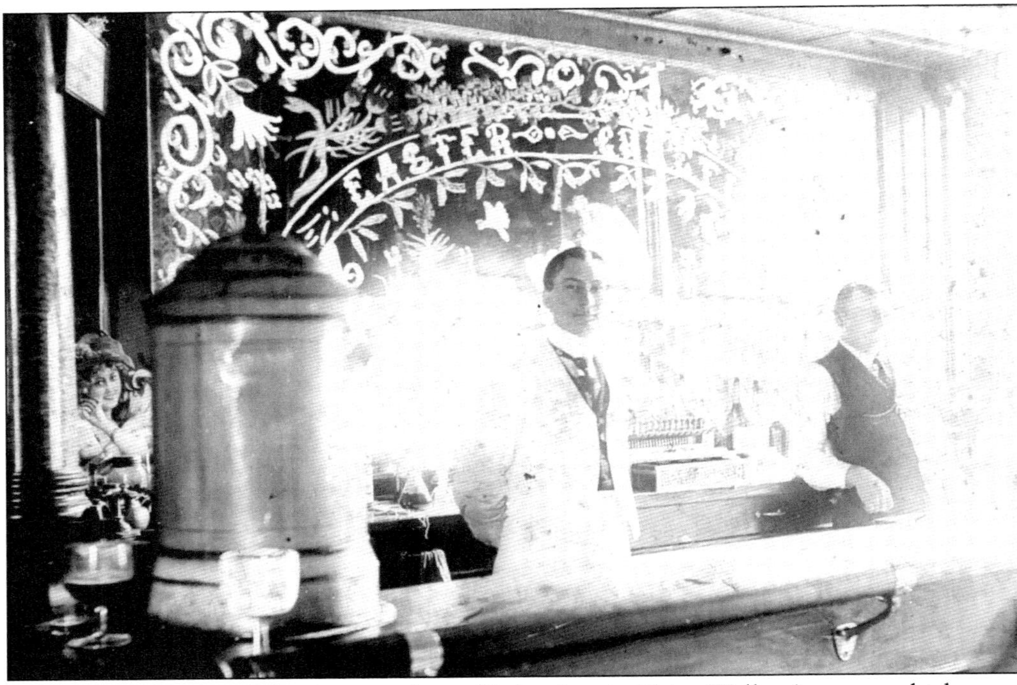

INTERIOR OF SALOON. The photograph was likely taken in Chine Wallace's tavern, which seems to be celebrating, of all things, Easter. The tavern was located in the building that stood on the southeast corner of Main and Second Streets. This business was razed about 2001 to allow for the expansion of the filling station.

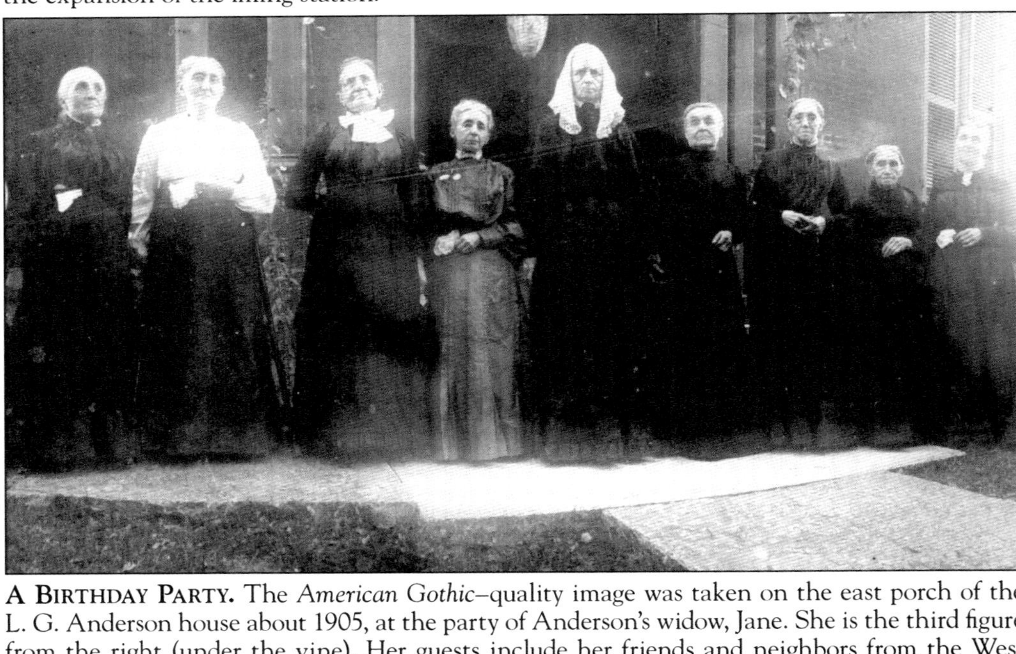

A BIRTHDAY PARTY. The *American Gothic*–quality image was taken on the east porch of the L. G. Anderson house about 1905, at the party of Anderson's widow, Jane. She is the third figure from the right (under the vine). Her guests include her friends and neighbors from the West Side. The tall figure at center, with the piece of lace covering her bald head, is the very ill Ruth Schenck, who built the house at 219 Oxford Road.

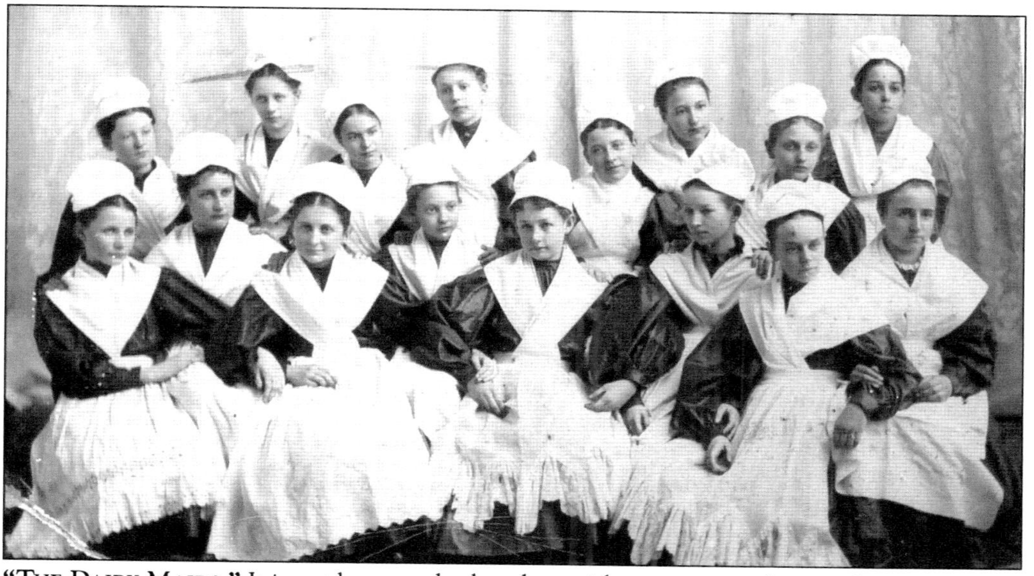

"THE DAIRY MAIDS." It is not known whether these girls are wearing this peculiar costume for a school play or function, or as part of an extracurricular activity. American adults at the turn of the 20th century were inclined to membership in a wide variety of clubs and organizations, which often had their own distinctive getups.

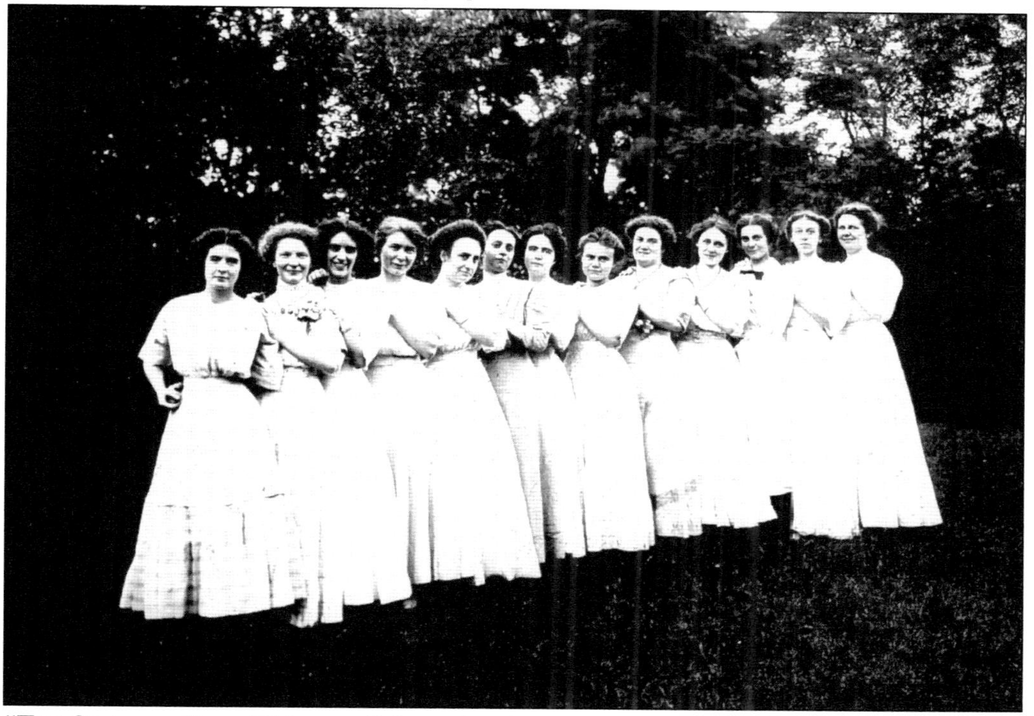

"THE COOKING CLUB." These well-dressed and grown-up young ladies must have been regarded as some of the most eligible females in the community. At far left is May Gaynor, daughter of Patrick Gaynor, the lawyer who lived on River Street. May later married Justin Harding of the paper making family.

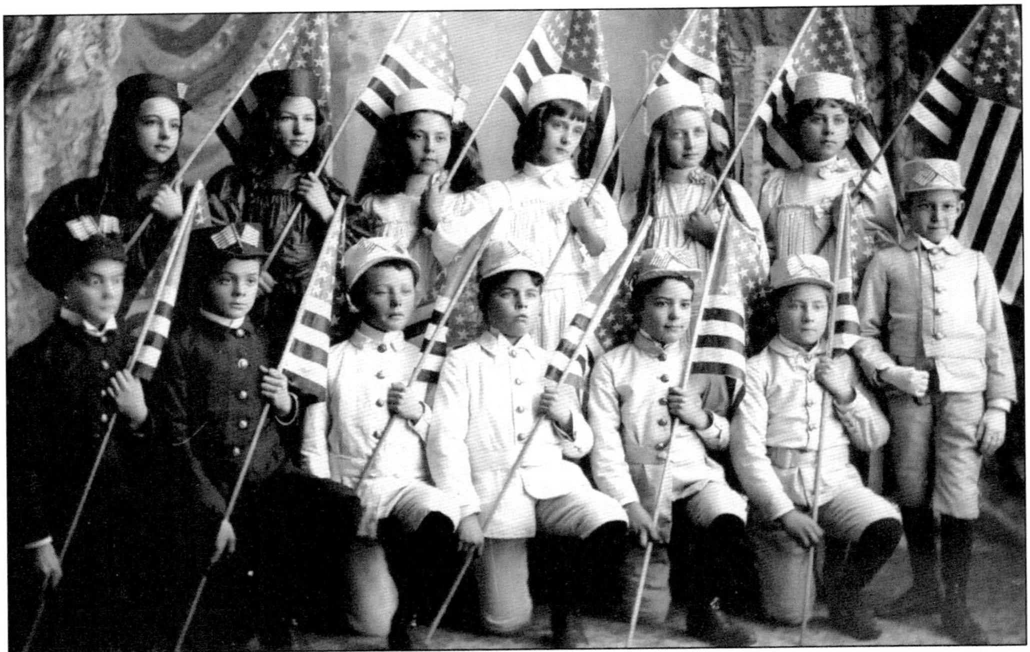

A PATRIOTIC TABLEAU. This image captures a celebration of George Washington's birthday in 1898 by students in the sixth grade. The children shown are wearing red, white, and blue uniforms. Kneeling in the front row at far left is Arthur Spader, named for a Civil War veteran who had been captured at Bull Run. At center front are West Side neighbors Edwin Forrest Harding and Walter Cromer Anderson. Anderson later headed Franklin's Anderson Lumber Company, and Harding made the U.S. Army his career.

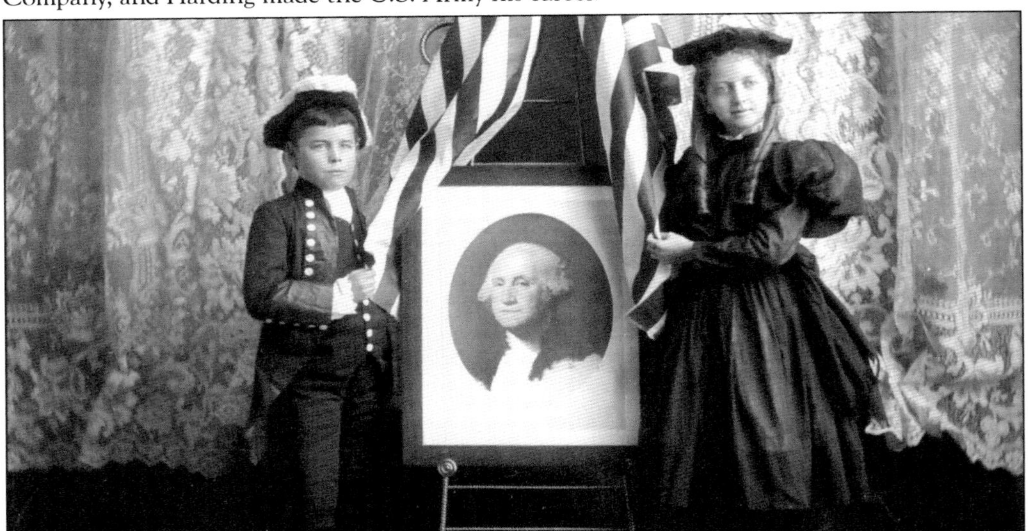

A PARTY FOR GEORGE. Here fifth-grade students celebrate George Washington's birthday in 1897. The boy is Edwin Forrest Harding (again) and the girl is Marguerite Gallaher, the daughter of professor J. J. Gallaher, who owned a towered Main Street house. Harding later made a successful military career and lived to be an old man. Marguerite Gallaher died of tuberculosis within three years of this photograph.

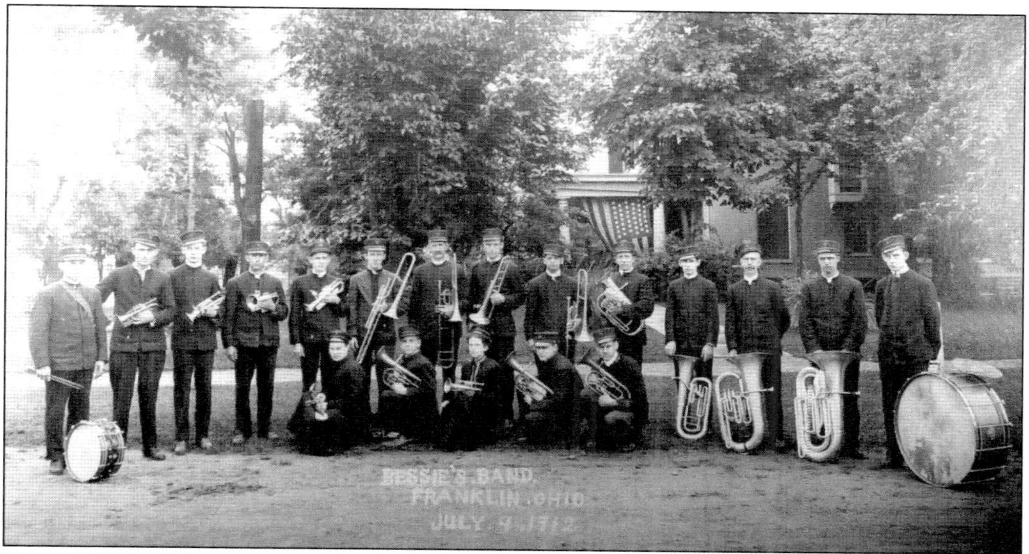

BESSIE'S BAND. Bessie Whiteman was a cornet player who, at age 16, formed a band in 1908. The organization had between 13 to 30 members and included Bessie's sister and her husband. The band lasted for 20 years. Eden Thirkield's home, located at the northeast corner of River and Fourth Streets, is in the background. The photograph looks north.

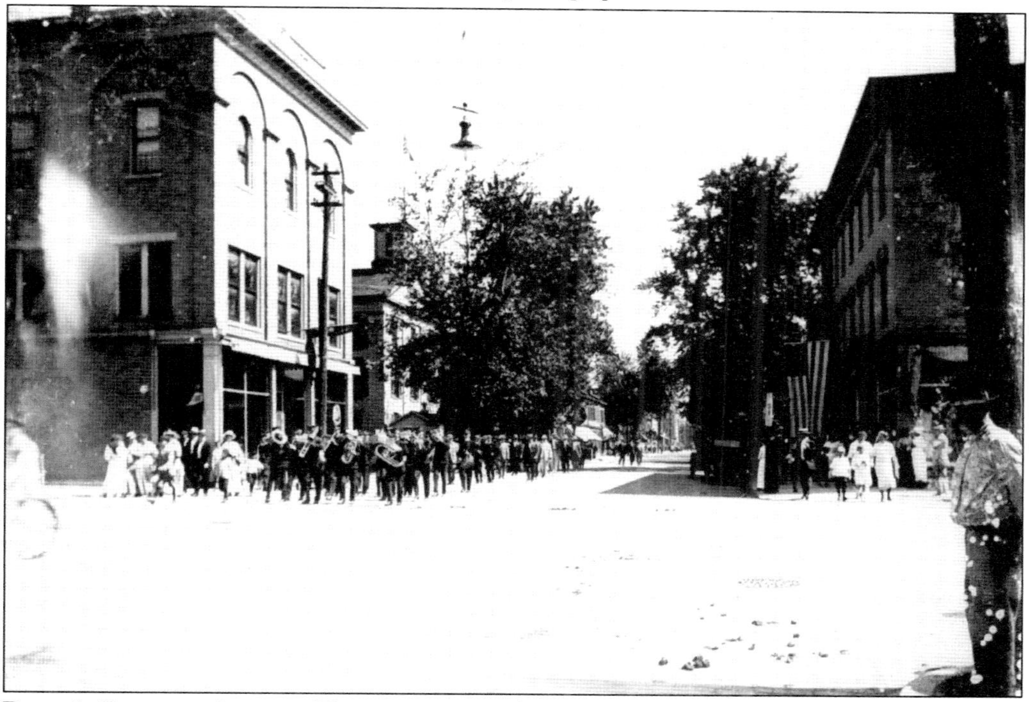

BESSIE'S BAND IN ACTION. The group is marching south on Main Street, near the corner of Fourth Street. Bessie's band was also on the scene when William H. Taft rode through Franklin while campaigning for the presidency in 1908. Though Taft said little, the crowd thoroughly enjoyed the performance after Taft had finished speaking. The Conover Hardware Store is at left and Thirkfield's is at right.

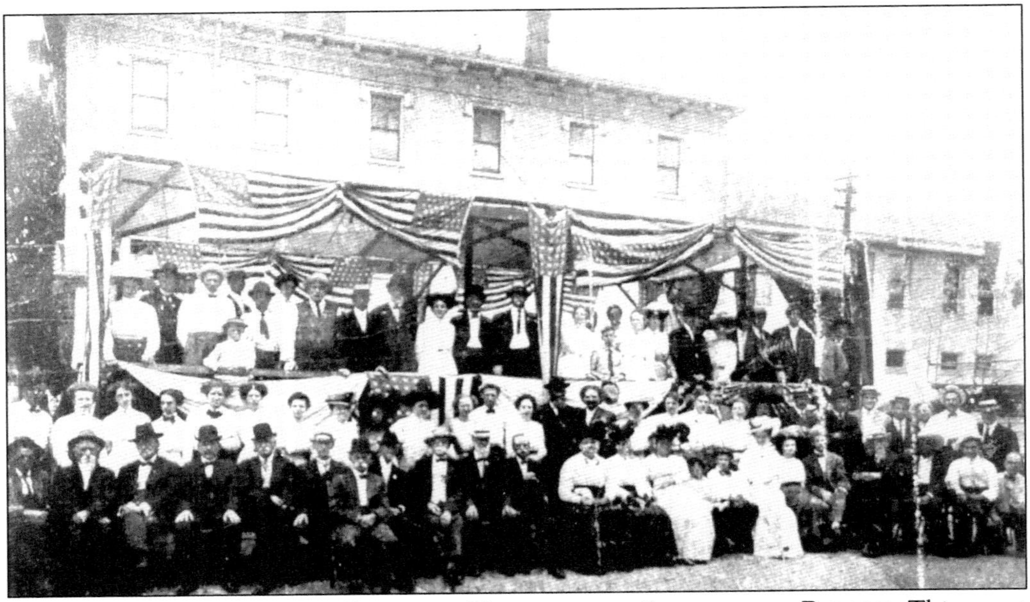

Reviewing Stand for the Franklin Homecoming Celebration Parade. This event occurred July 12–14, 1910. Three bands, including Bessie's and one from the Knights of Pythias, were present, and a song especially composed by Harry C. Eldridge was performed. The festival also led to the compilation of two wonderful collections of photographs from this period. This view is looking north with the Thirkield Department Store in the background. Several Civil War veterans are present amongst the reviewers.

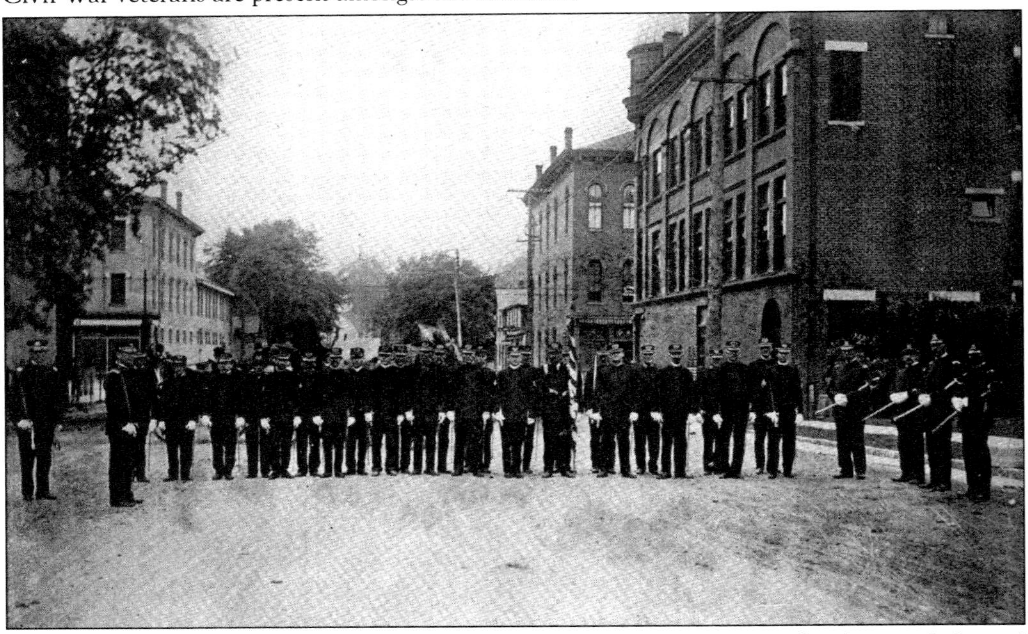

Company No. 99, United Royal Knights of Pythias. This fraternal order was dedicated to friendship, charity, and benevolence. They were also exceptionally well turned out in their tailored uniforms, white gloves, and sabers. This photograph was taken on West Fourth Street, looking east. The Hamilton Building, with its domed tower, is at right.

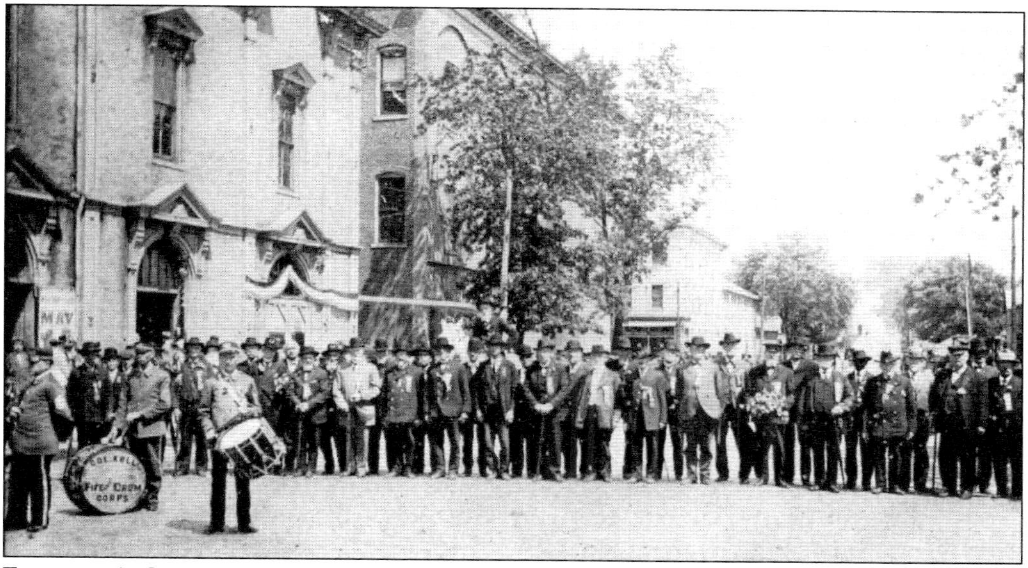

FRANKLIN'S CIVIL WAR VETERANS. This photograph shows remaining veterans about 30 years later, in front of the city building on Fourth Street that housed the veterans' organization, the John Kell Post #241 of the Grand Army of the Republic (GAR), formed in June 1882 with 80 members. In their GAR hall, the aging soldiers would adopt military titles and ranks, use the old terms and expressions, relive their youthful experiences, remember departed comrades, and celebrate their patriotism together.

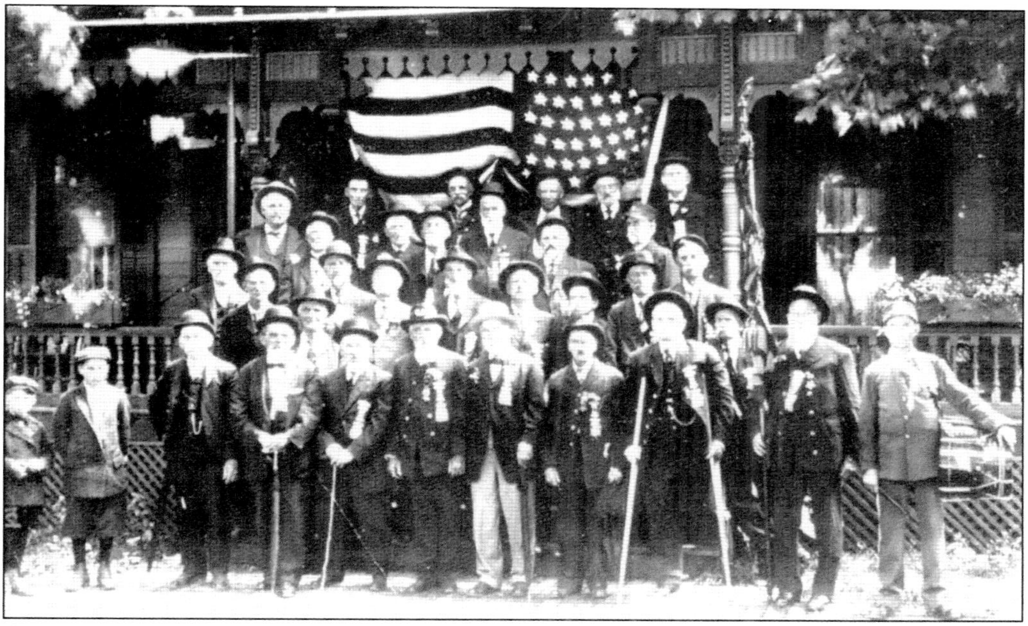

FRANKLIN'S AGING CIVIL WAR VETERANS. The photograph was taken about 1910 on the front porch of Dr. Firman Evans's Eastlake-style home on River Street. Among the non-veterans in the picture is the young and clean-shaven Dr. Evans himself, standing in the rear row, far left. To his right stands county probate judge Alex Boxwell, who while serving in the state legislature created the Boxwell Exam, which allowed rural students to attend city high schools.

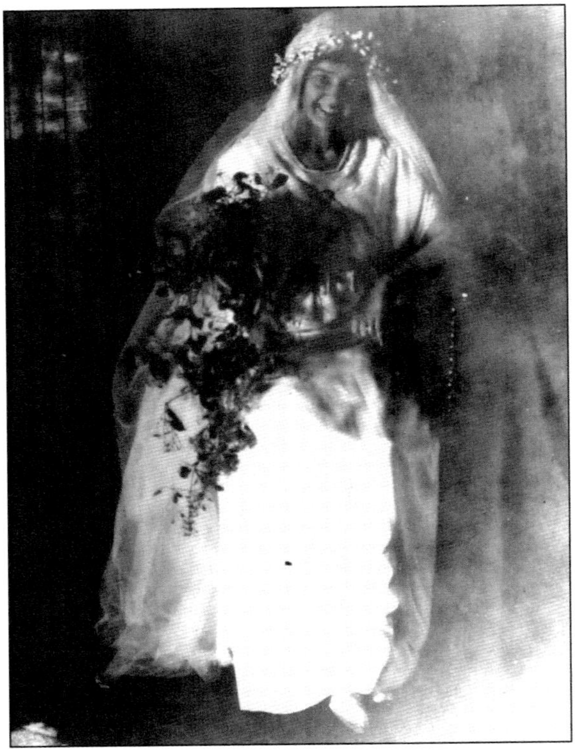

ELEANOR HOOD IN HER WEDDING DRESS. The photograph was taken on the occasion of her September 1913 wedding to Franklin's Lt. Edwin Forrest Harding. Hood was from Engle's Corner, today a part of south Middletown, and was described as one of the prettiest girls in the state. Lieutenant Harding was a graduate of West Point, but his home was at 302 Park Avenue. The newlyweds would soon proceed to Lieutenant Harding's duty station at Fort Missoula, Montana.

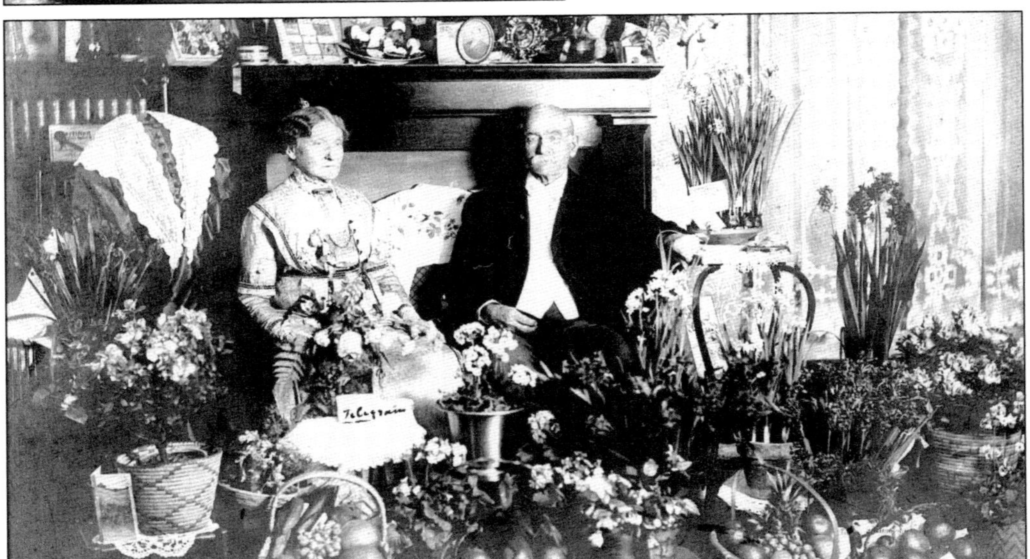

THE GOLDEN WEDDING ANNIVERSARY CELEBRATION OF THE OBEDIAH DENISES. Among the accompanying 50 surprises the couple received on their 50th wedding anniversary were baked goods, fruit, plants, and bouquets of flowers. Martha Denise's wedding dress stands at her right shoulder. Obediah Denise was a dentist from Franklin, who served in three different Ohio regiments during the Civil War. After the war, he moved to Davenport, Iowa, where this photograph was taken. (Courtesy of Patty Frazee.)

EMMA ROBBINS IN HER OLD WEDDING DRESS. The photograph was taken in the early 20th century in front of the Evans-Schenck house, located at the corner of Main and Third Streets. Emma's dress suggests that she got married in the 1870s, when brides typically wore their best dress rather than white. Ben Robbins, Emma's husband, was a bookkeeper at a coal yard, and the couple lived on East Sixth Street.

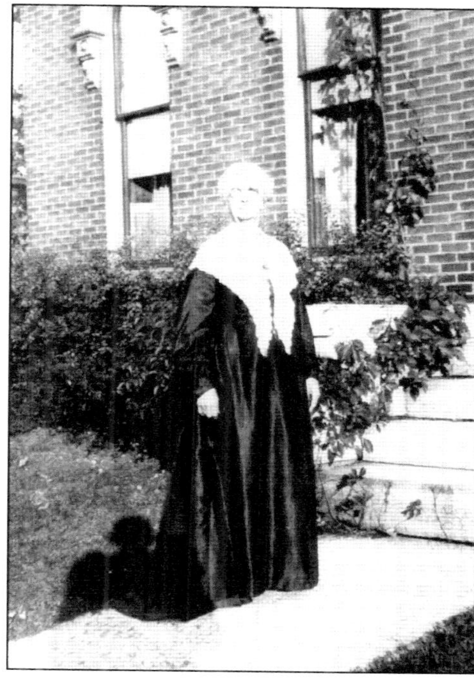

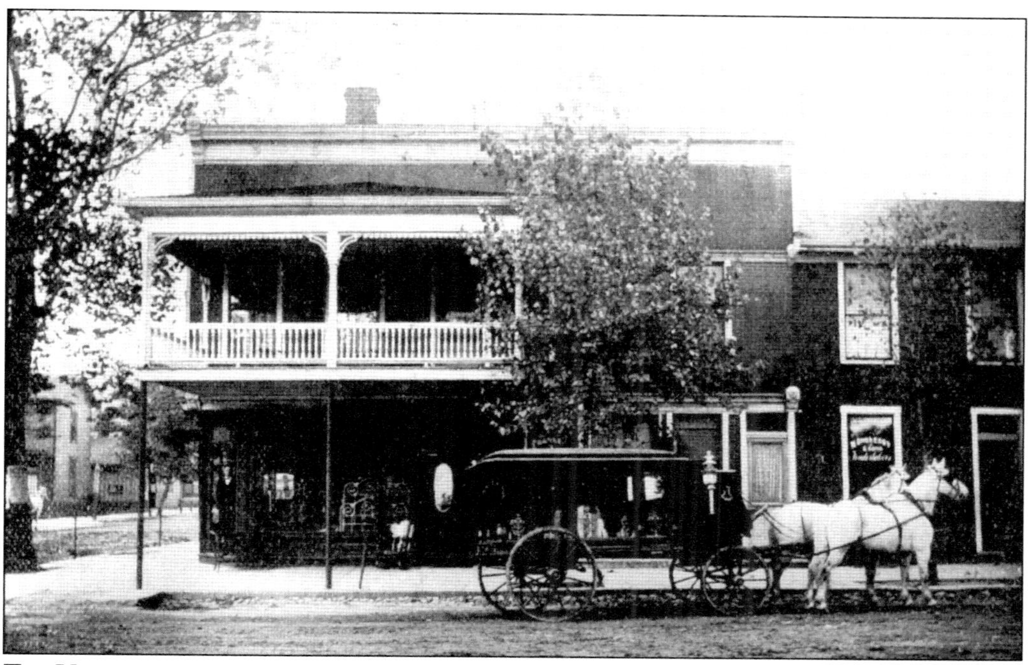

THE UNGLESBY FUNERAL HOME AND HEARSE. Eventually most Franklin residents, irrespective of their wealth or status, were compelled to deal with this establishment, located at the northeast corner of Main and Second Streets. Unglesby's provided the coffin, headstone, transportation to the cemetery, and any other frills that the mourning family desired. During this period, though, visitations were customarily conducted in the parlors of the homes of the dearly departed.

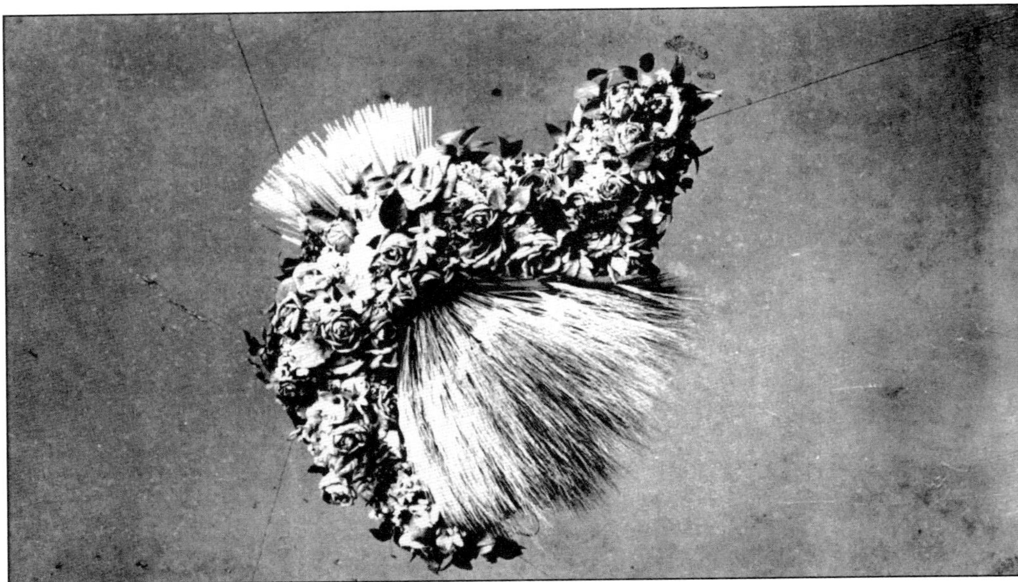

A Funeral Wreath. This illustrated card is from the funeral of L. G. Anderson in July 1889. The Victorians reveled in mourning and keepsakes were important. Photographs of the dead were commonly produced, not only to serve as souvenirs of grief, but also to send to relatives who could not travel to the funeral. The local newspaper said that the granite monument over L. G. Anderson's grave, in Franklin's Woodhill Cemetery, was the largest private monument in the county at the time of its construction.

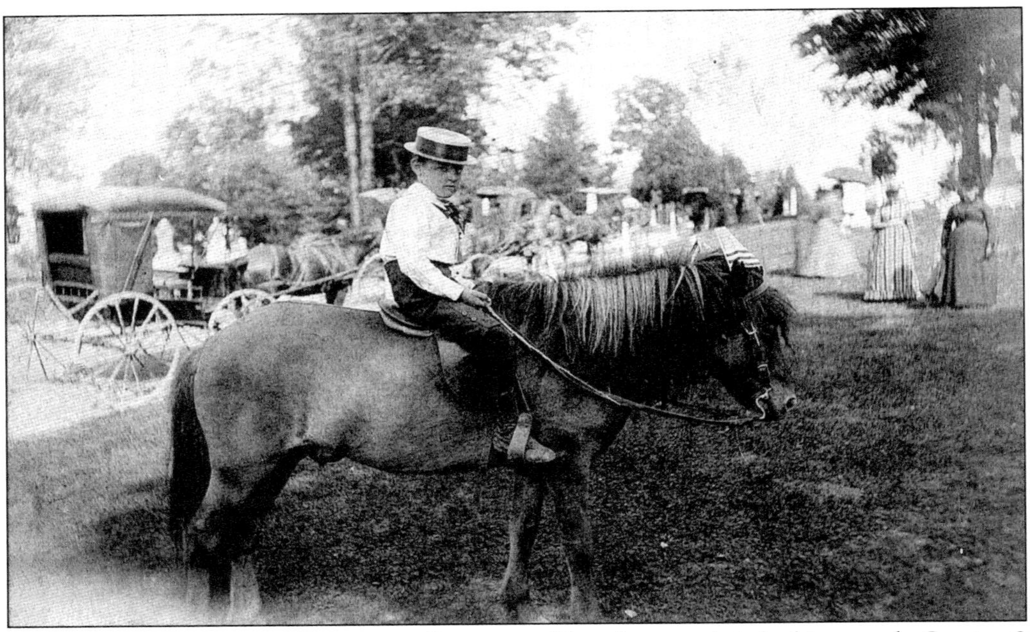

Memorial Day 1884 in Woodhill Cemetery. The photograph is looking north. Section 9 of the cemetery is on the left and Section 6 is on the right. Young Richard Woolley is mounted on his horse, Felix. At the time, Master Woolley lived at 205 Oxford Road. (Courtesy of Patty Frazee.)

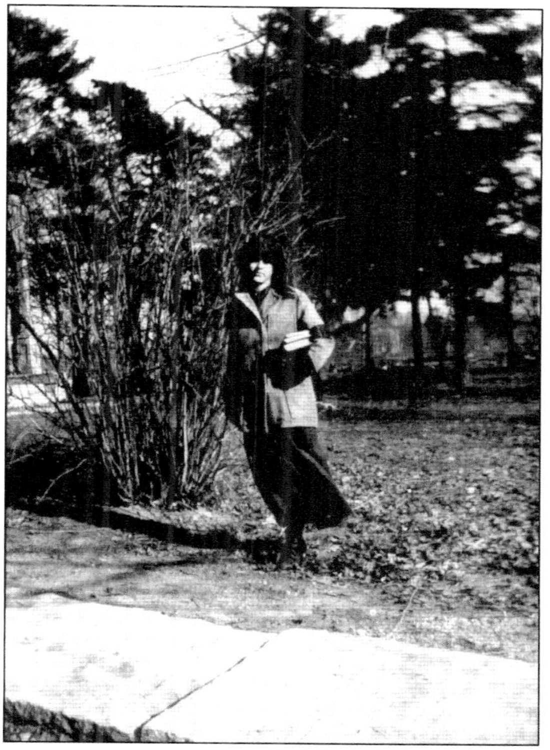

BARBARA ANDERSON WEARING MOURNING ARMBAND. Anderson is standing on the sidewalk to the south entrance of her grandmother's home at 49 Miami Avenue. Barbara lived across the street at 302 Lake Avenue. The photograph was taken in late 1911, and the armband is a symbol of Anderson's mourning for her sister Sarah Bernice, who had just died of an intestinal illness at age 20.

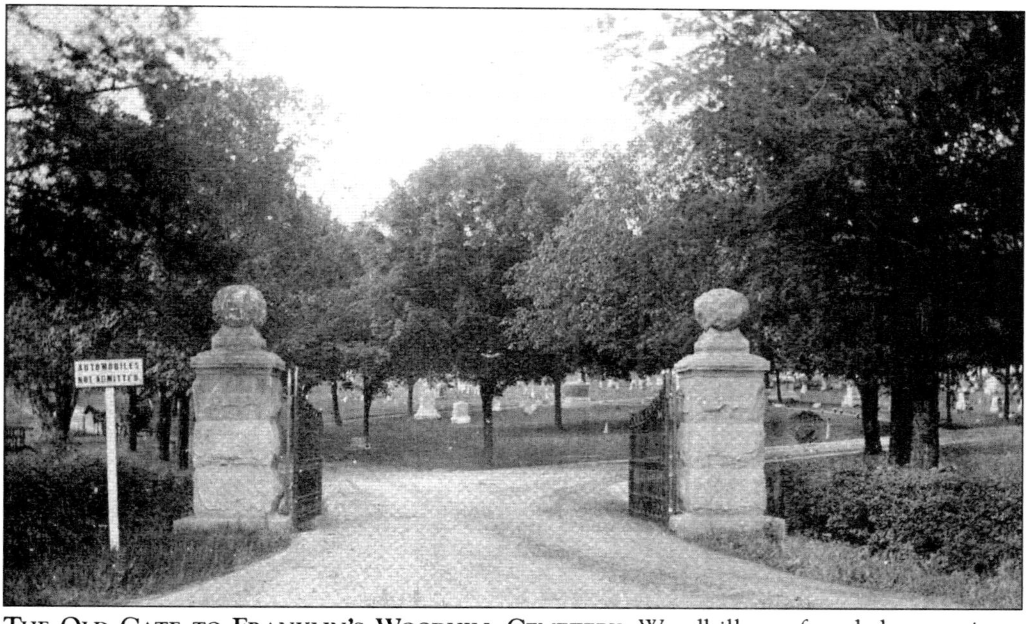

THE OLD GATE TO FRANKLIN'S WOODHILL CEMETERY. Woodhill was founded as a private cemetery in 1856 on the hills well south of the village. When it opened, there were already two cemeteries in the village downtown along Fourth Street. By the 1880s, Woodhill had gone bankrupt when an employee embezzled its funds, and the cemetery was taken over by the township.

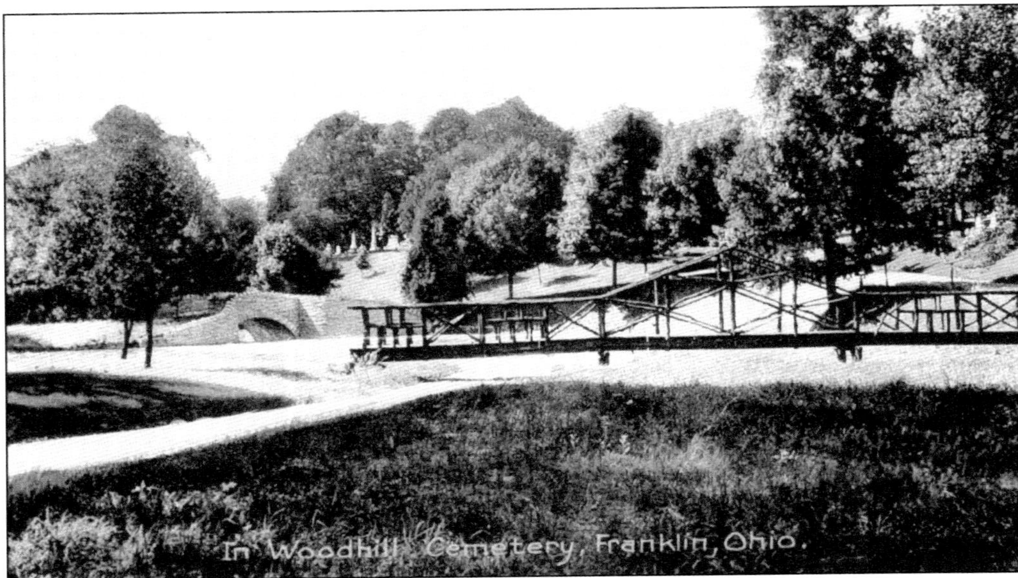

A Tranquil Scene in Woodhill Cemetery. The appropriately picturesque pond and bridge are located at the south end of Woodhill Cemetery. In 1876, the graves in the village's original burial yard were moved, many of them to Woodhill. And during the late 19th century and early 20th century, burial remains were periodically moved from Hillside Cemetery, the remaining downtown cemetery. Finally, in 1931, the last of the graves from Hillside were moved to Woodhill. (Courtesy of William Moses.)

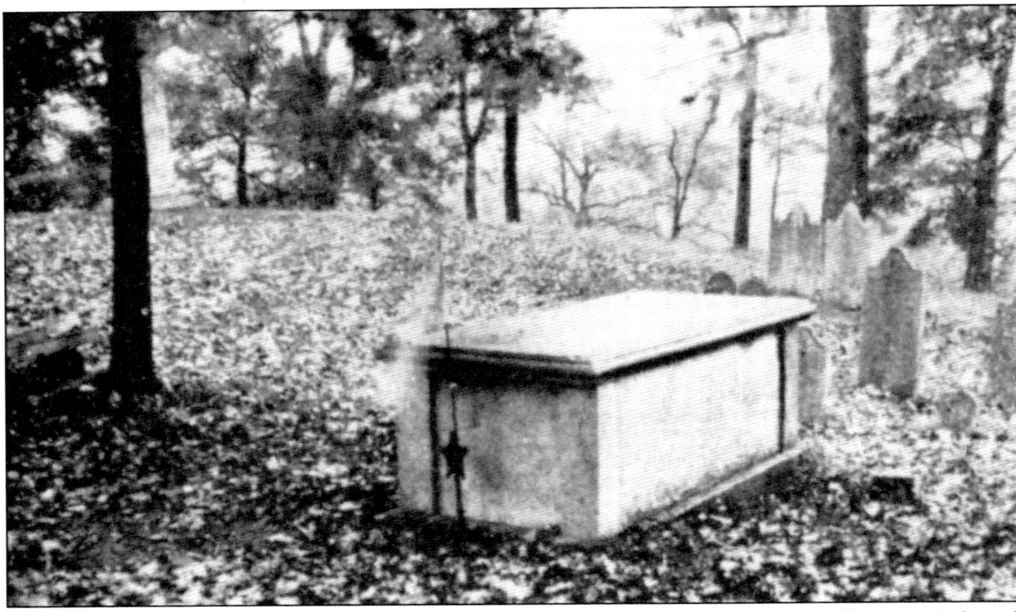

The Grave of William Cortenus Schenck in Woodhill Cemetery. William C. Schenck was the skilled land surveyor credited with laying out the village in 1796. Later he and other members of his family came from New Jersey to live in this community of cabins along the river. Schenck died at the state capital in 1821, probably of malaria, while serving in the legislature. He was originally buried in the Franklin Graveyard downtown.

Six

Neighbors and Notables

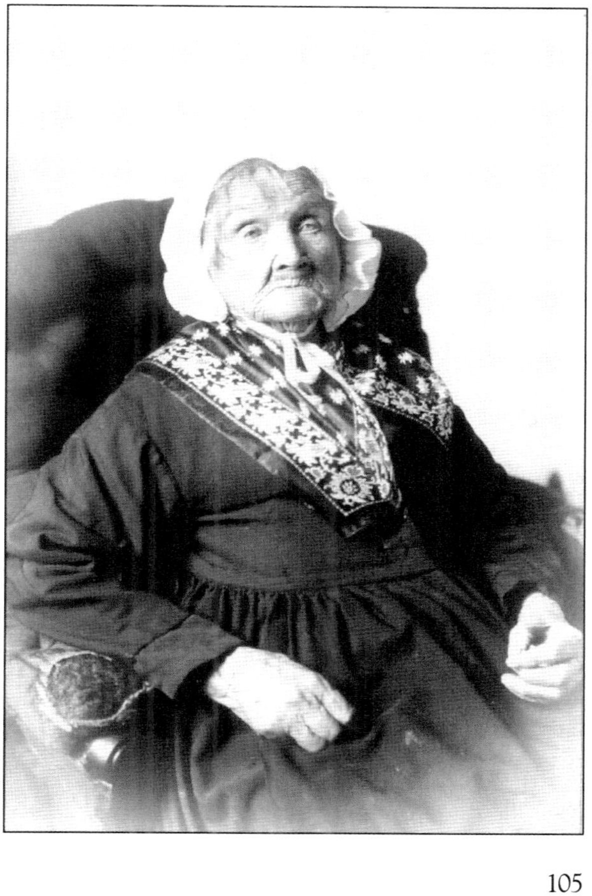

Mary Small Campbell. This photograph shows Mary on her 100th Birthday in 1886. During the span of her life, she saw the world change beyond recognition. When Mary arrived in Ohio by flatboat at age 10, American Indians were common visitors to her cabin home. At age 20 she married Samuel Campbell, a wheelwright, and they lived in a cabin at the northwest corner of Main and Second Streets. A few years before her death, this cabin was torn down and the brick Rossman Grocery erected in its place. Two of Mary's sons became U.S. congressmen, and a grandson served as governor of Ohio. By the time of her death, the railroad, with its travel opportunities, was taken for granted, and the quiet collection of cabins she had grown up among had becoming crowded with belching factories.

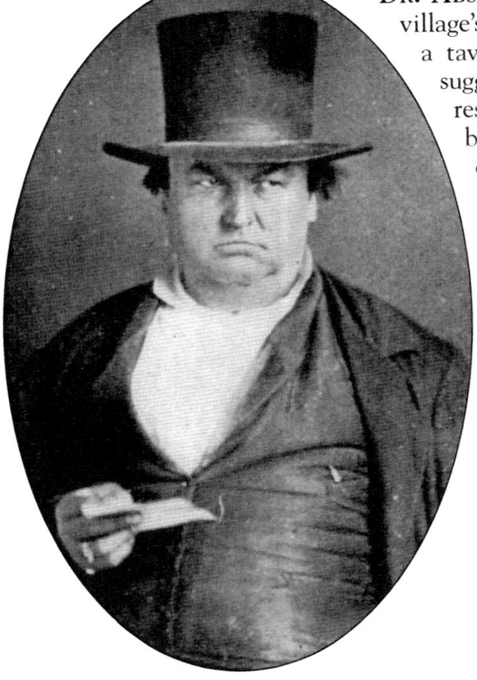

DR. ABSALOM DEATH. This Dr. Death (one of two in the village's history) was elected the village's first mayor at a tavern meeting in 1837. His menacing appearance suggests he was the very determined embodiment of responsibility, sobriety, and frontier justice, unalloyed by a whiff of mercy. Later he became the director of a medical college in Cincinnati. He was buried in Middletown.

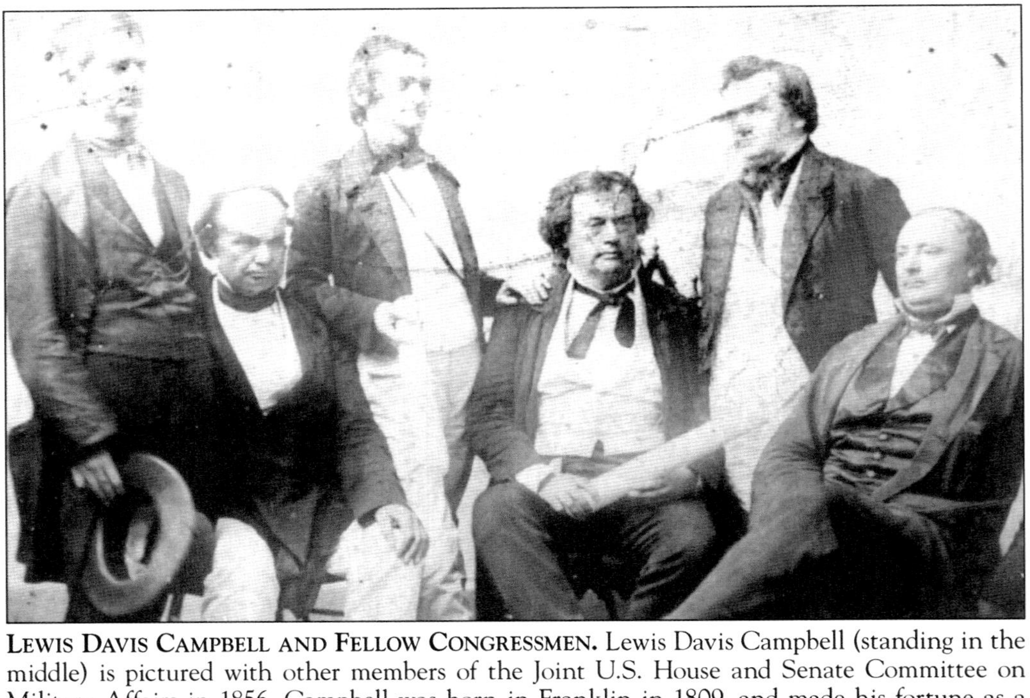

LEWIS DAVIS CAMPBELL AND FELLOW CONGRESSMEN. Lewis Davis Campbell (standing in the middle) is pictured with other members of the Joint U.S. House and Senate Committee on Military Affairs in 1856. Campbell was born in Franklin in 1809, and made his fortune as a newspaper editor in Hamilton before going to Congress. Also pictured are political giants of the era, Sens. Stephen Douglas of Illinois (standing right), Howell Cobb of Georgia (sitting center), and William Seward of New York (standing left).

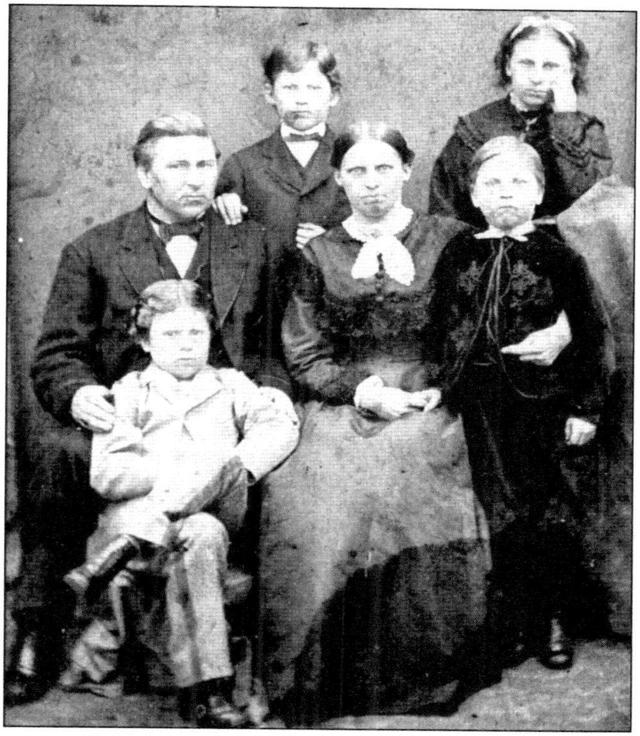

THE ABRAHAM EBENEZER (A. E.) HARDING FAMILY. Harding was an immigrant who brought from his native England the art and science of the manufacture of fine writing paper. He established paper mills both at Excello, south of Middletown, and in Franklin. Shown are Harding, his wife Adelaide (née Bridge), and their sons. At right, in the embroidered jacket, is Clarence. Behind Harding is Charles, and in front sits John Eugene. The latter became a U.S. congressman representing Middletown.

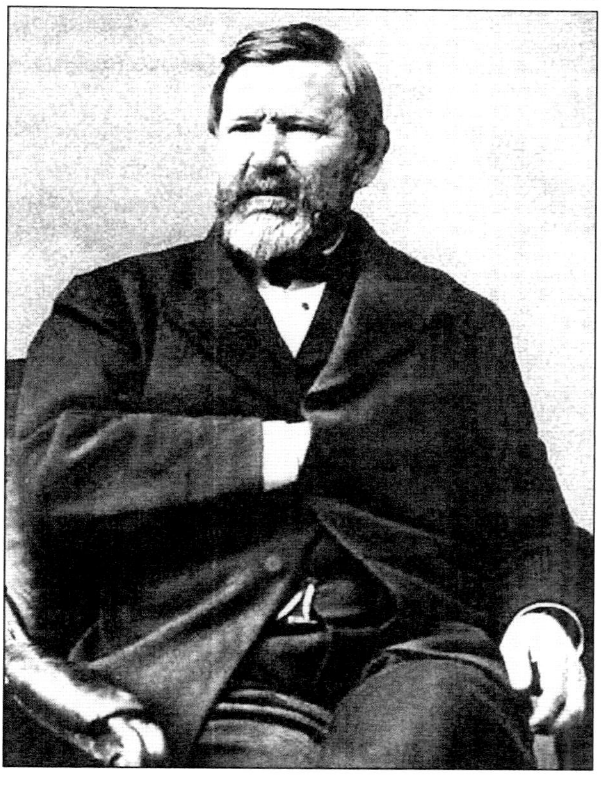

ROBERT CUMMING SCHENCK. Schenck was the son of William C. Schenck, founder of Franklin, and was born in a cabin (now gone) that stood on River Street in 1811. Among the first students at Miami University, Robert became a lawyer in Dayton, was a general during the Civil War (where he was wounded), was a member of the House of Representatives before and after the war, and served as an ambassador before his public life was destroyed by scandal.

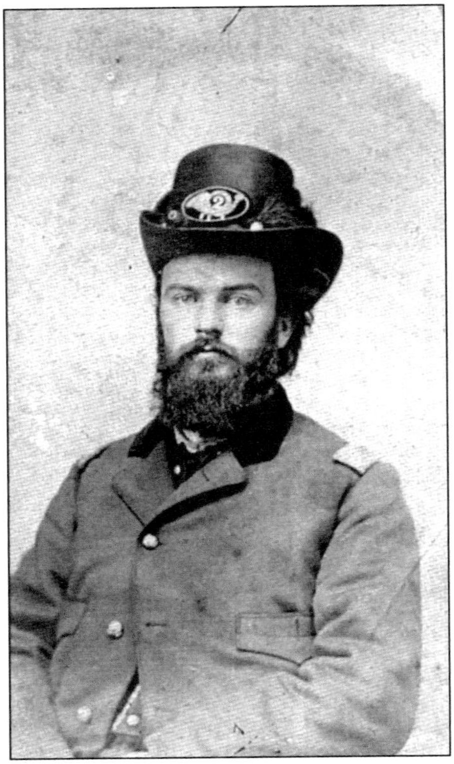

Brevet Brig. Gen. Obediah C. Maxwell. At the outbreak of the Civil War, Maxwell was a village shoe merchant, but he quickly rose to become lieutenant colonel and commanding officer of the Second Ohio Infantry. Wounded three times during the war, he was awarded a brevet (honorary rank) of brigadier general of volunteers in 1865. After initial postwar success, he fell into despair and killed himself at the Phillips House hotel in Dayton. (Courtesy of Larry Strayer.)

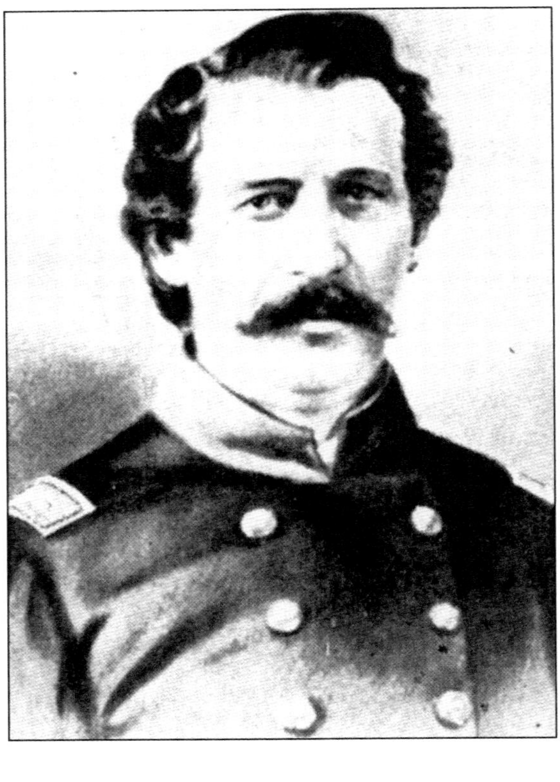

Lt. Col. John Kell. An immigrant from Germany and a tailor by trade, Kell was the village's postmaster and leader of its local militia company, which he commanded when it became Company F, First Ohio Infantry (90-day enlistment) at First Bull Run. He rose to become lieutenant colonel in the Second Ohio Volunteer Infantry. Kell was commanding this regiment when he was killed in action at the battle of Stone's River on December 31, 1862.

CAPT. BEN MORGAN. An immigrant from England, Morgan was a married farmer living south of Franklin at the outbreak of the Civil War. Pictured here in 1861, he raised Company F, 75th Ohio Infantry, and was promoted to become lieutenant colonel of that regiment. Wounded at Gettysburg, Morgan was captured in 1864 in Florida and suffered in prison. After the war, he served as the village's mayor and later returned to farming on Manchester Road, within today's Middletown. (Courtesy of Jackie Lane.)

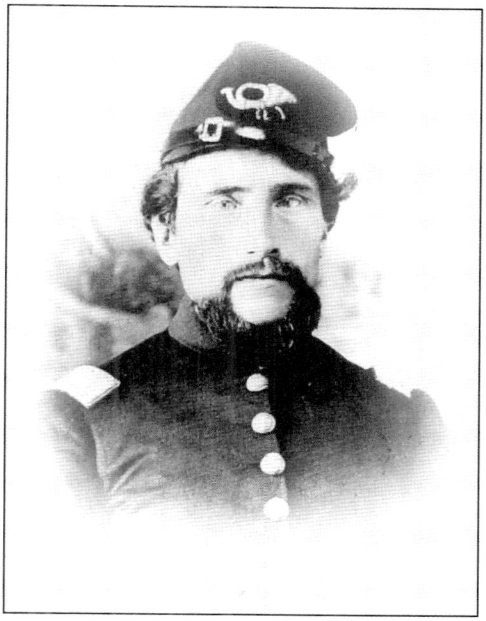

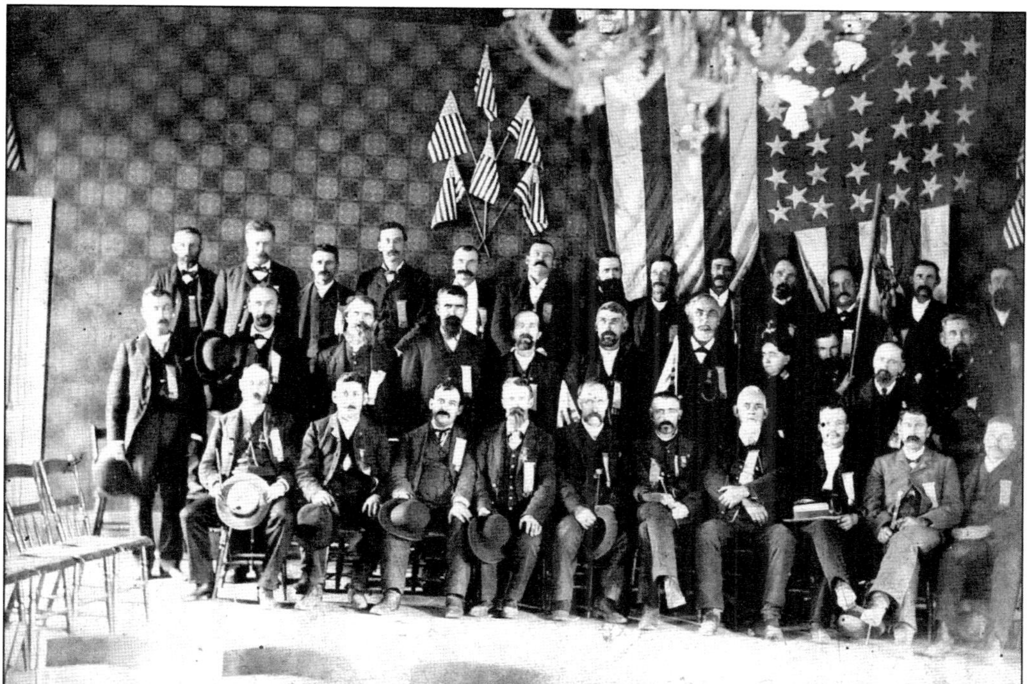

FRANKLIN'S CIVIL WAR VETERANS. This photograph shows the veterans in their vigorous middle age prior to 1881, and was probably taken in the old city building or the Odd Fellows building. More than 220 men from the township served in the Union forces during the war. At least 100 of them were in three-year regiments, such as the 2nd, 75th, and 79th Ohio Infantry Regiments. Among these Franklin soldiers, there were 40 sets of brothers and 5 fathers with their sons. (Courtesy of Patty Frazee.)

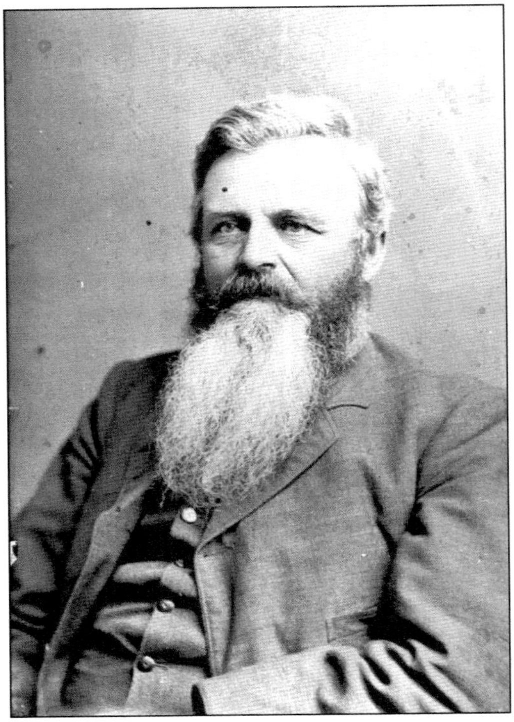

LEVI CROLL. Croll and partner Hugh Death were co-owners of a flour mill that prospered during the Civil War. When Croll sold off his share, he became the richest man in the township. He used his money to open a bank, start a grain and lumber business, purchase a 194-acre farm on the West Side, and build a Second Empire mansion at the center of the farm. (Courtesy of Bob Croll)

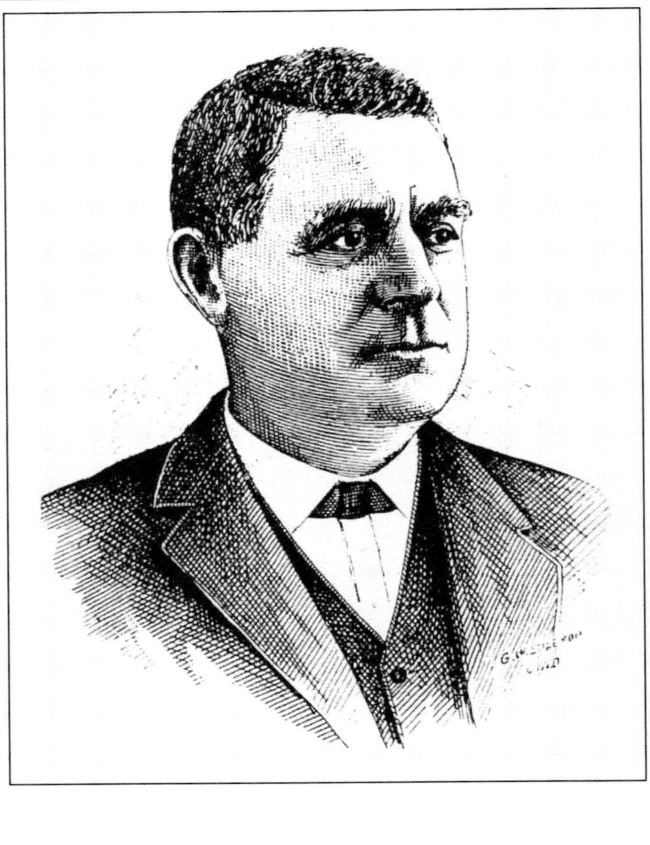

LEWIS GASTON ANDERSON. L. G. Anderson purchased 156 acres on the West Side in 1857, and by the mid-1860s, had built a large Italianate villa on the property. In the early 1870s he established a grain and lumber company downtown that operated until the 1960s. Anderson was a county commissioner and served one term in the state senate. Before his death, Anderson created the Mackinaw Development Corporation, which divided up his farm into lots for future houses.

JOHN L. THIRKIELD. John Thirkield was the co-founder of the Thirkield Department Store in 1836, which operated in the village for over a hundred years at the northeast corner of Main and Fourth Streets. He lived in a small Federal-style home just behind the store on the north side of Fourth Street that later housed the village's telephone exchange. His daughter was the mother of longtime local school teacher Nan Carpenter.

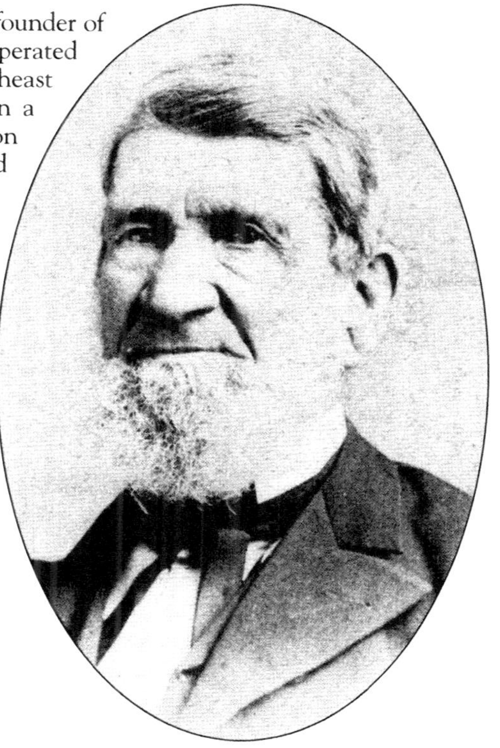

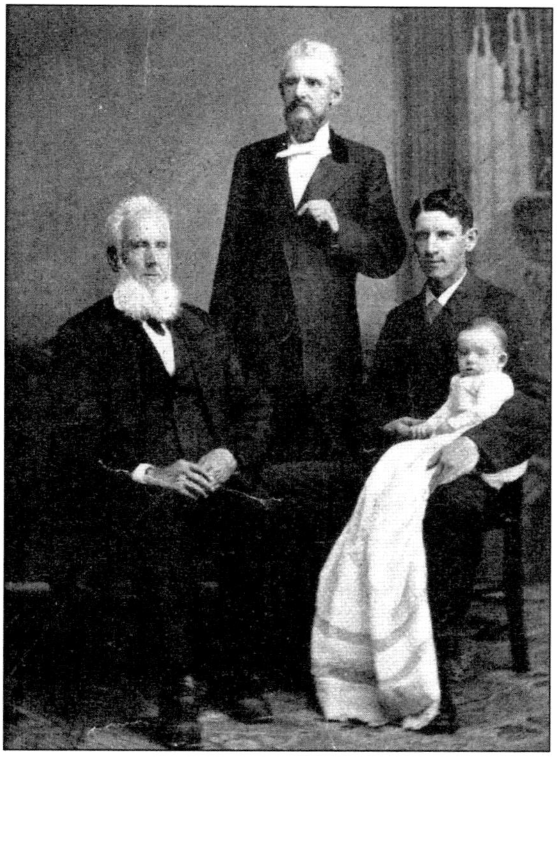

THE DOCTORS OF THE EVANS FAMILY. Standing is Dr. Richard P. Evans, the father of Firman Evans. Sitting at left is Dr. Otho Evans Jr., who served in the Civil War and lived in an Italianate house on Main Street. Otho Evans's son, George (not pictured), also became a doctor. Sitting at right is Dr. Firman Evans, who built an Eastlake home on River Street. In his arms is his son, the future doctor, Rice Evans.

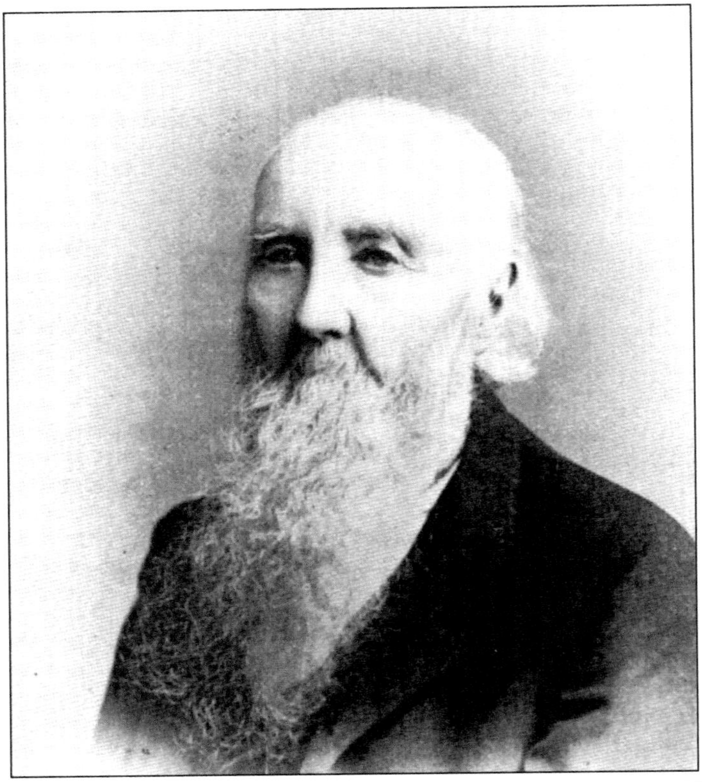

WILLIAM A. S. VAN HORNE. Van Horne was an industrialist and visionary who gave his name to the hydraulic that channeled water from the Chautauqua Dam to power his planing mill and other factories in Franklin. He built a richly detailed Queen Anne–style house at the northwest corner of Jackson and River Streets. One of Van Horne's sons served in the 69th Ohio Volunteer Infantry during the Civil War and was killed late in that conflict.

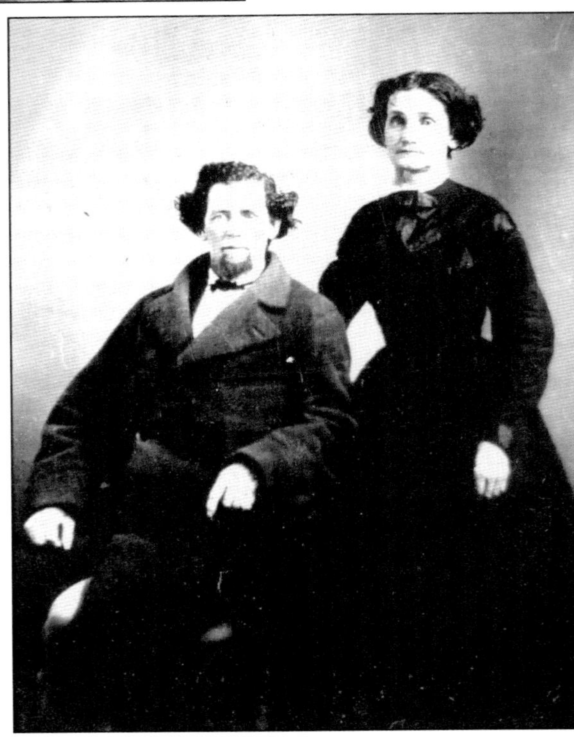

JOSEPH BEAUCHAMP WOODWARD AND MARY CAMPBELL WOODWARD. Joseph Woodward was a farmer, developer, and one-time village postmaster. His wife, Mary, was the sister of congressman Lewis Davis Campbell. The Woodwards lived in a elegant Italianate house on Lebanon Road. One of their daughters, Lilly, married Clarence Harding, an heir to the Harding Paper Mills.

PATRICK GAYNOR. Gaynor was Irish-born lawyer and a prominent local Democrat. He lived in the Alamo-shaped concrete home that he designed himself, and that still stands at 324 River Street. Both of his sons served in World War I. Gaynor's daughter, May, married Justin Harding. Harding was also a lawyer and served as a judge during the Nuremberg Trials after World War II.

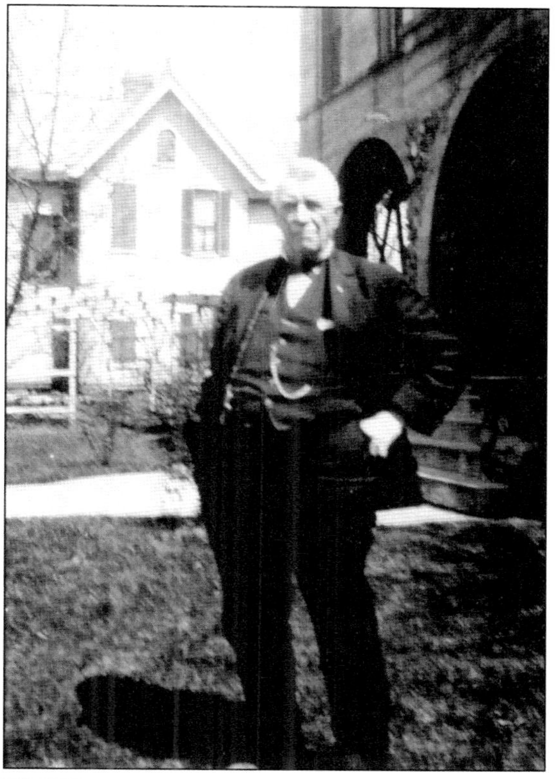

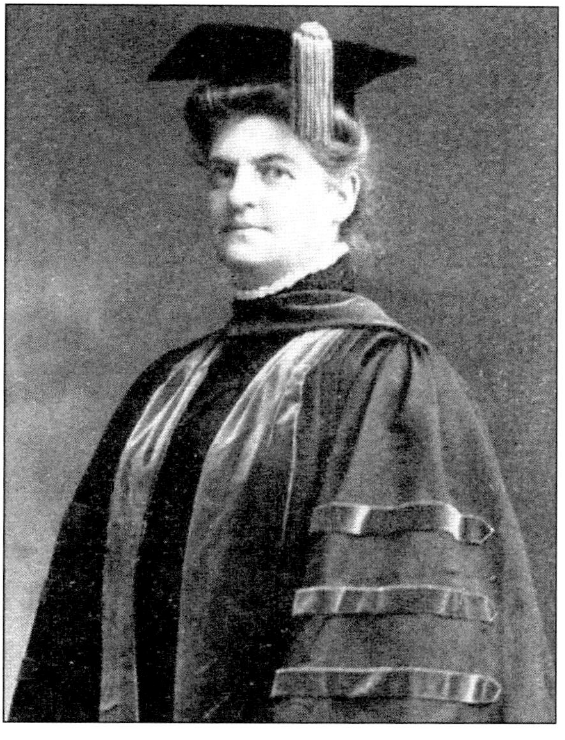

JANE SHERZER. Named Jennie by her parents, but calling herself Jane because the name gave her more gravity, she was the daughter of Main Street harness maker Jacob Sherzer. After serving as principal of the Franklin High School, in 1899 Jane Sherzer earned her doctorate in German literature, an educational accomplishment quite rare for that time. She ended her career as president of the Oxford (Ohio) College for Women. Her salient quality was said to have been her lack of a sense of humor.

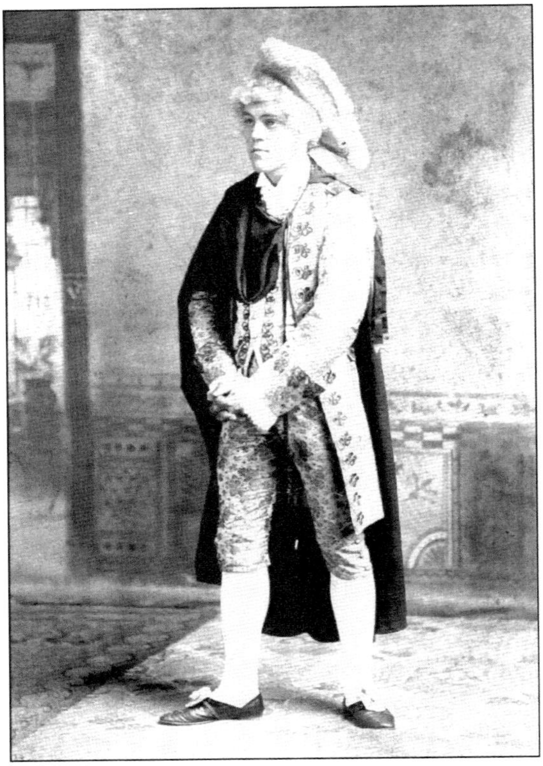

SEYMOUR S. TIBBALS. This is an image of Tibbals dressed for a theatrical function. He was the longtime editor of the local newspaper, the *Franklin Chronicle*. In the late 1920s, he became president and manager of the Miami Valley Chautauqua.

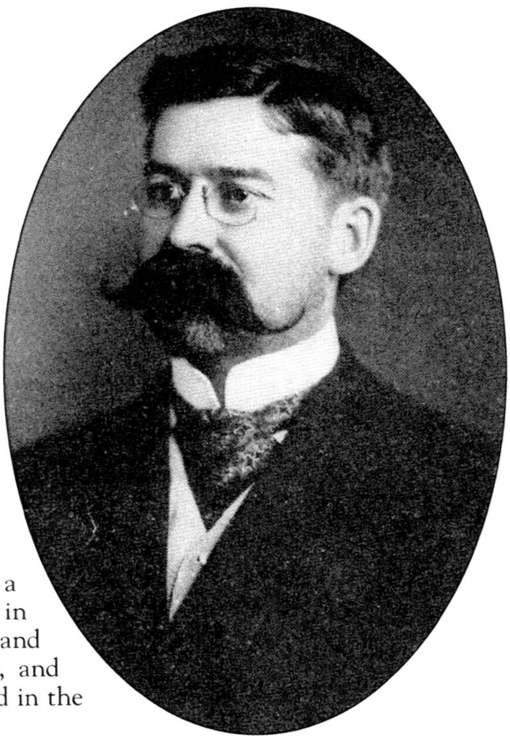

DR. SILAS STERLING STAHL. Stahl had a medical practice on Main Street and lived in the Italianate house built by Ruth Schenck and located at 219 Oxford Road. In middle age, and shorn of his luxuriant moustache, Stahl served in the army in World War I.

GEORGE ROSSMAN. When his father died in 1875, George Rossman took over the family business. In 1881, he built a new brick store at the northwest corner of Main and Second Streets, on the site of the old Campbell log cabin. In 1888, he married Lueza Denise, and they lived in a turreted Queen Anne house that still stands at 127 East Second Street. The store operated until 1949. (Courtesy of Patty Frazee.)

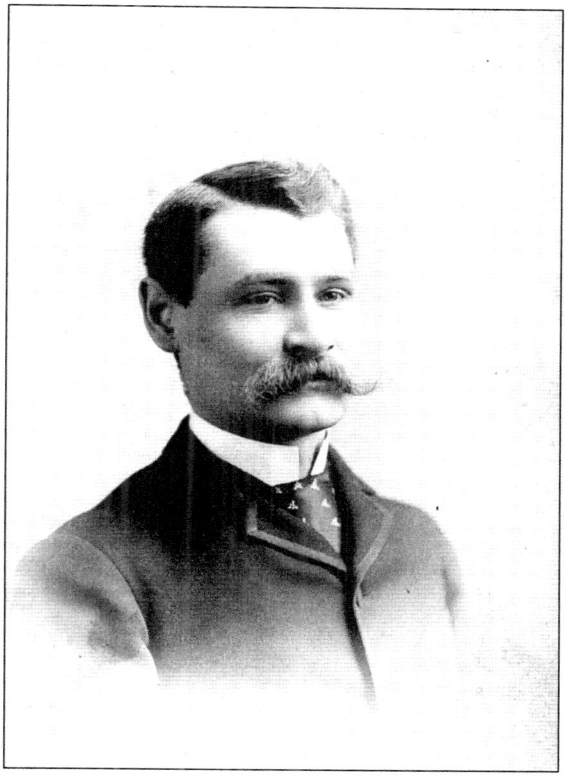

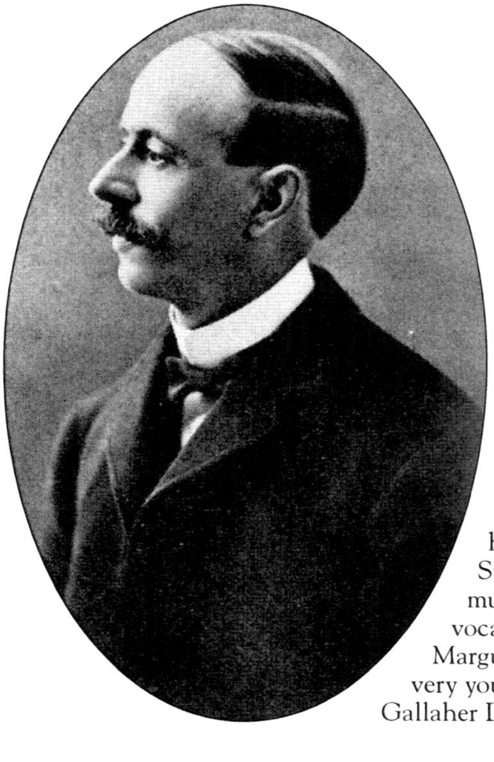

PROF. JAMES JUDSON GALLAHER. Professor Gallaher was a man of independent wealth who purchased Frank Deardoff's Second Empire house located on Main Street, south of Sixth Street. Gallaher lived there for over 60 years, much of that time teaching instrumental and vocal music to young local students. His daughter Marguerite was stricken with tuberculosis and died very young, but his son, J. Frank, established a chain of Gallaher Drug Stores in Dayton.

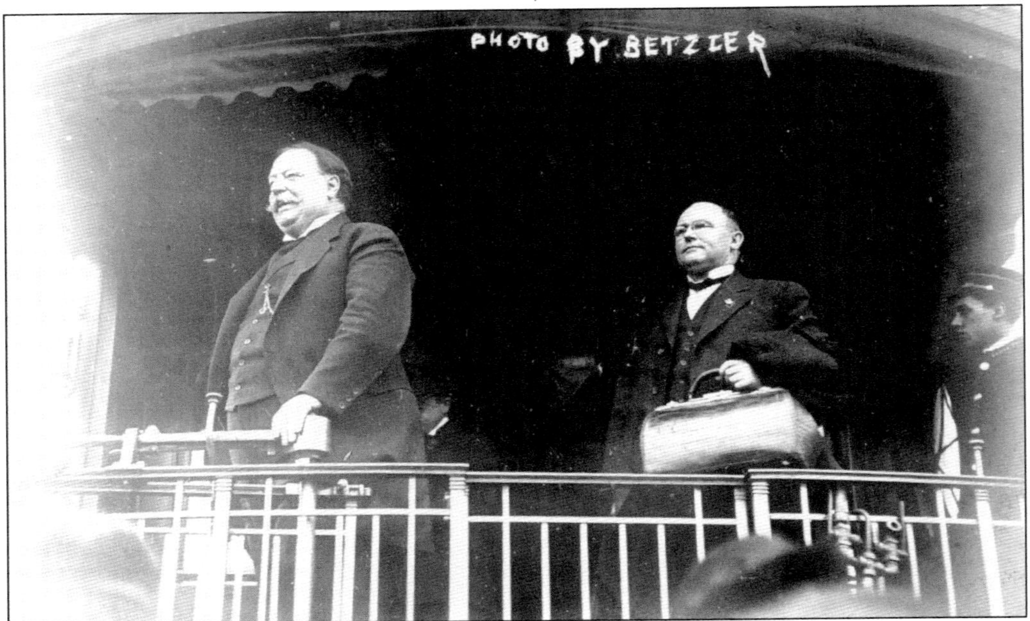

WILLIAM HOWARD TAFT IN FRANKLIN. The image was taken by local photographer William Betzler at the Big Four Railroad Station, near Fourth Street, on September 10, 1908, as Taft was campaigning for the U.S. presidency. Taft, who was Theodore Roosevelt's secretary of war, easily defeated Democratic candidate William Jennings Bryan, who was a frequent visitor to Franklin's Miami Valley Chautauqua. It was said that Taft only got 14 words out of his mouth during his visit, but Bessie's band kept the crowd entertained anyway.

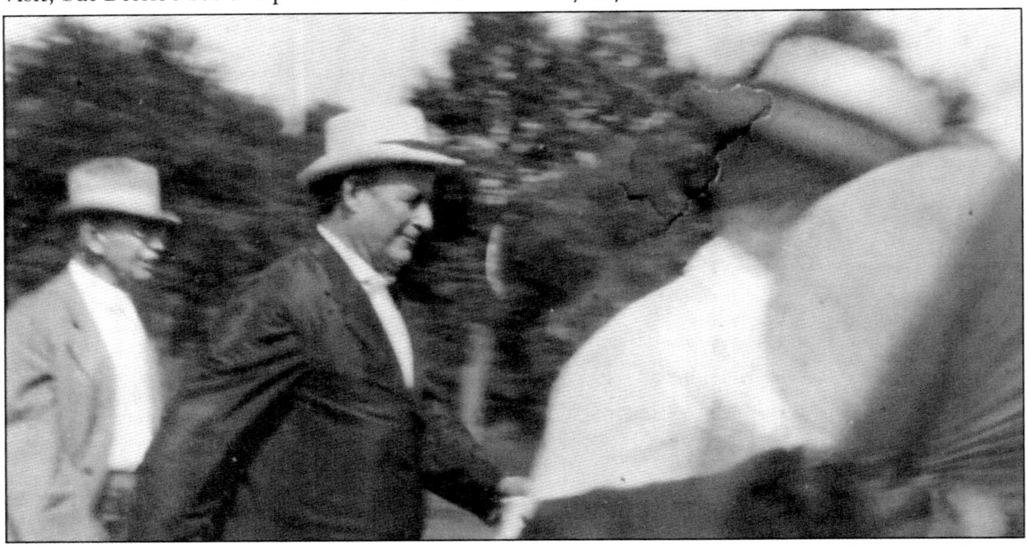

WILLIAM JENNINGS BRYAN AT THE MIAMI VALLEY CHAUTAUQUA. Pictured in 1911, Bryan (right) was the Democratic Party's presidential nominee in 1896, 1900, and 1908. Though unsuccessful in those elections, he was a hit on the Chautauqua circuit and spoke here between 1899 and 1916. The man with the moustache and glasses behind Bryan is Joseph D. Miller, a lawyer and the village's most prominent Democrat. When in town, Bryan stayed at Miller's large home, Valeridge, located at 258 Hill Avenue.

Seven

The Flood

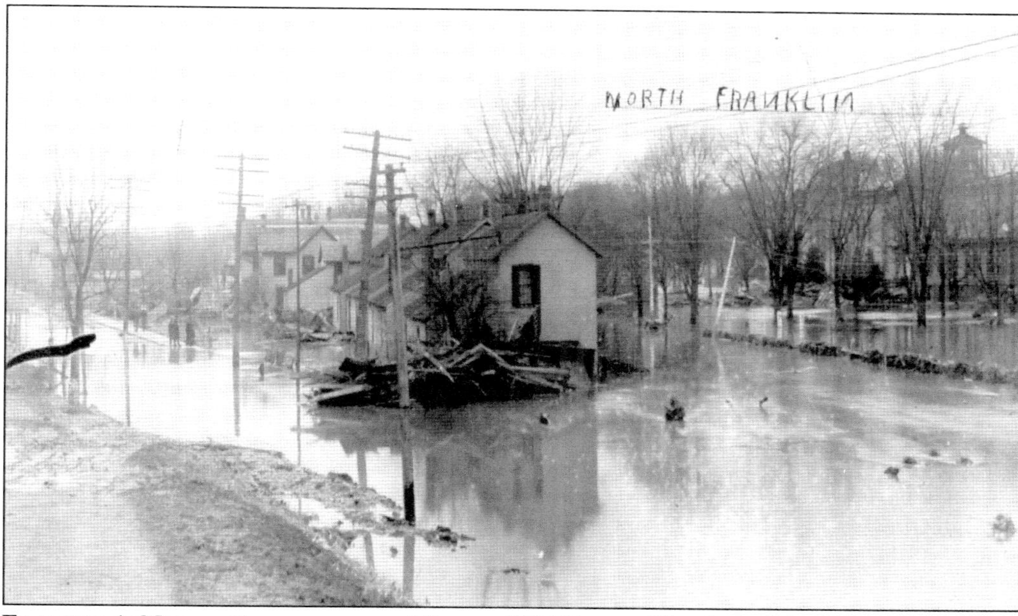

Franklin's North End after the March 1913 Flood. Flooding of the Great Miami River was commonplace, occurring in 1828, 1847, 1866, and 1898. But the 1913 flood was much worse than anything experienced before, and it inundated Dayton, Miamisburg, Middletown, and Hamilton. By the evening of March 25, the river was over its banks and rising. The greatest damage was done on the outer edge of Franklin's West Side, where 9 houses were washed from their foundations and another 13 were badly damaged. In that part of town, eight people drowned. This photograph is looking south from the hill on the eastern end of Van Horne Avenue, near where the golf course is today. During the flood, many families gathered on the hill for safety. The tower at right marks the Harding Paper Mill on River Street. Although it was catastrophic to the community in many ways, the flood did contain a very wide silver lining in that the numerous photographs taken of the devastation did provide a lasting record of the appearance of many buildings that would soon be long gone or irrevocably changed.

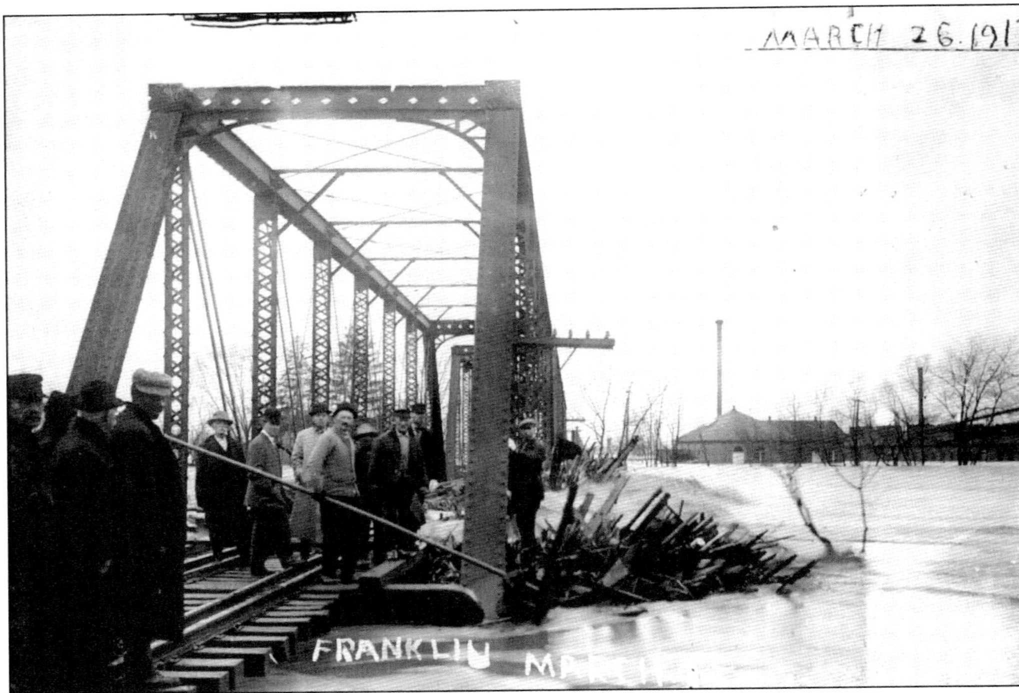

The Big Four Railroad Bridge during the Flood. This view is from the east and was photographed on March 26, 1913. The picture shows the river's great height and captures the helplessness of Franklin's citizens. In the distance, on the west side of the river, are the Franklin Water Works (left) and the Franklin Wheel Company (right).

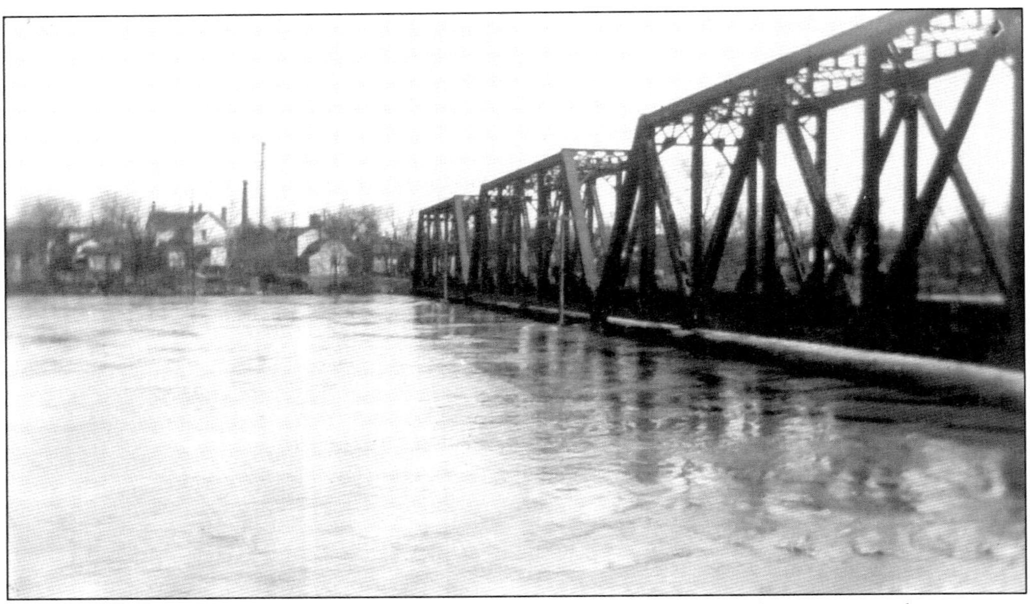

The Railroad Bridge during the Flood. In the distance of this view to the east are the smokestacks of Franklin's paper mills and other factories that were clustered around the intersection of Sixth Street and the Canal.

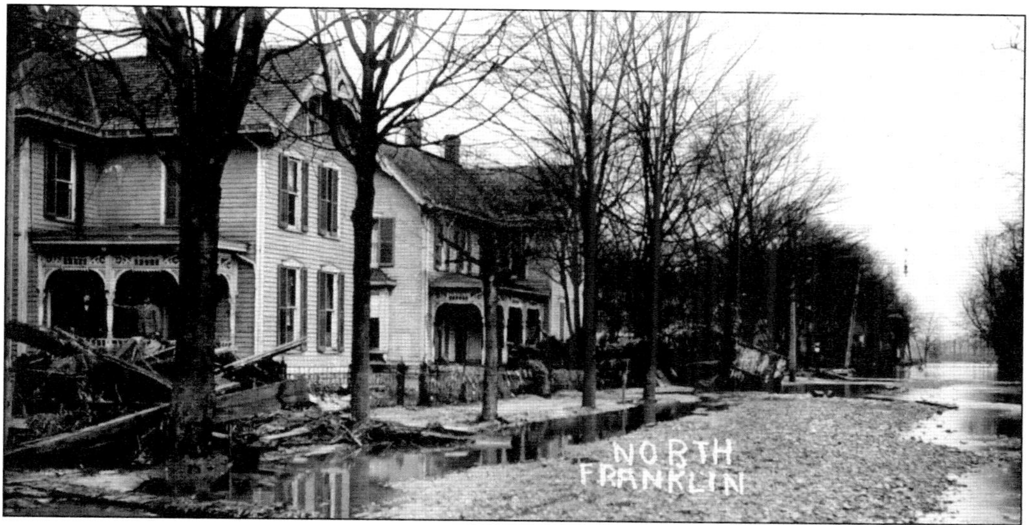

HOUSES ON RIVER STREET. The view is looking north. The house at left, 25 North River Street, still stands but the porch has changed. The home to the rear, to its north, is gone. Note the ornate porches and iron-fence railing, once so prevalent among village homes and now almost all vanished. In the distance there also appears to be an outhouse left behind by the flood waters.

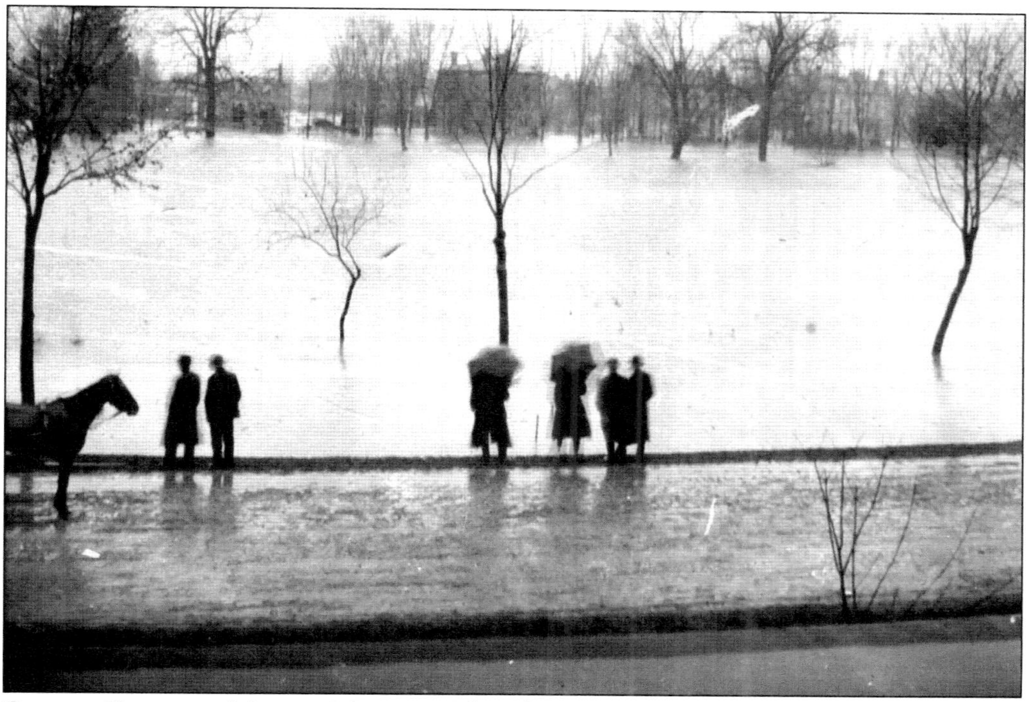

OXFORD ROAD ON MARCH 26, 1913. This photograph was taken from an upper floor of 45 West Third Street, on the east side of the river. Visible in the distance are, from right to left, Nos. 205, 209, and 219 Oxford Road. The small pile to the south of 219 Oxford Road is what had previously been the house at 225 Oxford Road under construction. One local person remembers that the flood waters carried away many of the wooden beams intended for the new house.

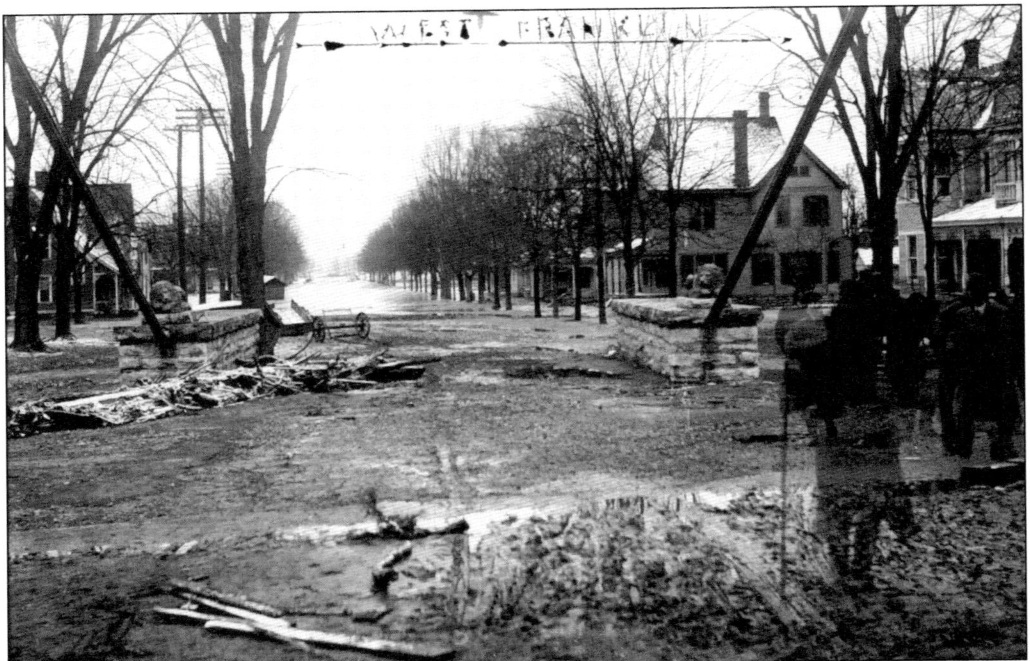

THE WEST END OF THE SUSPENSION BRIDGE. This is a view to the west along Park Avenue. Off of the image to the far left is 205 Park Avenue, and behind it is 222 Park Avenue. At far right is 137 Miami Avenue, and to its rear are Nos. 219 and 217 Park Avenue. (Courtesy of William Moses.)

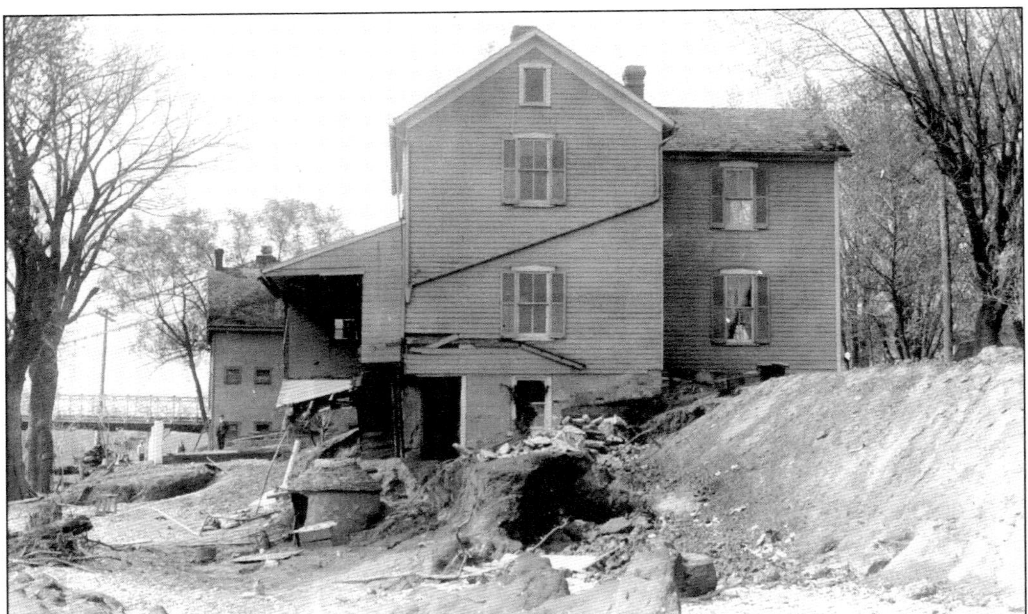

THE HEAVILY DAMAGED JOSEPH REED HOUSE. The view is looking south. This house, built before 1867, stood on the riverbank just north of the west end of the suspension bridge. In the general cleanup and levee construction that followed in the wake of the flood, the house was moved from the bank to the northwest corner of Maple Street and Spring Avenue.

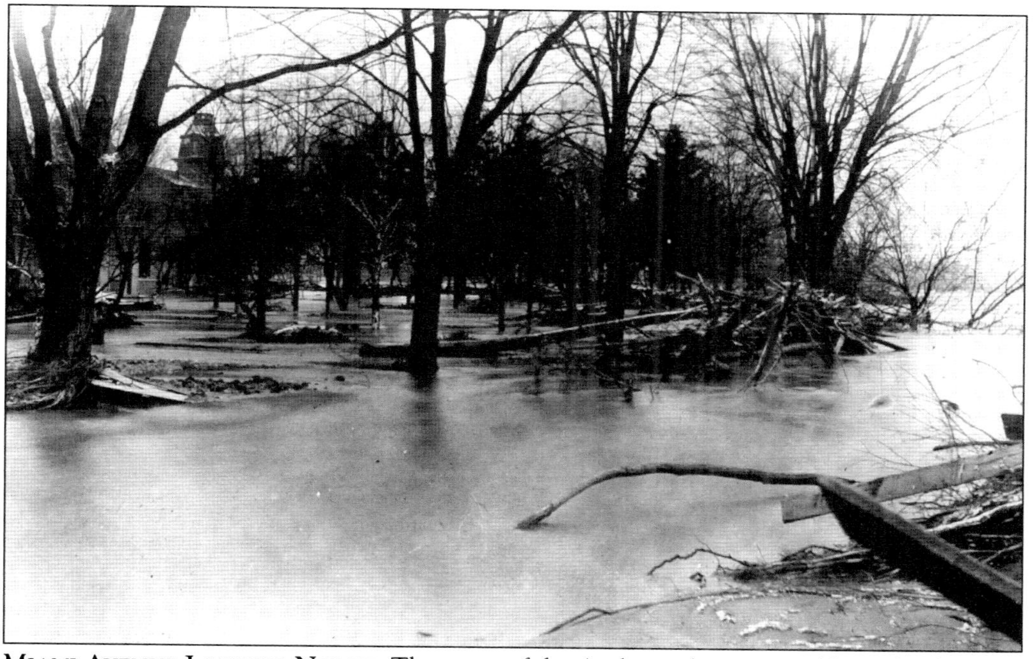

MIAMI AVENUE LOOKING NORTH. The tower of the Anderson house is visible in the distance. The flood waters reached a depth of five feet on the West Side.

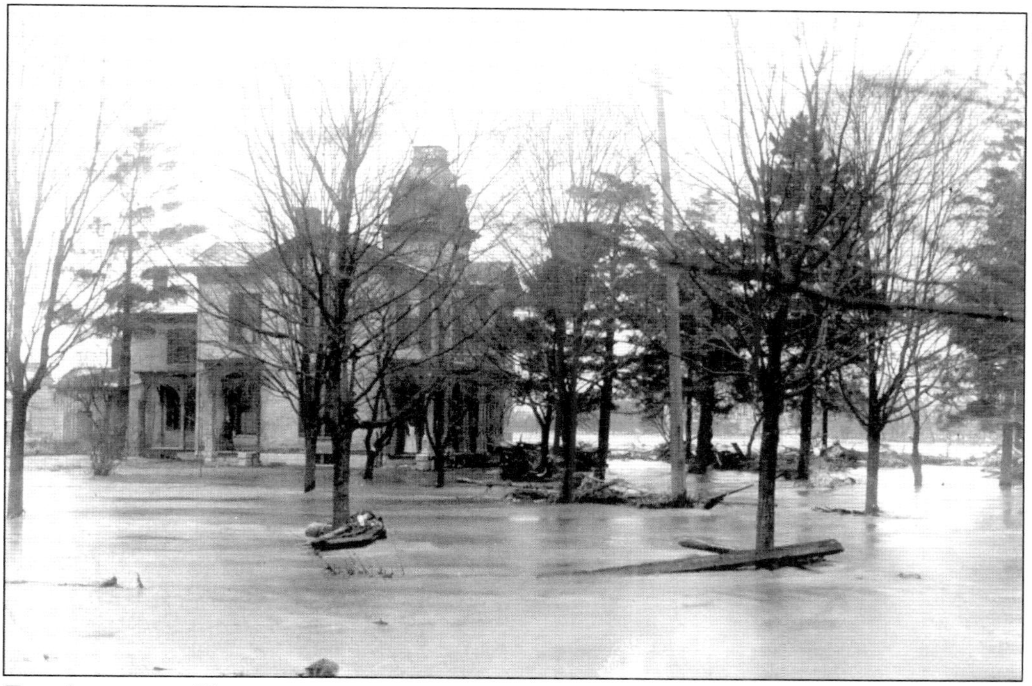

THE ANDERSON HOME AT 49 MIAMI AVENUE. Although the waters are receding, they still cover Lake Avenue in the foreground of this view to the north. William G. Anderson, in bow tie and homburg hat, with valise under his arm, stands on the south porch. On the front porch is an unidentified woman in an apron.

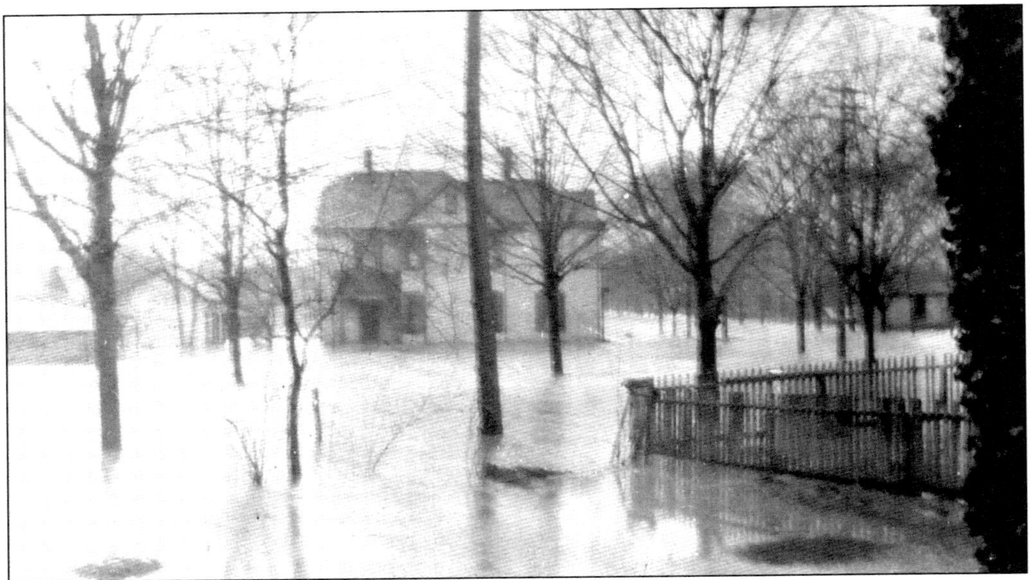

The West Side after the Flood. The flood water recedes as one looks south along Elm Street from the kitchen porch of the Anderson home at 49 Miami Avenue. In the foreground at right is all that remains of the picket fence washed away by the flood. Behind the section of fence appears to be a pet cemetery. The building at center is 108–110 Elm Street.

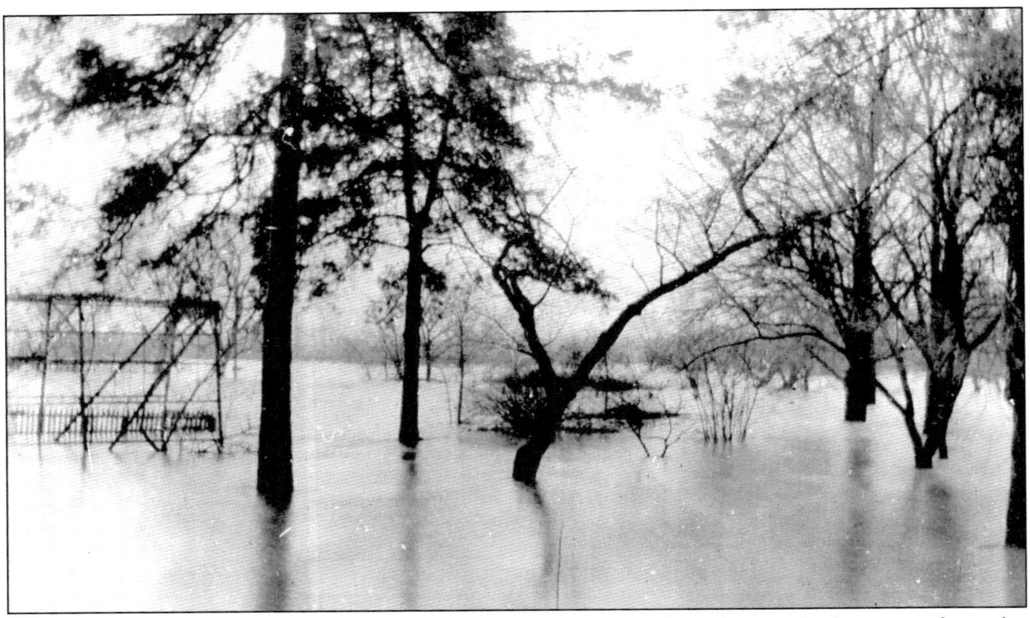

View of the Flood from a West Side Home. This is the dismal scene looking east from the front porch of the Anderson home at 49 Miami Avenue. Lost in the haze is the Great Miami River and beyond it the village of Franklin. The Andersons spent two days imprisoned in the upper floor of their home. At the height of the flood, their piano was said to have been floating in their parlor.

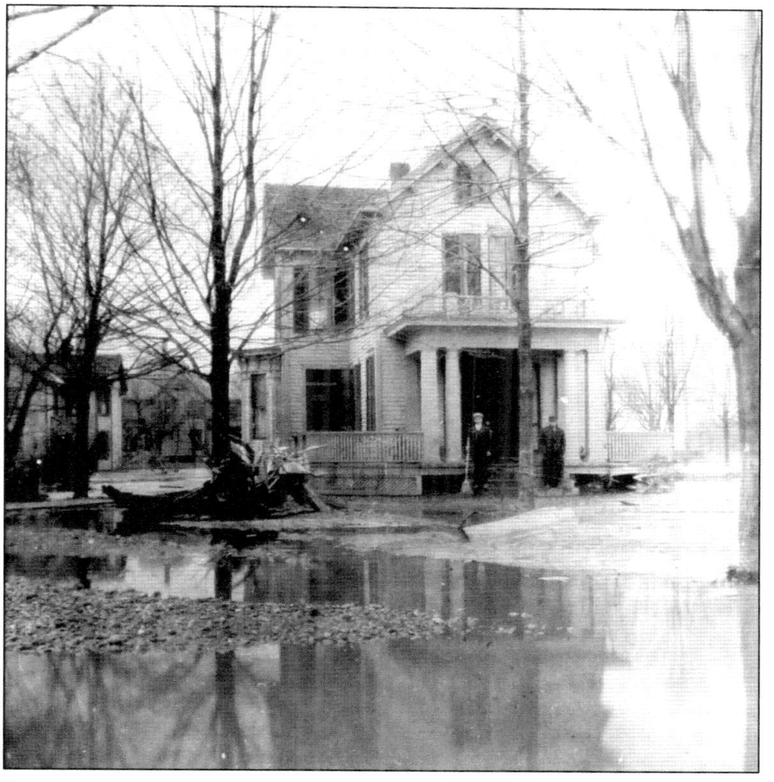

THE MALONEY HOUSE DURING FLOOD CLEANUP. This Italianate house had been built in 1879 by Derrick Anderson, the oldest of L. G. Anderson's children. In his prime, Derrick was a bank director, proprietor of a paper mill, and owner of Nightingale, the successful trotting horse that lived in a barn behind this house. But almost simultaneously in the mid-1890s, the bank crashed, the mill failed, and the horse lost a race, altogether destroying Anderson's fortunes.

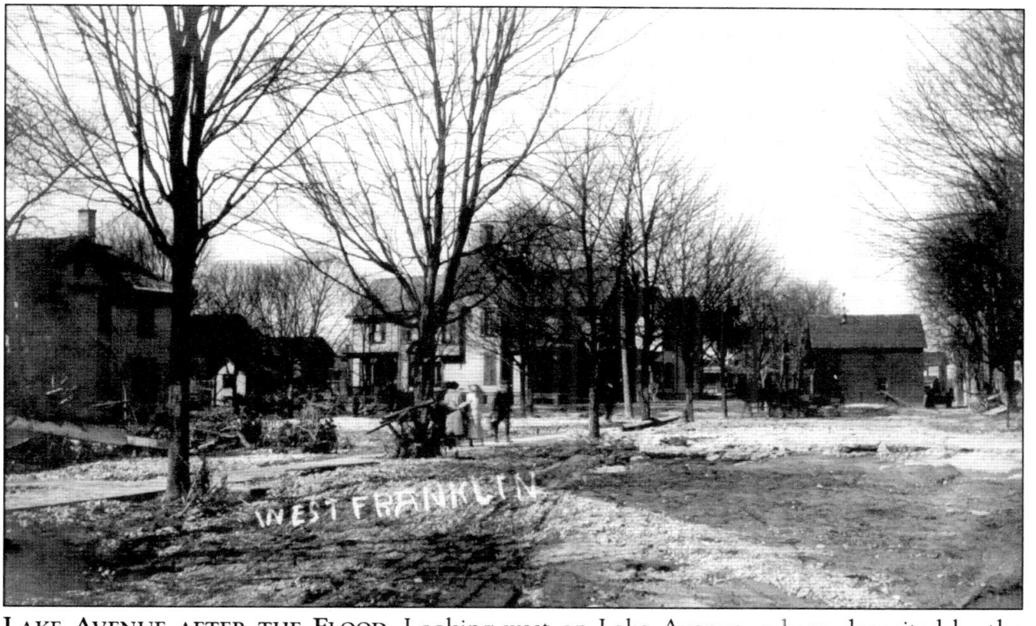

LAKE AVENUE AFTER THE FLOOD. Looking west on Lake Avenue, a barn deposited by the flood waters sits in the middle of the road. On the far left is 108–110 Elm Street, where Derrick Anderson spent his last years. Across Elm Street is 302 Lake Avenue, the home of his brother, Howard B. Anderson.

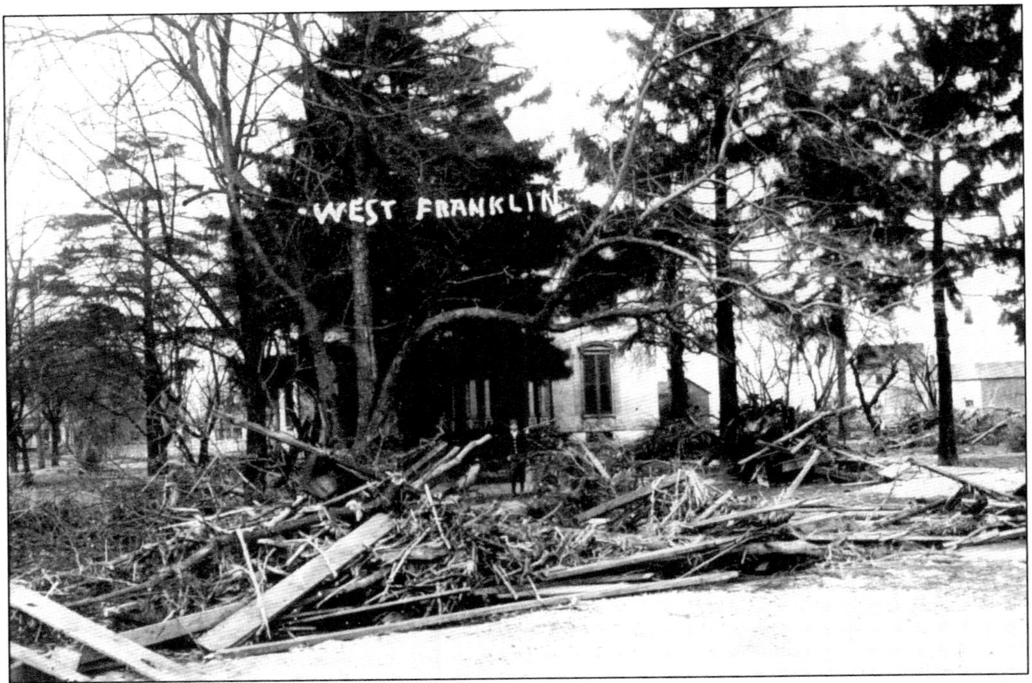

FLOOD DEBRIS IN FRONT OF 49 MIAMI AVENUE. Photographed on March 27, 1913, this is the Anderson home on Miami Avenue, as viewed from the east. Standing in the shade of the front porch is Bob Anderson, the grandson of the home's builder. Huge piles of debris deposited by flood lay against the porch and nearby trees. Many of the evergreen trees prominent in this photograph are still alive and healthy today.

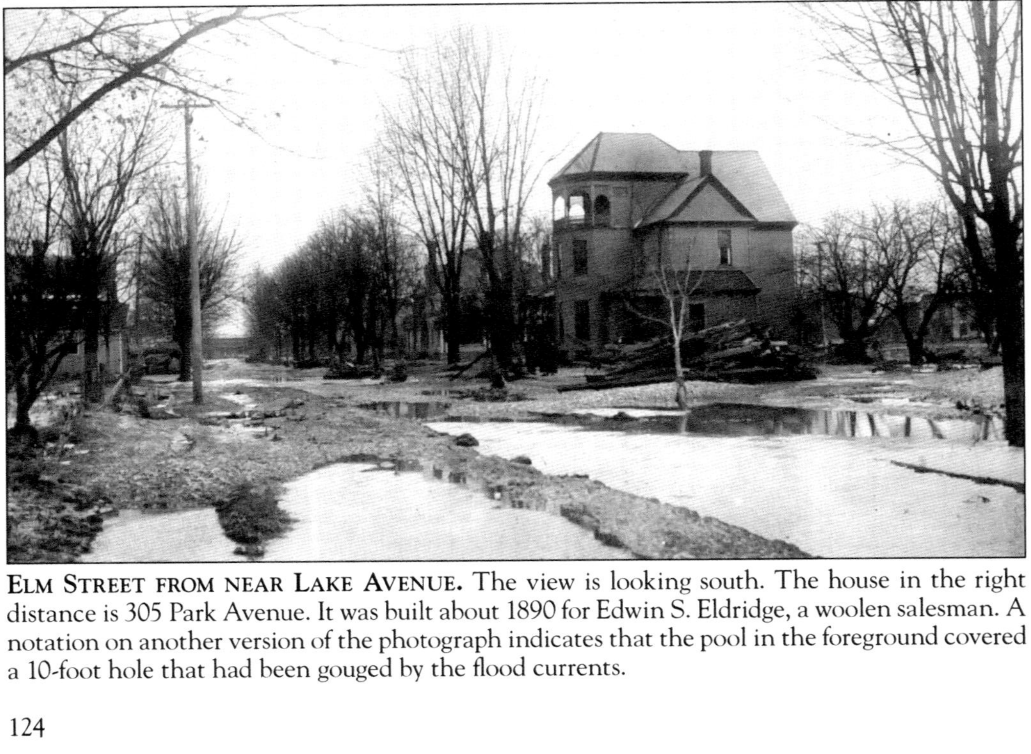

ELM STREET FROM NEAR LAKE AVENUE. The view is looking south. The house in the right distance is 305 Park Avenue. It was built about 1890 for Edwin S. Eldridge, a woolen salesman. A notation on another version of the photograph indicates that the pool in the foreground covered a 10-foot hole that had been gouged by the flood currents.

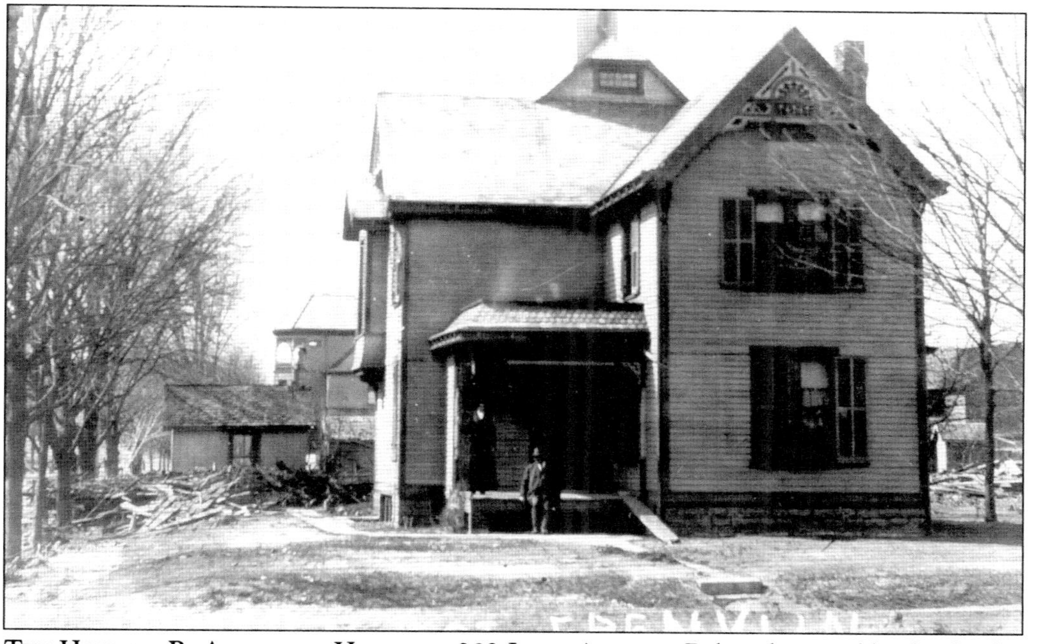

THE HOWARD B. ANDERSON HOUSE AT 302 LAKE AVENUE. Debris deposited by the flood is seen everywhere in this southward view along Elm Street. The shed in the left distance also appears out of place and may have been deposited there by the flood waters.

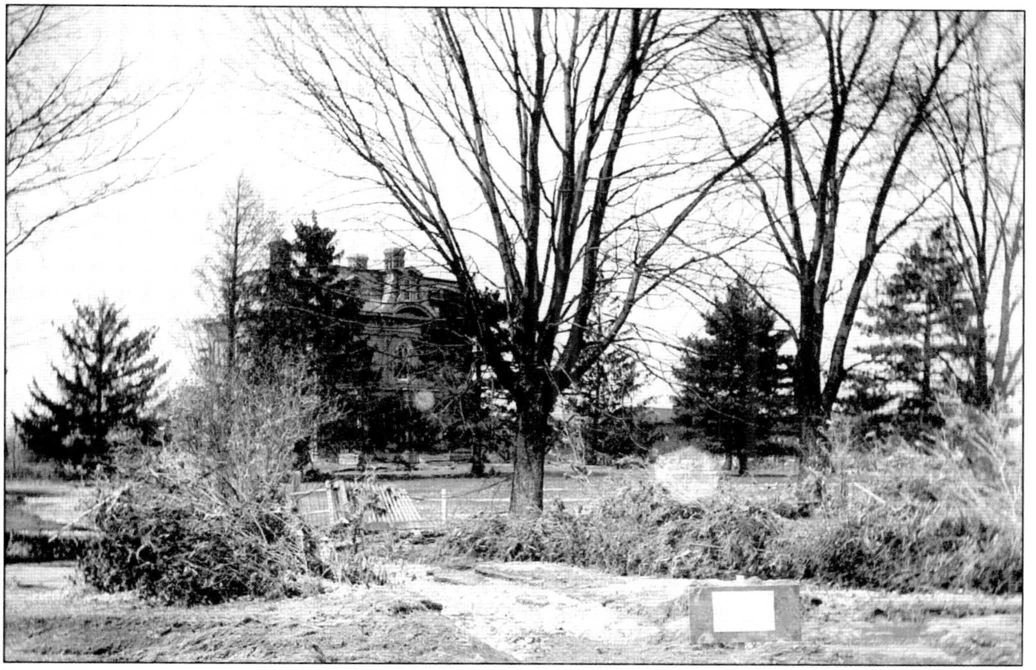

LEVI CROLL MANSION IN THE FLOOD AFTERMATH. An eyewitness account from a girl who lived at the far-western edge of the Franklin suburbs described how on the evening of March 25 the entire contents of the Croll farm (implements, supplies, and livestock) floated past her home. The power of the water is evidenced in the gouging seen in the foreground.

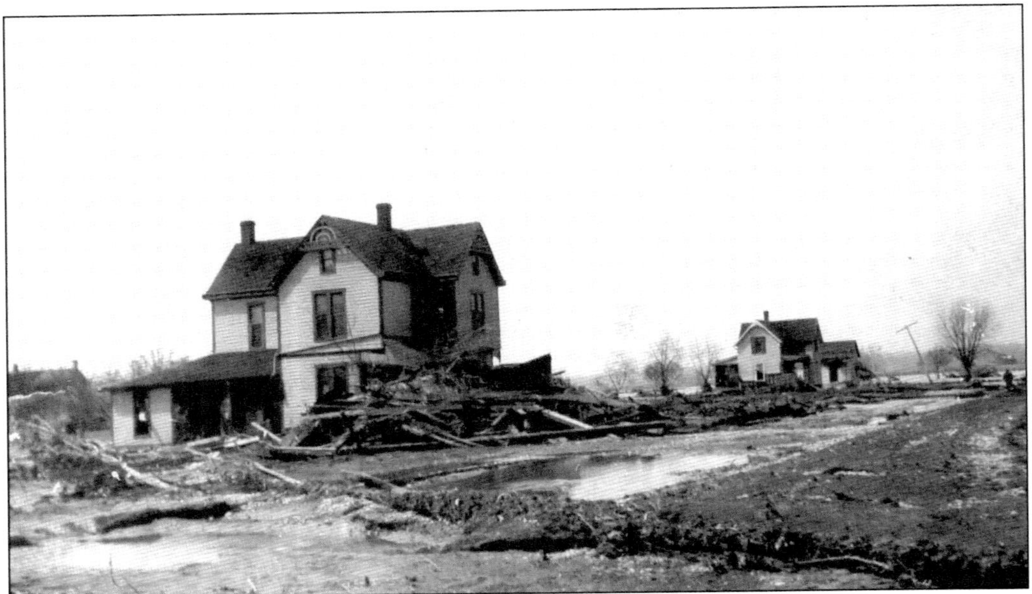

FLOOD CLEANUP AT 600 PARK AVENUE. This view looks toward the southwest. A note made on the original photograph states that a dead cow was found in this home's living room.

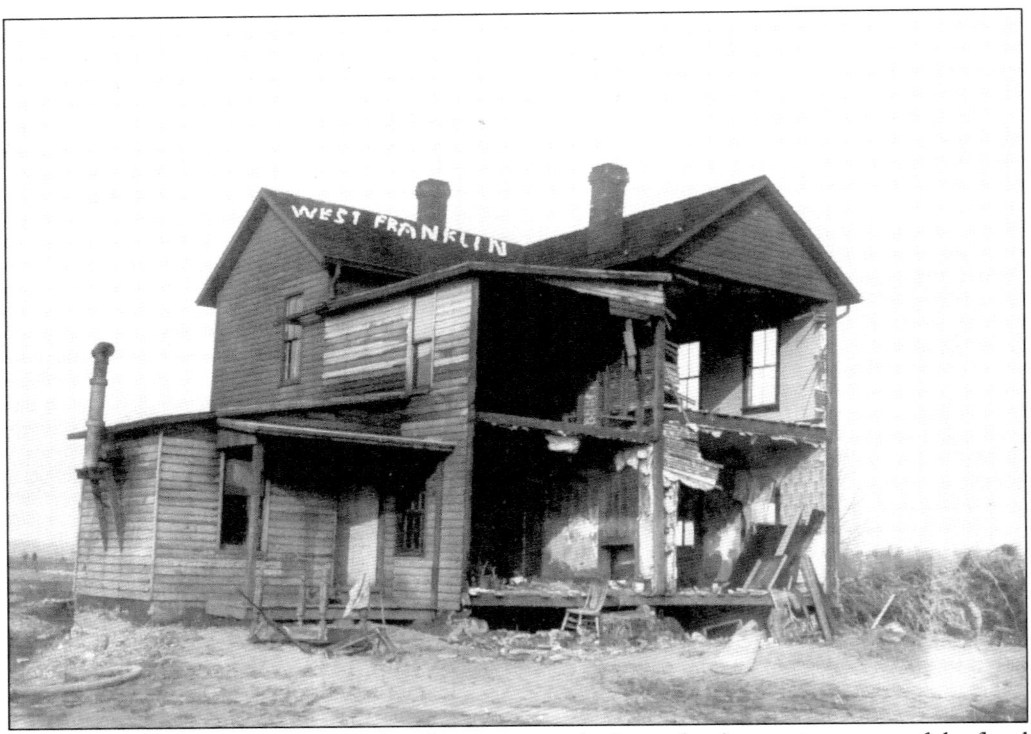

THE ALONZO MILLARD HOUSE. This close-up not only shows the destructive power of the flood waters but also provides insight into turn-of-the-century interior decoration. This house was not repaired after the flood.

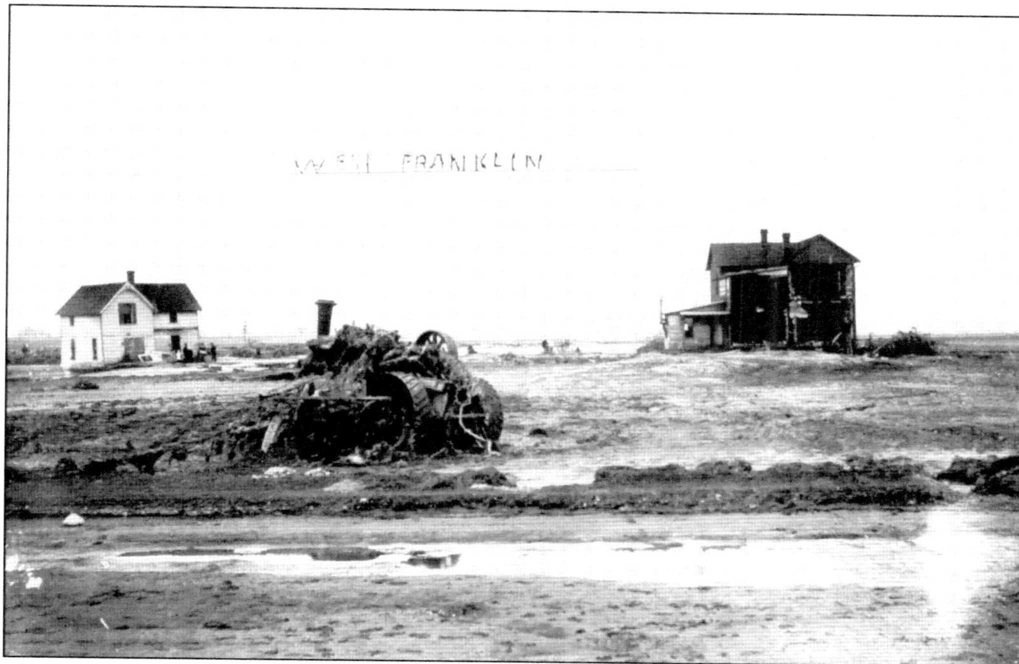

WEST SIDE FLOOD DEVASTATION. This photograph is looking approximately north. The wet surface in the foreground appears to be South Street. The Millard House is in the right distance. In the foreground is a farm tractor. A note on the original photograph asserts the tractor was pushed 30 feet by the flood surge.

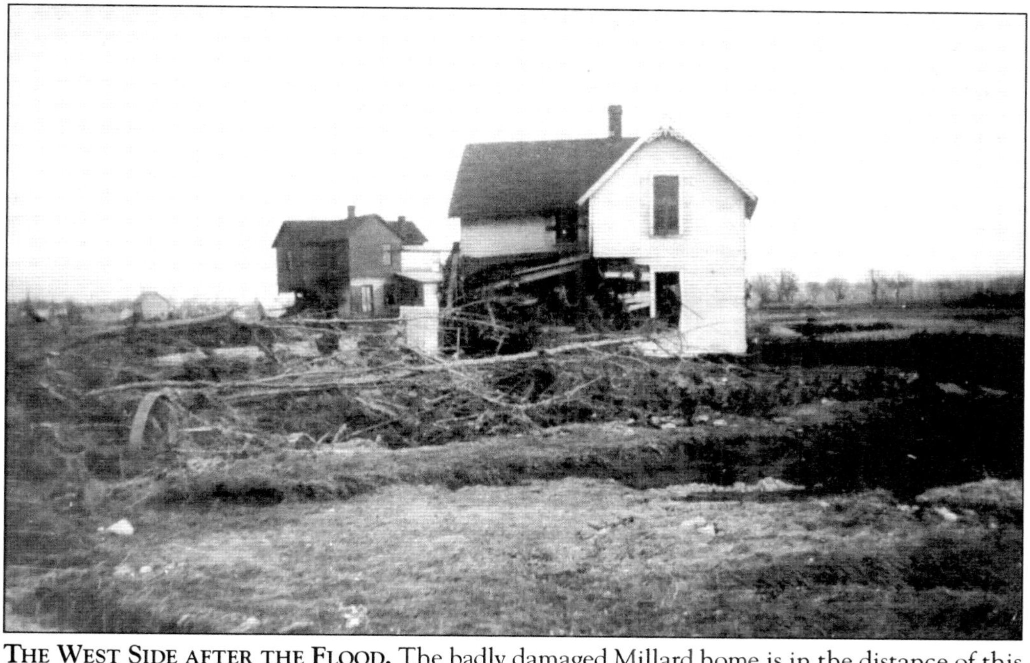

THE WEST SIDE AFTER THE FLOOD. The badly damaged Millard home is in the distance of this view, looking approximately south from near the 700 block of Park Avenue. Both of these homes were moved or destroyed when the levee was constructed around the West Side.

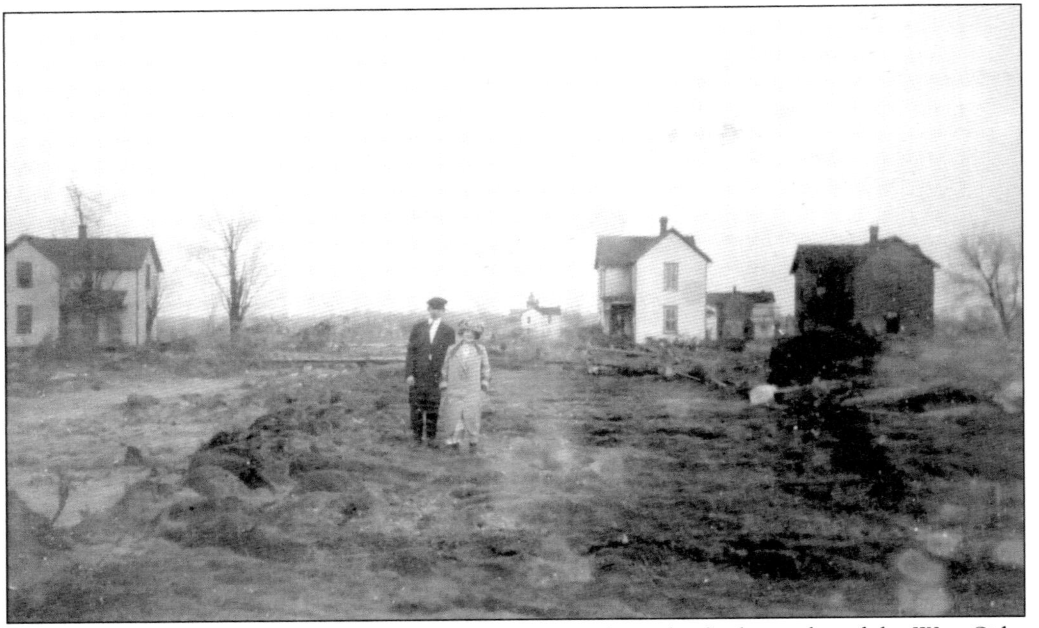

WEST SIDE DESTRUCTION. This photograph looks east from the farthest edge of the West Side. In the center distance is the high school on Maple Street. The couple in the foreground is probably Justin and May Harding, who had just experienced the flood while living in 302 Park Avenue. All the houses shown in the photograph were moved or destroyed when the Miami Conservancy levee was constructed around the West Side.

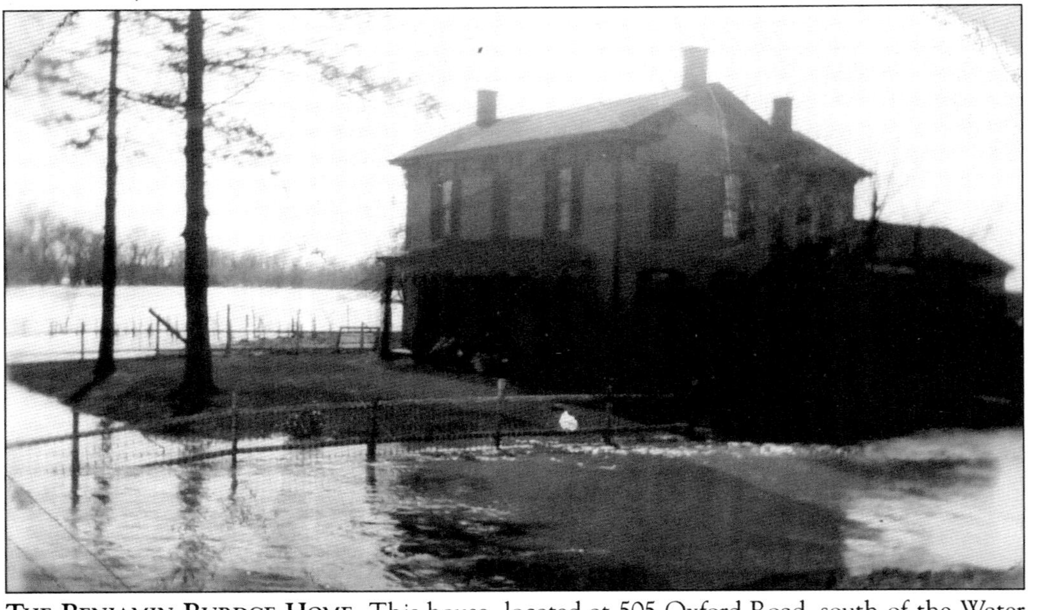

THE BENJAMIN BURDGE HOME. This house, located at 505 Oxford Road, south of the Water Works and West Side residences, was surrounded for two days by the flood waters. The Burdges had lived in the house since about 1900. Prior to that, the home and surrounding farmland had been the property of several generations of Barkalows since 1804, when William P. Barkalow first settled here in the wilderness.